סדר תפלות ישראל

# The Union Prayerbook

*for*

# JEWISH WORSHIP

NEWLY REVISED EDITION

EDITED AND PUBLISHED BY

THE CENTRAL CONFERENCE OF AMERICAN RABBIS

## PART I

NEW YORK

1961

PRINTED IN THE UNITED STATES OF AMERICA

# TABLE OF CONTENTS

And ye shall seek Me, and find Me when ye shall search for Me with all your heart.

—Jeremiah xxix: 13

Worship the Lord in the beauty of holiness.

—Psalm xcvi: 9

The Lord is nigh unto all that call upon Him, unto all that call upon Him in truth.

—Psalm cxlv: 18

Know thou the God of thy father, and serve Him with a whole heart, and with a willing mind; for the Lord searcheth all hearts, and understandeth all the imaginings of the thoughts; if thou seek Him, He will be found by thee.

—I Chronicles xxviii: 9

In the midst of a congregation at prayer, God's presence will be found.

—Berachot 6a

The Merciful One desires our heart.

—Sanhedrin 106b

What is the service of the heart? It is prayer.

—Taanit 2a

We should not rise to pray in the spirit of gloom or of idleness, of levity or idle talk, but only in the joy of religious duty.

—Berachot 31a

When you pray do not make your prayer mere routine, but a plea before God for mercy and grace.

—Abot ii: 13

3

When you pray, pray in the synagog of your city; if you are unable to pray in the synagog, pray in your field; if you are unable to pray in your field, pray in your home; if you are unable to pray in your home, pray on your couch; and if you are unable to pray on your couch, meditate in your heart. This is the meaning of the verse: "Commune with your own heart upon your bed, and be still."

—Midrash Tehillim on Psalm iv: 5

Prayer without devotion is like a body without a soul.

—Medieval Proverb

It is proper for you to know, my brother, that the aim of our devotion in prayer consists in naught save the soul's longing for God, humbling itself before Him, and extolling the Creator with praise and gratitude unto His name, and casting all burdens upon Him.

—Bahia ibn Pakkudah, *Duties of the Heart*, iii

# שבת

# Services for the Sabbath

---

Evening Services
Morning Service
Afternoon Service

# RITUAL FOR LIGHTING SABBATH CANDLES

Come, let us welcome the Sabbath. May its radiance illumine our hearts as we kindle these tapers.

Light is the symbol of the divine. The Lord is my light and my salvation.

Light is the symbol of the divine in man. The spirit of man is the light of the Lord.

Light is the symbol of the divine law. For the commandment is a lamp and the law is a light.

Light is the symbol of Israel's mission. I, the Lord, have set thee for a covenant of the people, for a light unto the nations.

Therefore, in the spirit of our ancient tradition that hallows and unites Israel in all lands and all ages, do we now kindle the Sabbath lights.

בָּרוּךְ אַתָּה יְיָ אֱלֹהֵינוּ מֶלֶךְ הָעוֹלָם אֲשֶׁר קִדְּשָׁנוּ בְּמִצְוֹתָיו וְצִוָּנוּ לְהַדְלִיק נֵר שֶׁל־שַׁבָּת:

Blessed art Thou, O Lord our God, King of the universe, who hast sanctified us by Thy laws and commanded us to kindle the Sabbath light.

May the Lord bless us with Sabbath joy.

May the Lord bless us with Sabbath holiness.

May the Lord bless us with Sabbath peace.

Amen.

# Evening Services for the Sabbath

## I

*Choir*

(Psalm xcii)

מִזְמוֹר שִׁיר לְיוֹם הַשַּׁבָּת:

It is good to give thanks to the Lord and to sing praises to Thy name, O Most High; to declare Thy lovingkindness in the morning, and Thy faithfulness in the night seasons, with an instrument of ten strings and with the psaltery; with a solemn sound upon the harp. For Thou, Lord, hast made me glad through Thy work; I will rejoice in the works of Thy hands. How great are Thy works, O Lord! Thy thoughts are very deep. A brutish man knoweth not, nei-

טוֹב לְהֹדוֹת לַיהֹוָה
וּלְזַמֵּר לְשִׁמְךָ עֶלְיוֹן:
לְהַגִּיד בַּבֹּקֶר חַסְדֶּךָ
וֶאֱמוּנָתְךָ בַּלֵּילוֹת: עֲלֵי־
עָשׂוֹר וַעֲלֵי־נָבֶל עֲלֵי
הִגָּיוֹן בְּכִנּוֹר: כִּי שִׂמַּחְתַּנִי
יְהֹוָה בְּפָעֳלֶךָ בְּמַעֲשֵׂי
יָדֶיךָ אֲרַנֵּן: מַה־גָּדְלוּ
מַעֲשֶׂיךָ יְהֹוָה מְאֹד עָמְקוּ
מַחְשְׁבֹתֶיךָ: אִישׁ־בַּעַר לֹא
יֵדָע וּכְסִיל לֹא יָבִין אֶת־
זֹאת: בִּפְרֹחַ רְשָׁעִים כְּמוֹ

8

ther doth a fool under-
stand this. When the
wicked spring up as the
grass, and when all the
workers of iniquity flourish, it is that they may
be destroyed forever.
But Thou, O Lord, art
exalted evermore. For
lo, Thine enemies, O
Lord, for lo, Thine ene-
mies shall perish; all the
workers of iniquity shall
be scattered. The right-
eous shall blossom like
the palm-tree, and grow
like a cedar in Lebanon.
Rooted in the house of
the Lord, they shall
flower in the courts of
our God. They shall be
sturdy in old age, flour-
ishing and verdant; to
declare that the Lord is
upright, my Rock, in
whom there is no un-
righteousness.

עֵשֶׂב וַיָּצִיצוּ כָּל־פְּעֲלֵי אָוֶן
לְהִשָּׁמְדָם עֲדֵי־עַד: וְאַתָּה
מָרוֹם לְעֹלָם יְהֹוָה. כִּי
הִנֵּה אֹיְבֶיךָ יְהֹוָה כִּי־הִנֵּה
אֹיְבֶיךָ יֹאבֵדוּ יִתְפָּרְדוּ
כָּל־פְּעֲלֵי אָוֶן: וַתָּרֶם
כִּרְאֵים קַרְנִי בַּלֹּתִי בְּשֶׁמֶן
רַעֲנָן: וַתַּבֵּט עֵינִי בְּשׁוּרָי
בַּקָּמִים עָלַי מְרֵעִים
תִּשְׁמַעְנָה אָזְנָי: צַדִּיק
כַּתָּמָר יִפְרָח כְּאֶרֶז
בַּלְּבָנוֹן יִשְׂגֶּה: שְׁתוּלִים
בְּבֵית יְהֹוָה. בְּחַצְרוֹת
אֱלֹהֵינוּ יַפְרִיחוּ: עוֹד
יְנוּבוּן בְּשֵׂיבָה. דְּשֵׁנִים
וְרַעֲנַנִּים יִהְיוּ: לְהַגִּיד
כִּי־יָשָׁר יְהֹוָה. צוּרִי וְלֹא־
עַוְלָתָה בּוֹ:

*Silent Prayer*

### Reader

Lord of the universe, we lift up our hearts to Thee who made heaven and earth. The infinite heavens and the quiet stars tell of Thine endless power. We turn from our daily toil, from its difficulties and its conflicts, from its clamor and its weariness, to meditate on the serene calm of Thy presence which pervades all creation and hallows our life with the blessing of Sabbath peace.

Father of Peace, bless Thou our worship on this Sabbath day. Enlighten our eyes to behold Thy guiding power in all nature from the remotest star to our inmost soul. Inspire our hearts to love Thee and to make Thy will the law of our life. Grant us comfort in sorrow, strength in trial and the courage to serve Thee in all our ways. May our words of prayer and our unspoken meditations be acceptable unto Thee, our Creator and Redeemer. Amen.

### Responsive Reading

**Reader**

O come, let us sing unto the Lord; let us raise our voice in joy to the Rock of our salvation.

**Congregation**

O sing unto the Lord a new song; sing unto the Lord, all the earth.

Sing unto the Lord; bless His name; proclaim His salvation from day to day.

*Honor and majesty are before Him; strength and beauty are in His sanctuary.*

Worship the Lord in the beauty of holiness; tremble before Him, all the earth.

*The Lord reigneth; the world is established that it cannot be moved.*

Let the heavens be glad, and the earth rejoice; let the field exult, and all that is therein.

*He will judge the world with righteousness; and the peoples in His faithfulness.*

O ye that love the Lord, hate evil; He preserveth the souls of His servants.

*Light is sown for the righteous, and gladness for the upright in heart.*

Be glad in the Lord, ye righteous; and give thanks to His holy name.

*He hath remembered His mercy and His faithfulness toward the house of Israel.*

All the ends of the earth have seen the salvation of our God.

*The Lord our God is holy.*

(Congregation rises)

### Reader

Praise ye the Lord, to whom all praise is due.

### Choir and Congregation

Praised be the Lord to whom all praise is due forever and ever.

(Congregation is seated)

### Reader

Praised be Thou, O Lord our God, ruler of the world, by whose law the shadows of evening fall and the gates of morn are opened. In wisdom Thou hast established the changes of times and seasons and ordered the ways of the stars in their heavenly courses. Creator of heaven and earth, O living God, rule Thou over us forever. Praised be Thou, O Lord, for the day and its work and for the night and its rest.

### Congregation and Reader

Infinite as is Thy power, even so is Thy love. Thou didst manifest it through Israel, Thy people. By laws and commandments, by statutes and ordinances hast Thou led us in the way of righteousness and brought us to the light of truth. Therefore at our lying down and our rising up, we will meditate on Thy teachings and find in Thy laws true life and length of days. O that Thy love may never depart from our hearts. Praised be Thou, O Lord, who hast revealed Thy love through Israel.

(Congregation rises)

Reader

בָּרְכוּ אֶת־יְיָ הַמְבֹרָךְ:

Choir and Congregation

בָּרוּךְ יְיָ הַמְבֹרָךְ לְעוֹלָם וָעֶד:

(Congregation is seated)

Reader

בָּרוּךְ אַתָּה יְיָ אֱלֹהֵינוּ מֶלֶךְ הָעוֹלָם. אֲשֶׁר
בִּדְבָרוֹ מַעֲרִיב עֲרָבִים. בְּחָכְמָה פּוֹתֵחַ שְׁעָרִים.
וּבִתְבוּנָה מְשַׁנֶּה עִתִּים וּמַחֲלִיף אֶת־הַזְּמַנִּים.
וּמְסַדֵּר אֶת־הַכּוֹכָבִים בְּמִשְׁמְרוֹתֵיהֶם בָּרָקִיעַ
כִּרְצוֹנוֹ. בּוֹרֵא יוֹם וָלָיְלָה. יְיָ צְבָאוֹת שְׁמוֹ. אֵל
חַי וְקַיָּם תָּמִיד יִמְלֹךְ עָלֵינוּ לְעוֹלָם וָעֶד. בָּרוּךְ
אַתָּה יְיָ הַמַּעֲרִיב עֲרָבִים:

אַהֲבַת עוֹלָם בֵּית יִשְׂרָאֵל עַמְּךָ אָהָבְתָּ. תּוֹרָה
וּמִצְוֹת חֻקִּים וּמִשְׁפָּטִים אוֹתָנוּ לִמַּדְתָּ. עַל־כֵּן יְיָ
אֱלֹהֵינוּ בְּשָׁכְבֵנוּ וּבְקוּמֵנוּ נָשִׂיחַ בְּחֻקֶּיךָ. וְנִשְׂמַח
בְּדִבְרֵי תוֹרָתֶךָ וּבְמִצְוֹתֶיךָ לְעוֹלָם וָעֶד. כִּי הֵם
חַיֵּינוּ וְאֹרֶךְ יָמֵינוּ. וּבָהֶם נֶהְגֶּה יוֹמָם וָלָיְלָה.
וְאַהֲבָתְךָ אַל־תָּסִיר מִמֶּנּוּ לְעוֹלָמִים. בָּרוּךְ אַתָּה
יְיָ אוֹהֵב עַמּוֹ יִשְׂרָאֵל:

(Congregation rises)

### Reader

Hear, O Israel: The Lord our God, the Lord is One. Praised be His name whose glorious kingdom is forever and ever.

(Congregation is seated)

### Congregation and Reader

Thou shalt love the Lord, thy God, with all thy heart, with all thy soul, and with all thy might. And these words, which I command thee this day, shall be upon thy heart. Thou shalt teach them diligently unto thy children, and shalt speak of them when thou sittest in thy house, when thou walkest by the way, when thou liest down, and when thou risest up. Thou shalt bind them for a sign upon thy hand, and they shall be for frontlets between thine eyes. Thou shalt write them upon the doorposts of thy house and upon thy gates: That ye may remember and do all My commandments and be holy unto your God.

### Responsive Reading

Reader

Eternal truth it is that Thou alone art God, and there is none else.

Congregation

And through Thy power alone has Israel been redeemed from the hand of oppressors.

Great deeds hast Thou wrought in our behalf and wonders without number.

(Congregation rises)

Reader, then Choir and Congregation

שְׁמַע יִשְׂרָאֵל יְהוָה אֱלֹהֵינוּ יְהוָה אֶחָד:

בָּרוּךְ שֵׁם כְּבוֹד מַלְכוּתוֹ לְעוֹלָם וָעֶד:

(Congregation is seated)

Reader

וְאָהַבְתָּ אֵת יְיָ אֱלֹהֶיךָ בְּכָל־לְבָבְךָ וּבְכָל־נַפְשְׁךָ

וּבְכָל־מְאֹדֶךָ: וְהָיוּ הַדְּבָרִים הָאֵלֶּה אֲשֶׁר אָנֹכִי

מְצַוְּךָ הַיּוֹם עַל־לְבָבֶךָ: וְשִׁנַּנְתָּם לְבָנֶיךָ וְדִבַּרְתָּ

בָּם. בְּשִׁבְתְּךָ בְּבֵיתֶךָ וּבְלֶכְתְּךָ בַדֶּרֶךְ וּבְשָׁכְבְּךָ

וּבְקוּמֶךָ: וּקְשַׁרְתָּם לְאוֹת עַל־יָדֶךָ. וְהָיוּ לְטֹטָפֹת

בֵּין עֵינֶיךָ: וּכְתַבְתָּם עַל־מְזֻזוֹת בֵּיתֶךָ וּבִשְׁעָרֶיךָ:

לְמַעַן תִּזְכְּרוּ וַעֲשִׂיתֶם אֶת־כָּל־מִצְוֹתָי וִהְיִיתֶם

קְדֹשִׁים לֵאלֹהֵיכֶם: אֲנִי יְיָ אֱלֹהֵיכֶם:

Responsive Reading

אֱמֶת וֶאֱמוּנָה כָּל־זֹאת וְקַיָּם עָלֵינוּ. כִּי הוּא יְיָ

אֱלֹהֵינוּ וְאֵין זוּלָתוֹ. וַאֲנַחְנוּ יִשְׂרָאֵל עַמּוֹ:

הַפּוֹדֵנוּ מִיַּד מְלָכִים. מַלְכֵּנוּ הַגּוֹאֲלֵנוּ מִכַּף

כָּל־הֶעָרִיצִים:

הָעֹשֶׂה גְדֹלוֹת עַד־אֵין חֵקֶר. וְנִפְלָאוֹת עַד־אֵין

מִסְפָּר:

*Thou hast kept us in life; Thou hast not let our foot-steps falter.*

Thy love has watched over us in the night of oppression;

*Thy mercy has sustained us in the hour of trial.*

And now that we live in a land of freedom, may we continue to be faithful to Thee and Thy word.

*May Thy law rule the life of all Thy children and Thy truth unite their hearts in fellowship.*

O God, our refuge and our hope, we glorify Thy name now as did our fathers in ancient days:

### Choir

Who is like unto Thee, O Lord, among the mighty? Who is like unto Thee, glorious in holiness, awe-inspiring, working wonders?

### Reader

Thy children acknowledged Thy sovereign power, and exclaimed:

### Choir

The Lord shall reign forever and ever.

### Reader

As Thou hast redeemed Israel and saved him from arms stronger than his own, so mayest Thou redeem all who are oppressed and persecuted. Praised be Thou, O Lord, Redeemer of Israel.

הַשָּׁם נַפְשֵׁנוּ בַּחַיִּים. וְלֹא נָתַן לַמּוֹט רַגְלֵנוּ:

הָעֹשֶׂה לָנוּ נִסִּים בְּמִצְרָיִם. אוֹתוֹת וּמוֹפְתִים
בְּאַדְמַת בְּנֵי־חָם:

וַיּוֹצֵא אֶת־עַמּוֹ יִשְׂרָאֵל מִתּוֹכָם לְחֵירוּת עוֹלָם.
וְרָאוּ בָנָיו גְּבוּרָתוֹ. שִׁבְּחוּ וְהוֹדוּ לִשְׁמוֹ:

וּמַלְכוּתוֹ בְּרָצוֹן קִבְּלוּ עֲלֵיהֶם מֹשֶׁה וּבְנֵי
יִשְׂרָאֵל:

לְךָ עָנוּ שִׁירָה בְּשִׂמְחָה רַבָּה וְאָמְרוּ כֻלָּם:

Choir

מִי־כָמֹכָה בָּאֵלִם יְיָ. מִי כָּמֹכָה נֶאְדָּר בַּקֹּדֶשׁ
נוֹרָא תְהִלֹּת עֹשֵׂה פֶלֶא:

Reader

מַלְכוּתְךָ רָאוּ בָנֶיךָ. זֶה אֵלִי עָנוּ וְאָמְרוּ:

Choir

יְיָ יִמְלֹךְ לְעֹלָם וָעֶד:

Reader

וְנֶאֱמַר כִּי־פָדָה יְהֹוָה אֶת־יַעֲקֹב וּגְאָלוֹ מִיַּד חָזָק
מִמֶּנּוּ. בָּרוּךְ אַתָּה יְיָ גָּאַל יִשְׂרָאֵל:

## Choir

The children of Israel shall keep the Sabbath, to observe the Sabbath throughout their generations as a perpetual covenant. It is a sign between Me and the children of Israel forever.

## Reader

Praised be Thou, O Lord, God of our fathers, God of Abraham, Isaac and Jacob, great, mighty, and exalted. Thou bestowest lovingkindness upon all Thy children. Thou rememberest the devotion of the fathers. In Thy love, Thou bringest redemption to their descendants for the sake of Thy name. Thou art our King and Helper, our Savior and Protector. Praised be Thou, O Lord, Shield of Abraham.

Eternal is Thy power, O Lord, Thou art mighty to save. In lovingkindness Thou sustainest the living; in the multitude of Thy mercies, Thou preservest all. Thou upholdest the falling and healest the sick; freest the captives and keepest faith with Thy children in death as in life. Who is like unto Thee, Almighty God, Author of life and death, Source of salvation? Praised be Thou, O Lord, who hast implanted within us eternal life.

Thou art holy, Thy name is holy and Thy worshipers proclaim Thy holiness. Praised be Thou, O Lord, the holy God.

(Prayers for Special Sabbaths, pp. 79–84)

Choir

וְשָׁמְרוּ בְנֵי־יִשְׂרָאֵל אֶת־הַשַׁבָּת לַעֲשׂוֹת אֶת־
הַשַׁבָּת לְדֹרֹתָם בְּרִית עוֹלָם: בֵּינִי וּבֵין בְּנֵי יִשְׂרָאֵל
אוֹת הִוא לְעֹלָם׃

Reader

בָּרוּךְ אַתָּה יְיָ אֱלֹהֵינוּ וֵאלֹהֵי אֲבוֹתֵינוּ. אֱלֹהֵי
אַבְרָהָם אֱלֹהֵי יִצְחָק וֵאלֹהֵי יַעֲקֹב. הָאֵל הַגָּדוֹל
הַגִּבּוֹר וְהַנּוֹרָא. אֵל עֶלְיוֹן. גּוֹמֵל חֲסָדִים טוֹבִים.
וְקֹנֵה הַכֹּל וְזוֹכֵר חַסְדֵי אָבוֹת. וּמֵבִיא גֹאֵל לִבְנֵי
בְנֵיהֶם. לְמַעַן שְׁמוֹ בְּאַהֲבָה: מֶלֶךְ עוֹזֵר וּמוֹשִׁיעַ
וּמָגֵן. בָּרוּךְ אַתָּה יְיָ מָגֵן אַבְרָהָם:

אַתָּה גִּבּוֹר לְעוֹלָם אֲדֹנָי. רַב לְהוֹשִׁיעַ. מְכַלְכֵּל
חַיִּים בְּחֶסֶד. מְחַיֶּה הַכֹּל בְּרַחֲמִים רַבִּים. סוֹמֵךְ
נוֹפְלִים וְרוֹפֵא חוֹלִים וּמַתִּיר אֲסוּרִים. וּמְקַיֵּם
אֱמוּנָתוֹ לִישֵׁנֵי עָפָר. מִי כָמוֹךָ בַּעַל גְּבוּרוֹת. וּמִי
דּוֹמֶה לָּךְ. מֶלֶךְ מֵמִית וּמְחַיֶּה. וּמַצְמִיחַ יְשׁוּעָה:
בָּרוּךְ אַתָּה יְיָ נֹטֵעַ בְּתוֹכֵנוּ חַיֵּי עוֹלָם:

אַתָּה קָדוֹשׁ וְשִׁמְךָ קָדוֹשׁ וּקְדוֹשִׁים בְּכָל־יוֹם
יְהַלְלוּךָ סֶּלָה. בָּרוּךְ אַתָּה יְיָ הָאֵל הַקָּדוֹשׁ:

### Reader

Heavenly Father, we rejoice that amid the ceaseless cares and anxieties, the vain desires and wearisome struggles of our earthly life, Thy holy Sabbath has been given us as a day of rest and refreshment of soul. We thank Thee for all Thy mercies unto us during the past week, for the preservation of our lives, of our health, and our strength; for the blessings of home, of love, of friendship, and for all good influences which support us in the hour of trial and temptation. Thou sendest us the joys that brighten our days; from Thy hand also come the sorrows that cast their shadows over them. In all our experiences we recognize Thy guidance and praise Thy wisdom. O may this Sabbath bring rest to every disquieted heart and be a healing balm to every wounded soul.

Thou who hearest prayer, we beseech Thee to endow us with a contented disposition. When we pray for new blessings, may we come to Thee in the spirit of humility and submission, remembering that we cannot know whether what we ask is really for our good. Thou alone knowest and orderest all things well, whether Thou grantest our petitions or deniest them. When we sing Thy praise, may our souls rise with our songs to Thee, and when we render Thee our homage, may we remember that only by obedience to Thy commandments, by faithfulness to our duties, by the goodness of our deeds, can we make our worship acceptable to Thee.

Look with compassion upon Thy children and grant us strength of love and purity of purpose, that we may live together in unity and work together in peace and concord, so that the well-being of all may be promoted, and Thy name, O God, be glorified in all the earth. Amen.

### Congregation and Reader

Our God and God of our fathers, grant that our worship on this Sabbath be acceptable to Thee. Sanctify us through Thy commandments that we may share in the blessings of Thy word. Teach us to be satisfied with the gifts of Thy goodness and gratefully to rejoice in all Thy mercies. Purify our hearts that we may serve Thee in truth. O help us to preserve the Sabbath as Israel's heritage from generation to generation, that it may bring rest and joy, peace and comfort to the dwellings of our brethren, and through it Thy name be hallowed in all the earth. Praised be Thou, O Lord, who sanctifiest the Sabbath.

### Reader

Grant us peace, Thy most precious gift, O Thou eternal source of peace, and enable Israel to be its messenger unto the peoples of the earth. Bless our country that it may ever be a stronghold of peace, and its advocate in the council of nations. May contentment reign within its borders, health and happiness within its homes. Strengthen the bonds of friendship and fellowship among the inhabitants of all lands. Plant virtue in every soul, and may the love of Thy name hallow every home and every heart. Praised be Thou, O Lord, Giver of peace.

### Choir: Amen.

Congregation and Reader

אֱלֹהֵינוּ וֵאלֹהֵי אֲבוֹתֵינוּ רְצֵה בִמְנוּחָתֵנוּ קַדְּשֵׁנוּ

בְּמִצְוֹתֶיךָ וְתֵן חֶלְקֵנוּ בְּתוֹרָתֶךָ שַׂבְּעֵנוּ מִטּוּבֶךָ

וְשַׂמְּחֵנוּ בִּישׁוּעָתֶךָ וְטַהֵר לִבֵּנוּ לְעָבְדְּךָ בֶּאֱמֶת

וְהַנְחִילֵנוּ יְיָ אֱלֹהֵינוּ בְּאַהֲבָה וּבְרָצוֹן שַׁבַּת קָדְשֶׁךָ

וְיָנוּחוּ בָהּ יִשְׂרָאֵל מְקַדְּשֵׁי שְׁמֶךָ. בָּרוּךְ אַתָּה יְיָ

מְקַדֵּשׁ הַשַּׁבָּת:

Reader

שָׁלוֹם רַב עַל־יִשְׂרָאֵל עַמְּךָ תָּשִׂים לְעוֹלָם. כִּי

אַתָּה הוּא מֶלֶךְ אָדוֹן לְכָל־הַשָּׁלוֹם. וְטוֹב בְּעֵינֶיךָ

לְבָרֵךְ אֶת־עַמְּךָ יִשְׂרָאֵל בְּכָל־עֵת וּבְכָל־שָׁעָה

בִּשְׁלוֹמֶךָ:

## Silent Prayer

(or such other prayer as the heart may prompt)

O God, keep my tongue from evil and my lips from speaking guile.  Be my support when grief silences my voice, and my comfort when woe bends my spirit.  Implant humility in my soul, and strengthen my heart with perfect faith in Thee.  Help me to be strong in temptation and trial and to be patient and forgiving when others wrong me.  Guide me by the light of Thy counsel, that I may ever find strength in Thee, my Rock and my Redeemer.  Amen.

*(or the following Psalm)*

(Psalm xxiii)

The Lord is my shepherd, I shall not want.  He maketh me to lie down in green pastures; He leadeth me beside the still waters.  He restoreth my soul; He guideth me in straight paths for His name's sake.  Yea, though I walk through the valley of the shadow of death, I will fear no evil, for Thou art with me; Thy rod and Thy staff, they comfort me.  Thou preparest a table before me in the presence of mine enemies; Thou hast anointed my head with oil; my cup runneth over.  Surely goodness and mercy shall follow me all the days of my life, and I shall dwell in the house of the Lord forever.

## Choir

May the words of my mouth and the meditation of my heart be acceptable unto Thee, O Lord, my Rock and my Redeemer.

(Those congregations which read the Torah, turn to page 94)

### READING FROM SCRIPTURE

(For ADORATION and KADDISH, turn to page 71)

*Silent Prayer*

אֱלֹהַי נְצוֹר לְשׁוֹנִי מֵרָע וּשְׂפָתַי מִדַּבֵּר מִרְמָה:
וְלִמְקַלְלַי נַפְשִׁי תִדּוֹם וְנַפְשִׁי כֶּעָפָר לַכֹּל תִּהְיֶה:
פְּתַח לִבִּי בְּתוֹרָתֶךָ וּבְמִצְוֹתֶיךָ תִּרְדּוֹף נַפְשִׁי: וְכֹל
הַחוֹשְׁבִים עָלַי רָעָה מְהֵרָה הָפֵר עֲצָתָם וְקַלְקֵל
מַחֲשַׁבְתָּם. לְמַעַן יֵחָלְצוּן יְדִידֶיךָ הוֹשִׁיעָה יְמִינְךָ
וַעֲנֵנִי: יִהְיוּ לְרָצוֹן אִמְרֵי פִי וְהֶגְיוֹן לִבִּי לְפָנֶיךָ יְיָ
צוּרִי וְגוֹאֲלִי:

מִזְמוֹר לְדָוִד יְהֹוָה רֹעִי לֹא אֶחְסָר: בִּנְאוֹת
דֶּשֶׁא יַרְבִּיצֵנִי עַל־מֵי מְנוּחוֹת יְנַהֲלֵנִי: נַפְשִׁי יְשׁוֹבֵב
יַנְחֵנִי בְמַעְגְּלֵי־צֶדֶק לְמַעַן שְׁמוֹ: גַּם כִּי־אֵלֵךְ בְּגֵיא
צַלְמָוֶת לֹא־אִירָא רָע כִּי־אַתָּה עִמָּדִי עֲמָדִי שִׁבְטְךָ
וּמִשְׁעַנְתֶּךָ הֵמָּה יְנַחֲמֻנִי: תַּעֲרֹךְ לְפָנַי שֻׁלְחָן נֶגֶד
צֹרְרָי דִּשַּׁנְתָּ בַשֶּׁמֶן רֹאשִׁי כּוֹסִי רְוָיָה: אַךְ טוֹב
וָחֶסֶד יִרְדְּפוּנִי כָּל־יְמֵי חַיָּי וְשַׁבְתִּי בְּבֵית יְהֹוָה
לְאֹרֶךְ יָמִים:

## II

### Choir

לְכָה דוֹדִי לִקְרַאת כַּלָּה. פְּנֵי שַׁבָּת נְקַבְּלָה:

לִקְרַאת שַׁבָּת לְכוּ וְנֵלְכָה. כִּי הִיא מְקוֹר
הַבְּרָכָה. מֵרֹאשׁ מִקֶּדֶם נְסוּכָה. סוֹף מַעֲשֶׂה
בְּמַחֲשָׁבָה תְּחִלָּה:

לְכָה דוֹדִי לִקְרַאת כַּלָּה. פְּנֵי שַׁבָּת נְקַבְּלָה:

הִתְעוֹרְרִי הִתְעוֹרְרִי. כִּי בָא אוֹרֵךְ קוּמִי אוֹרִי.
עוּרִי עוּרִי שִׁיר דַּבֵּרִי. כְּבוֹד יְיָ עָלַיִךְ נִגְלָה:

לְכָה דוֹדִי לִקְרַאת כַּלָּה. פְּנֵי שַׁבָּת נְקַבְּלָה:

בּוֹאִי בְשָׁלוֹם עֲטֶרֶת בַּעְלָהּ. גַּם בְּשִׂמְחָה
וּבְצָהֳלָה. תּוֹךְ אֱמוּנֵי עַם סְגֻלָּה. בּוֹאִי כַלָּה. בּוֹאִי
כַלָּה:

לְכָה דוֹדִי לִקְרַאת כַּלָּה. פְּנֵי שַׁבָּת נְקַבְּלָה:

Beloved, come, the bride to meet,
The Princess Sabbath let us greet.

Come, to the Sabbath greetings bring,
For it is blessing's constant spring:
Of old ordained, divinely taught,
Last in creation, first in thought.

Beloved, come, the bride to meet,
The Sabbath Princess let us greet.

> Arouse thyself, awake and shine,
> Thy light has come, the light divine;
> Awake and sing, and over thee
> The glory of the Lord shall be.

Beloved, come, the bride to meet,
The Sabbath Princess let us greet.

> Crown of thy husband, come in peace;
> Let joy and gladsome song increase.
> Among His faithful, sorrow-tried,
> His chosen people,—come, O bride.

Beloved, come, the bride to meet,
The Sabbath Princess let us greet.

### Reader

On this day, holy unto Israel, we enter this sanctuary to unite with our brethren in worship. We come unto Thee, O God, with joyous gratitude for the strength Thou hast given us to do our work during the past week, and for the fortitude to meet trials and temptations. May this hour of devotion awaken within us the consciousness of Thy presence, and bring peace and rest to our spirits. Aid us to banish all anxiety and fear, all fretting and complaining, and sustain our hearts with faith. Send forth Thy light that we may walk in the way of Thy commandments. Draw our spirits toward Thee, and let Thy truth lead us. Help us to become instruments of Thy will. Through days of labor and Sabbaths of rest, through our daily tasks and our worship, we would minister unto Thee. Let the beauty of Thy holiness shine into our hearts that we may grow more steadfast in our faith and in our love of Thee and of our fellowmen. Amen.

## Responsive Reading

Reader

Only for God doth my soul wait in stillness; from Him cometh my hope.

Congregation

*He alone is my rock and my salvation, I shall not be moved.*

Show me Thy ways, O Lord; teach me Thy paths, guide me in Thy truth.

*Whom have I in heaven but Thee? And having Thee I desire none else upon earth.*

My flesh and my heart fail, but God is my strength and my portion forever.

*Wait for the Lord, be strong, and let thy heart take courage.*

Create in me a clean heart, O God; and renew a steadfast spirit within me.

*When many cares perplex me, Thy comfort delights my soul.*

My times are in Thy hand, and Thou wilt guide and sustain me even unto the end.

*With Thee is the fountain of life; in Thy light do we see light.*

(Congregation rises)

### Reader

בָּרְכוּ אֶת־יְיָ הַמְבֹרָךְ:

Praise ye the Lord, to whom all praise is due.

### Choir and Congregation

בָּרוּךְ יְיָ הַמְבֹרָךְ לְעוֹלָם וָעֶד:

Praised be the Lord to whom all praise is due forever and ever.

(Congregation is seated)

### Reader

Ever-living God! Thy majesty is proclaimed by the marvels of earth and sky. Sun, moon and stars testify of Thy power and wisdom. Day follows day in endless succession and the years vanish, but Thy sovereignty endures. Though all things pass, let not Thy glory depart from us. Help us to become co-workers with Thee and endow our fleeting days with abiding worth.

### Congregation and Reader

All goodness and truth are Thine, O Lord. May no evil estrange us from Thee, nor error darken our vision of Thy purposes. Help us to discern Thy justice and to understand Thy will. In adversity and in prosperity, let Thy law be a lamp unto our feet to illumine our path. May we so labor in Thy service that our lives become a hymn of praise unto Thee.

(Congregation rises)

## Congregation and Reader

שְׁמַע יִשְׂרָאֵל יְהֹוָה אֱלֹהֵינוּ יְהֹוָה אֶחָד:

Hear, O Israel: The Lord our God, the Lord is One.

בָּרוּךְ שֵׁם כְּבוֹד מַלְכוּתוֹ לְעוֹלָם וָעֶד:

Praised be His name whose glorious kingdom is forever and ever.

(Congregation is seated)

## Reader

וְאָהַבְתָּ אֵת יְיָ אֱלֹהֶיךָ בְּכָל־לְבָבְךָ וּבְכָל־נַפְשְׁךָ
וּבְכָל־מְאֹדֶךָ: וְהָיוּ הַדְּבָרִים הָאֵלֶּה אֲשֶׁר אָנֹכִי
מְצַוְּךָ הַיּוֹם עַל־לְבָבֶךָ: וְשִׁנַּנְתָּם לְבָנֶיךָ וְדִבַּרְתָּ
בָּם. בְּשִׁבְתְּךָ בְּבֵיתֶךָ וּבְלֶכְתְּךָ בַדֶּרֶךְ וּבְשָׁכְבְּךָ
וּבְקוּמֶךָ: וּקְשַׁרְתָּם לְאוֹת עַל־יָדֶךָ. וְהָיוּ לְטֹטָפֹת
בֵּין עֵינֶיךָ: וּכְתַבְתָּם עַל־מְזֻזוֹת בֵּיתֶךָ וּבִשְׁעָרֶיךָ:
לְמַעַן תִּזְכְּרוּ וַעֲשִׂיתֶם אֶת־כָּל־מִצְוֹתָי וִהְיִיתֶם
קְדֹשִׁים לֵאלֹהֵיכֶם: אֲנִי יְיָ אֱלֹהֵיכֶם:

## Congregation and Reader

Thou shalt love the Lord, thy God, with all thy heart, with all thy soul, and with all thy might. And

these words, which I command thee this day, shall
be upon thy heart. Thou shalt teach them diligently
unto thy children, and shalt speak of them when thou
sittest in thy house, when thou walkest by the way,
when thou liest down, and when thou risest up. Thou
shalt bind them for a sign upon thy hand, and they shall
be for frontlets between thine eyes. Thou shalt write
them upon the doorposts of thy house and upon thy
gates: That ye may remember and do all My commandments and be holy unto your God.

## Responsive Reading

**Reader**
In truth, the Lord of the universe is our redeemer.

**Congregation**
*He is the refuge of the oppressed, the deliverer of
the persecuted.*

Let us praise Him who giveth rest unto the weary and
hope unto the despondent.

*Let us enthrone Him as our King and hold fast unto
His law.*

Blessed be the Sabbath, the queen of days, which
brings unto Israel enrichment of soul.

*Even as Israel has kept the Sabbath, so the Sabbath
has kept Israel.*

Happy are they who remember the Sabbath and sanctify it with prayer and song.

*They rejoice in the Lord, and delight in the heritage
of their fathers.*

Their homes are filled with light and gladness, their
hearts are steadfast, trusting in the Lord.
*The joy of the Lord is their strength.*

### Choir

יִשְׂמְחוּ בְמַלְכוּתְךָ שׁוֹמְרֵי שַׁבָּת וְקוֹרְאֵי עֹֽנֶג עַם
מְקַדְּשֵׁי שְׁבִיעִי. כֻּלָּם יִשְׂבְּעוּ וְיִתְעַנְּגוּ מִטּוּבֶֽךָ.
וּבַשְּׁבִיעִי רָצִֽיתָ בּוֹ וְקִדַּשְׁתּוֹ חֶמְדַּת יָמִים אוֹתוֹ
קָרָֽאתָ זֵֽכֶר לְמַעֲשֵׂה בְרֵאשִׁית:

They who keep the Sabbath and call it a delight, rejoice in Thy kingdom. All who hallow the seventh
day shall be gladdened by Thy goodness. This day is
Israel's festival of the spirit, sanctified and blessed by
Thee, the most precious of days, a symbol of the joy
of creation.

Reader

בָּרוּךְ אַתָּה יְיָ אֱלֹהֵינוּ וֵאלֹהֵי אֲבוֹתֵינוּ. אֱלֹהֵי
אַבְרָהָם אֱלֹהֵי יִצְחָק וֵאלֹהֵי יַעֲקֹב. הָאֵל הַגָּדוֹל
הַגִּבּוֹר וְהַנּוֹרָא. אֵל עֶלְיוֹן. גּוֹמֵל חֲסָדִים טוֹבִים.
וְקֹנֵה הַכֹּל וְזוֹכֵר חַסְדֵי אָבוֹת. וּמֵבִיא גְאֻלָּה לִבְנֵי
בְנֵיהֶם. לְמַעַן שְׁמוֹ בְּאַהֲבָה: מֶלֶךְ עוֹזֵר וּמוֹשִׁיעַ
וּמָגֵן. בָּרוּךְ אַתָּה יְיָ מָגֵן אַבְרָהָם:

אַתָּה גִּבּוֹר לְעוֹלָם אֲדֹנָי. רַב לְהוֹשִׁיעַ. מְכַלְכֵּל
חַיִּים בְּחֶסֶד. מְחַיֶּה הַכֹּל בְּרַחֲמִים רַבִּים. סוֹמֵךְ
נוֹפְלִים וְרוֹפֵא חוֹלִים וּמַתִּיר אֲסוּרִים. וּמְקַיֵּם
אֱמוּנָתוֹ לִישֵׁנֵי עָפָר. מִי כָמוֹךְ בַּעַל גְּבוּרוֹת. וּמִי
דוֹמֶה־לָּךְ. מֶלֶךְ מֵמִית וּמְחַיֶּה. וּמַצְמִיחַ יְשׁוּעָה:
בָּרוּךְ אַתָּה יְיָ נֹטֵעַ בְּתוֹכֵנוּ חַיֵּי עוֹלָם:

Reader

Praised be Thou, O Lord, God of our fathers, God
of Abraham, Isaac and Jacob, great, mighty, and exalted. Thou bestowest lovingkindness upon all Thy
children. Thou rememberest the devotion of the
fathers. In Thy love, Thou bringest redemption to
their descendants for the sake of Thy name. Thou art
our King and Helper, our Savior and Protector. Praised
be Thou, O Lord, Shield of Abraham.

Eternal is Thy power, O Lord, Thou art mighty to save. In lovingkindness Thou sustainest the living; in the multitude of Thy mercies, Thou preservest all. Thou upholdest the falling and healest the sick; freest the captives and keepest faith with Thy children in death as in life. Who is like unto Thee, Almighty God, Author of life and death, Source of salvation? Praised be Thou, O Lord, who hast implanted within us eternal life.

### Reader

Almighty and merciful God, Thou hast called Israel to Thy service and found him worthy to bear witness unto Thy truth among the peoples of the earth. Give us grace to fulfil this mission with zeal tempered by wisdom and guided by regard for other men's faith. May our life prove the strength of our own belief in the truths we proclaim. May our bearing toward our neighbors, our faithfulness in every sphere of duty, our compassion for the suffering and our patience under trial show that He whose law we obey is indeed the God of all goodness, the Father of all men, that to serve Him is perfect freedom and to worship Him the soul's purest happiness.

O Lord, open our eyes that we may see and welcome all truth, whether shining from the annals of ancient revelations or reaching us through the seers of our own time; for Thou hidest not Thy light from any generation of Thy children that yearn for Thee and seek Thy guidance.

## Congregation and Reader

We pray for the masters and teachers in Israel that they may dispense Thy truth with earnestness and zeal, yet not without charity. May the law of love be found on their lips, and may they by precept and example lead many in the ways of righteousness.

Bless, O God, all endeavors, wherever made, to lift up the fallen, to redeem the sinful, to bring back those who wander from the right path and restore them to a worthy life.

Endow us with purity of heart and steadfastness of spirit that our lives may testify of Thee and sanctify Thy name. O satisfy us early with Thy mercy, that we may rejoice and be glad all our days. Amen.

## Silent Prayer
### (or such other prayer as the heart may prompt)

O God, who art the strength of all that trust in Thee, my soul is filled with gratitude for the numberless blessings Thou bestowest on me. With a father's tender care Thou rememberest me every day and every hour.

Teach me, O Lord, to obey Thy will, to be content with what, in Thy wisdom, Thou hast allotted to me, and to share Thy gifts with those who need my help. Guide me, O Father, with Thy good counsel, and hold in Thy keeping the lives of those dear to me. May Thy presence dwell within my home; may peace and happiness abide in it, and love unite all who live under its shadow. And when, in Thy wisdom, Thou sendest trials and sorrows, grant me strength to bear them patiently, and courage to trust in Thy help. Guard Thou my going out and my coming in, now and evermore. Amen.

*(or the following Psalm)*

(Psalm cxxi)

I lift up mine eyes unto the mountains, whence cometh my help. My help cometh from the Lord, who made heaven and earth. He will not suffer thy foot to be moved; He that keepeth thee will not slumber. Behold, He that keepeth Israel doth neither slumber nor sleep. The Lord is thy keeper; the Lord is thy shade upon thy right hand. The sun shall not smite thee by day, nor the moon by night. The Lord shall keep thee from all evil; He shall keep thy soul. The Lord shall guard thy going out and thy coming in, from this time forth and forever.

## Choir

May the words of my mouth and the meditation of my heart be acceptable unto Thee, O Lord, my Rock and my Redeemer.

(Those congregations which read the Torah, turn to page 94)

### READING FROM SCRIPTURE

(For ADORATION and KADDISH, turn to page 71)

## III

*Choir*

(Psalm xcvii)

The Lord reigneth; let the earth rejoice; let the multitude of isles be glad. Clouds and darkness are round about Him; righteousness and justice are the foundations of His throne. The heavens declare His righteousness, and all the peoples behold His glory. Zion heareth and is glad, and the daughters of Judah rejoice; because of Thy judgments, O Lord. O ye that love the Lord, hate evil; He preserveth the souls of His saints; He delivereth them out of the hand of the wicked. Light is sown for the righteous, and gladness for the upright in heart. Be glad in the Lord, ye righteous; and give thanks to His holy name.

יְיָ מָלָךְ תָּגֵל הָאָרֶץ
יִשְׂמְחוּ אִיִּים רַבִּים: עָנָן
וַעֲרָפֶל סְבִיבָיו צֶדֶק
וּמִשְׁפָּט מְכוֹן כִּסְאוֹ:
הִגִּידוּ הַשָּׁמַיִם צִדְקוֹ
וְרָאוּ כָל־הָעַמִּים כְּבוֹדוֹ:
שָׁמְעָה וַתִּשְׂמַח צִיּוֹן
וַתָּגֵלְנָה בְּנוֹת יְהוּדָה לְמַעַן
מִשְׁפָּטֶיךָ יְיָ: אֹהֲבֵי יְיָ
שִׂנְאוּ רָע שֹׁמֵר נַפְשׁוֹת
חֲסִידָיו מִיַּד רְשָׁעִים
יַצִּילֵם: אוֹר־זָרֻעַ לַצַּדִּיק
וּלְיִשְׁרֵי־לֵב שִׂמְחָה: שִׂמְחוּ
צַדִּיקִים בַּיְיָ וְהוֹדוּ לְזֵכֶר
קָדְשׁוֹ:

*Silent Prayer*

*Reader*

God and Father, we have entered Thy sanctuary on this Sabbath to hallow Thy name and to offer unto Thee prayers of thanksgiving. The week of toil is ended, the day of rest has come. Thou, Creator of all, hast given us the blessing of labor, so that by our work we may fashion things of use and beauty. May the fruit of our labor be acceptable unto Thee. May each new Sabbath find us going from strength to strength, so that by Thy grace we may be helped to even worthier work. Make us conscious of our obligation to Thee and of the opportunities for service which Thou hast put within our reach. Help us to use our powers for the benefit of our fellowmen, so that the hearts of Thy children may be gladdened by the work of our hands.

*Responsive Reading*

Reader

I rejoiced when they said unto me: Let us go unto the house of the Lord.

Congregation

Wherewith shall I come unto the Lord and bow before God on high?

It hath been told thee, O man, what is good, and what the Lord doth require of thee.

Only to do justice, and to love mercy, and to walk humbly with thy God.

Have we not all one Father? Hath not one God created us?

Why do we deal treacherously brother against brother?

Proclaim liberty throughout the land unto all the inhabitants thereof.

*Let justice well up as waters and righteousness like
a mighty stream.*
Seek good and not evil that ye may live.
*And so the Lord God of hosts shall be with us.*

(Congregation rises)

*Reader*

בָּרְכוּ אֶת־יְיָ הַמְבֹרָךְ:

Praise ye the Lord, to whom all praise is due.

*Choir and Congregation*

בָּרוּךְ יְיָ הַמְבֹרָךְ לְעוֹלָם וָעֶד:

Praised be the Lord to whom all praise is due forever
and ever.

(Congregation is seated)

*Reader*

O Lord, how can we know Thee? Where can we
find Thee? Thou art as close to us as breathing and
yet art farther than the farthermost star. Thou art as
mysterious as the vast solitudes of the night and yet
art as familiar to us as the light of the sun. To the
seer of old Thou didst say: Thou canst not see my
face, but I will make all My goodness pass before Thee.
Even so does Thy goodness pass before us in the realm
of nature and in the varied experiences of our lives.
When justice burns like a flaming fire within us, when
love evokes willing sacrifice from us, when, to the last
full measure of selfless devotion, we proclaim our belief
in the ultimate triumph of truth and righteousness, do
we not bow down before the vision of Thy goodness?
Thou livest within our hearts, as Thou dost pervade
the world, and we through righteousness behold Thy
presence.

(Congregation rises)

### Reader, then Choir and Congregation

שְׁמַע יִשְׂרָאֵל יְהֹוָה אֱלֹהֵינוּ יְהֹוָה אֶחָד:

Hear, O Israel: The Lord our God, the Lord is One.

בָּרוּךְ שֵׁם כְּבוֹד מַלְכוּתוֹ לְעוֹלָם וָעֶד:

Praised be His name whose glorious kingdom is forever and ever.

(Congregation is seated)

### Reader

וְאָהַבְתָּ אֵת יְיָ אֱלֹהֶיךָ בְּכָל־לְבָבְךָ וּבְכָל־נַפְשְׁךָ
וּבְכָל־מְאֹדֶךָ: וְהָיוּ הַדְּבָרִים הָאֵלֶּה אֲשֶׁר אָנֹכִי
מְצַוְּךָ הַיּוֹם עַל־לְבָבֶךָ: וְשִׁנַּנְתָּם לְבָנֶיךָ וְדִבַּרְתָּ
בָּם. בְּשִׁבְתְּךָ בְּבֵיתֶךָ וּבְלֶכְתְּךָ בַדֶּרֶךְ וּבְשָׁכְבְּךָ
וּבְקוּמֶךָ: וּקְשַׁרְתָּם לְאוֹת עַל־יָדֶךָ. וְהָיוּ לְטֹטָפֹת
בֵּין עֵינֶיךָ: וּכְתַבְתָּם עַל־מְזֻזוֹת בֵּיתֶךָ וּבִשְׁעָרֶיךָ:
לְמַעַן תִּזְכְּרוּ וַעֲשִׂיתֶם אֶת־כָּל־מִצְוֹתָי וִהְיִיתֶם
קְדֹשִׁים לֵאלֹהֵיכֶם: אֲנִי יְיָ אֱלֹהֵיכֶם:

### Congregation and Reader

Thou shalt love the Lord, thy God, with all thy
heart, with all thy soul, and with all thy might. And
these words, which I command thee this day, shall be
upon thy heart. Thou shalt teach them diligently unto
thy children, and shalt speak of them when thou sittest in thy house, when thou walkest by the way, when

thou liest down, and when thou risest up. Thou shalt bind them for a sign upon thy hand, and they shall be for frontlets between thine eyes. Thou shalt write them upon the doorposts of thy house and upon thy gates: That ye may remember and do all My commandments and be holy unto your God.

## Responsive Reading

Reader

Eternal truth it is that Thou alone art God and there is none else.

Congregation

*May the righteous of all nations rejoice in Thy grace and exult in Thy justice.*

Let them beat their swords into plowshares and their spears into pruning-hooks:

*Let nation not lift up sword against nation nor learn war any more.*

Righteousness exalteth a nation, but sin is a reproach to any people.

*Treasures of wickedness profit not but righteousness delivereth from death.*

Thou shalt not hate thy brother in thy heart:

*But thou shalt love thy neighbor as thyself.*

The stranger that sojourneth with you shall be unto you as the home-born.

*For ye were strangers in the land of Egypt.*

What mean ye that ye crush My people and grind the face of the poor, saith the Lord.

*I know that the Lord will maintain the cause of the poor. and the right of the needy.*

### Choir

Who is like unto Thee, O Lord? Who is like unto Thee, glorious in holiness, awe-inspiring, working wonders?

### Reader

Thy children acknowledged Thy sovereign power, and exclaimed:

### Choir

The Lord shall reign forever and ever.

### Reader

As Thou hast redeemed Israel and saved him from arms stronger than his own, so mayest Thou redeem all who are oppressed and persecuted. Praised be Thou, O Lord, Redeemer of Israel.

### Choir

The children of Israel shall keep the Sabbath, to observe the Sabbath throughout their generations, for a perpetual covenant. It is a sign between Me and the the children of Israel forever.

Choir

מִי־כָמֹכָה בָּאֵלִם יְיָ. מִי כָּמֹכָה נֶאְדָּר בַּקֹּדֶשׁ
נוֹרָא תְהִלֹּת עֹשֵׂה פֶלֶא:

Reader

מַלְכוּתְךָ רָאוּ בָנֶיךָ. זֶה אֵלִי עָנוּ וְאָמְרוּ:

Choir

יְיָ יִמְלֹךְ לְעֹלָם וָעֶד:

Reader

וְנֶאֱמַר כִּי־פָדָה יְהֹוָה אֶת־יַעֲקֹב וּגְאָלוֹ מִיַּד חָזָק
מִמֶּנּוּ. בָּרוּךְ אַתָּה יְיָ גָּאַל יִשְׂרָאֵל:

Choir

וְשָׁמְרוּ בְנֵי־יִשְׂרָאֵל אֶת־הַשַּׁבָּת לַעֲשׂוֹת אֶת־
הַשַּׁבָּת לְדֹרֹתָם בְּרִית עוֹלָם: בֵּינִי וּבֵין בְּנֵי יִשְׂרָאֵל
אוֹת הִוא לְעֹלָם:

Reader

בָּרוּךְ אַתָּה יְיָ אֱלֹהֵינוּ וֵאלֹהֵי אֲבוֹתֵינוּ. אֱלֹהֵי
אַבְרָהָם אֱלֹהֵי יִצְחָק וֵאלֹהֵי יַעֲקֹב. הָאֵל הַגָּדוֹל
הַגִּבּוֹר וְהַנּוֹרָא. אֵל עֶלְיוֹן. גּוֹמֵל חֲסָדִים טוֹבִים.
וְקֹנֵה הַכֹּל וְזוֹכֵר חַסְדֵי אָבוֹת. וּמֵבִיא גְאֻלָּה לִבְנֵי
בְנֵיהֶם. לְמַעַן שְׁמוֹ בְּאַהֲבָה: מֶלֶךְ עוֹזֵר וּמוֹשִׁיעַ

וּמָגֵן. בָּרוּךְ אַתָּה יְיָ מָגֵן אַבְרָהָם:

אַתָּה גִּבּוֹר לְעוֹלָם אֲדֹנָי. רַב לְהוֹשִׁיעַ. מְכַלְכֵּל
חַיִּים בְּחֶסֶד. מְחַיֵּה הַכֹּל בְּרַחֲמִים רַבִּים. סוֹמֵךְ
נוֹפְלִים וְרוֹפֵא חוֹלִים וּמַתִּיר אֲסוּרִים. וּמְקַיֵּם
אֱמוּנָתוֹ לִישֵׁנֵי עָפָר. מִי כָמוֹךָ בַּעַל גְּבוּרוֹת. וּמִי
דוֹמֶה־לָּךְ. מֶלֶךְ מֵמִית וּמְחַיֶּה. וּמַצְמִיחַ יְשׁוּעָה:
בָּרוּךְ אַתָּה יְיָ נֹטֵעַ בְּתוֹכֵנוּ חַיֵּי עוֹלָם:

### Reader

Praised be Thou, O Lord, God of our fathers, God
of Abraham, Isaac and Jacob, great, mighty, and exalted. Thou bestowest lovingkindness upon all Thy
children. Thou rememberest the devotion of the
fathers. In love Thou bringest redemption to their descendants for the sake of Thy name. Thou art our
King and Helper, our Savior and Protector. Praised be
Thou, O Lord, Shield of Abraham.

Eternal is Thy power, O Lord, Thou art mighty to
save. In lovingkindness Thou sustainest the living; in
the multitude of Thy mercies, Thou preservest all.
Thou upholdest the falling, and healest the sick; freest
the captives and keepest faith with Thy children in
death as in life. Who is like unto Thee, Almighty God,
Author of life and death, Source of salvation? Praised
be Thou, O Lord, who hast implanted within us eternal
life.

#### Reader

O Lord, though we are prone to seek favors for ourselves alone, yet when we come into Thy presence, we are lifted above petty thoughts of self. We become ashamed of our littleness and are made to feel that we can worship Thee in holiness only as we serve our brothers in love.

How much we owe to the labors of our brothers! Day by day they dig far away from the sun that we may be warm, enlist in outposts of peril that we may be secure and brave the terrors of the unknown for truths that shed light on our way. Numberless gifts and blessings have been laid in our cradles as our birth-right.

Let us then, O Lord, be just and great-hearted in our dealings with our fellowmen, sharing with them the fruit of our common labor, acknowledging before Thee that we are but stewards of whatever we possess. Help us to be among those who are willing to sacrifice that others may not hunger, who dare to be bearers of light in the dark loneliness of stricken lives, who struggle and even bleed for the triumph of righteousness among men. So may we be co-workers with Thee in the building of Thy kingdom which has been our vision and goal through the ages.

#### Congregation and Reader

Our God and God of our fathers, grant that our worship on this Sabbath be acceptable to Thee. Sanctify us through Thy commandments that we may share in the blessings of Thy word. Teach us to be satisfied with the gifts of Thy goodness and gratefully to rejoice in all Thy mercies. Purify our hearts that we may serve Thee in truth. O help us to preserve the Sabbath as Israel's heritage from generation to generation, that it may ever bring rest and joy, peace and comfort to the dwellings of our brethren, and through it Thy name be hallowed in all the earth. Praised be Thou, O Lord, who sanctifiest the Sabbath.

### Choir: Amen.

### Silent Prayer

(or such other prayer as the heart may prompt)

In this moment of silent communion with Thee, O Lord, a still, small voice speaks in the depth of my spirit. It speaks to me of the things I must do to attain holy kinship with Thee and to grow in the likeness of Thee. I must do my allotted task with unflagging faithfulness even though the eye of no taskmaster is on me. I must be gentle in the face of ingratitude or when slander distorts my noblest motives. I must come to the end of each day with a feeling that I have used its gifts gratefully and faced its trials bravely. O Lord, help me to be ever more like Thee, holy for Thou art holy, loving for Thou art love. Speak to me, then, O Lord, as I seek Thee again and again in the stillness of meditation, until Thy bidding shall at last become for me a hallowed discipline, a familiar way of life, so that I may live on in deeds that bless other lives and leave behind me the heritage of a good name. Amen.

*(or the following Psalm)*

(Psalm xv)

Lord, who shall sojourn in Thy tabernacle?  Who shall dwell upon Thy holy mountain?  He that walketh uprightly, and worketh righteousness, and speaketh truth in his heart; that hath no slander upon his tongue, nor doeth evil to his fellow, nor taketh up a reproach against his neighbor; in whose eyes a vile person is despised, but he honoreth them that fear the Lord; he that sweareth to his own hurt, and changeth not; he that putteth not out his money on interest, nor taketh a bribe against the innocent.  He that doeth these things shall never be moved.

## Choir

May the words of my mouth and the meditation of my heart, be acceptable unto Thee, O Lord, my Rock and my Redeemer.  Amen.

(Those congregations which read the Torah, turn to page 94)

### READING FROM SCRIPTURE

(For ADORATION and KADDISH, turn to page 71)

## IV

### Choir

(Psalm xcviii)

O sing unto the Lord a new song; for He hath done marvelous things; His right hand, and His holy arm, hath wrought salvation for Him. The Lord hath made known His salvation; His righteousness hath He revealed in the sight of the nations. He hath remembered His mercy and His faithfulness toward the house of Israel; all the ends of the earth have seen the salvation of our God. Shout unto the Lord, all the earth; break forth and sing for joy, yea, sing praises. Sing praises unto the Lord with the harp; with the harp and the voice of melody. With trumpets and sound of the horn before the Lord, for He

מִזְמוֹר שִׁירוּ לַיְיָ שִׁיר
חָדָשׁ כִּי־נִפְלָאוֹת עָשָׂה
הוֹשִׁיעָה־לּוֹ יְמִינוֹ וּזְרוֹעַ
קָדְשׁוֹ: הוֹדִיעַ יְיָ יְשׁוּעָתוֹ
לְעֵינֵי הַגּוֹיִם גִּלָּה צִדְקָתוֹ:
זָכַר חַסְדּוֹ וֶאֱמוּנָתוֹ לְבֵית
יִשְׂרָאֵל רָאוּ כָל־אַפְסֵי־
אֶרֶץ אֵת יְשׁוּעַת אֱלֹהֵינוּ:
הָרִיעוּ לַיְיָ כָּל־הָאָרֶץ
פִּצְחוּ וְרַנְּנוּ וְזַמֵּרוּ: זַמְּרוּ
לַיְיָ בְּכִנּוֹר בְּכִנּוֹר וְקוֹל
זִמְרָה: בַּחֲצֹצְרוֹת וְקוֹל
שׁוֹפָר הָרִיעוּ לִפְנֵי הַמֶּלֶךְ
יְיָ: יִרְעַם הַיָּם וּמְלֹאוֹ תֵּבֵל
וְיֹשְׁבֵי בָהּ: נְהָרוֹת יִמְחֲאוּ־
כָף יַחַד הָרִים יְרַנֵּנוּ: לִפְנֵי

is come to judge the earth; He will judge the world with righteousness, and the peoples with equity.

יְיָ כִּי בָא לִשְׁפֹּט הָאָרֶץ יִשְׁפֹּט תֵּבֵל בְּצֶדֶק וְעַמִּים בְּמֵישָׁרִים:

### Silent Prayer

### Reader

Gathered in Thy house, O God, now that the shadows of evening fall, we open our hearts to the sweet and comforting influences of the day hallowed for Thy worship.

We thank Thee for all Thy blessings, for the dispensations of Thy providence and for the tokens of Thy goodness toward us. Every day we receive of the fulness of Thy bounty; by Thy protection we have passed safely through the dangers that beset our paths. When we are tried by sorrow and days of anguish are allotted to us, it is not that Thou hast forsaken us. Thine eye is ever upon us and Thine arm still guides us. In Thine own time, O God, we shall say with the ancient seer: I thank Thee, that Thou has tried me; for now that Thy visitation is past, Thou comfortest me, and I draw waters of joy from the wells of salvation.

We pray for all people who at this hour are in tribulation, in sickness, in want, in danger of body or soul. We name in our hearts those who are near to us and in whose afflictions we are afflicted. Let them see Thy help and grant them a blessed release from their trials.

*Congregation and Reader*

O Lord, be merciful to us in our failings and trespasses and, when we have gone astray, help us to find our way back to Thee. Grant us vision and courage, that, unhindered and unafraid, we may pursue the paths of truth and duty. Enlighten our minds that we put to the highest use every gift of Thy hand; that we cherish a good conscience above worldly gain, and a healthy soul above sensual gratification. We need Thy help, O Father, in our endeavor to fulfil the deeper longings of our hearts. Be with us as Thou wast with our fathers, and help us so to live that in work or rest, in company or solitude, we may testify to our faith in Thee and Thy law.

(Congregation rises)

*Reader*

בָּרְכוּ אֶת־יְיָ הַמְבֹרָךְ׃

Praise ye the Lord, to whom all praise is due.

*Choir and Congregation*

בָּרוּךְ יְיָ הַמְבֹרָךְ לְעוֹלָם וָעֶד׃

Praised be the Lord to whom all praise is due forever and ever.

(Congregation is seated)

## Reader

Thou art our God and Father, the source whence life and all its blessings flow. Wherever we turn our gaze we behold signs of Thy goodness and grace. The fulness of Thy power is disclosed to us in Thy gracious dealings with Israel, in Thy constant shaping of human destiny, and in the marvelous works of Thy creation. The whole universe proclaims Thy glory. Thy loving spirit hovers over all Thy works, guiding and sustaining them. The harmony and grandeur of nature speak to us of Thee, our God, of Thine infinite might and majesty.

*(Congregation rises)*

## Reader, then Choir and Congregation

שְׁמַע יִשְׂרָאֵל יְהֹוָה אֱלֹהֵינוּ יְהֹוָה אֶחָד:

Hear, O Israel: The Lord our God, the Lord is One.

בָּרוּךְ שֵׁם כְּבוֹד מַלְכוּתוֹ לְעוֹלָם וָעֶד:

Praised be His name whose glorious kingdom is forever and ever.

*(Congregation is seated)*

*Reader*

וְאָהַבְתָּ אֵת יְיָ אֱלֹהֶיךָ בְּכָל־לְבָבְךָ וּבְכָל־נַפְשְׁךָ
וּבְכָל־מְאֹדֶךָ: וְהָיוּ הַדְּבָרִים הָאֵלֶּה אֲשֶׁר אָנֹכִי
מְצַוְּךָ הַיּוֹם עַל־לְבָבֶךָ: וְשִׁנַּנְתָּם לְבָנֶיךָ וְדִבַּרְתָּ
בָּם. בְּשִׁבְתְּךָ בְּבֵיתֶךָ וּבְלֶכְתְּךָ בַדֶּרֶךְ וּבְשָׁכְבְּךָ
וּבְקוּמֶךָ: וּקְשַׁרְתָּם לְאוֹת עַל־יָדֶךָ. וְהָיוּ לְטֹטָפֹת
בֵּין עֵינֶיךָ: וּכְתַבְתָּם עַל־מְזֻזוֹת בֵּיתֶךָ וּבִשְׁעָרֶיךָ׃
לְמַעַן תִּזְכְּרוּ וַעֲשִׂיתֶם אֶת־כָּל־מִצְוֹתָי וִהְיִיתֶם
קְדֹשִׁים לֵאלֹהֵיכֶם: אֲנִי יְיָ אֱלֹהֵיכֶם:

*Congregation and Reader*

Thou shalt love the Lord, thy God, with all thy
heart, with all thy soul, and with all thy might. And
these words, which I command thee this day, shall be
upon thy heart. Thou shalt teach them diligently unto
thy children, and shalt speak of them when thou
sittest in thy house, when thou walkest by the way,
when thou liest down, and when thou risest up. Thou
shalt bind them for a sign upon thy hand, and they
shall be for frontlets between thine eyes. Thou shalt
write them upon the doorposts of thy house and upon
thy gates: That ye may remember and do all My commandments and be holy unto your God.

## Responsive Reading

**Reader**

Trust in the Lord with all thy heart and lean not upon thine own understanding.

**Congregation**

For He is our God, and we are His people, consecrated to His service.

Remember all the commandments of the Lord, and do them; that ye go not about after your own heart and your own eyes.

It is He who redeemed us from the hand of oppressors, and revived our spirits when our own strength failed us.

His works and wonders surpass our understanding, His gifts and blessings are without number.

We rejoice in His sovereign power; we praise and give thanks unto His name:

## Choir

מִי־כָמֹכָה בָּאֵלִים יְיָ. מִי כָּמֹכָה נֶאְדָּר בַּקֹּדֶשׁ
נוֹרָא תְהִלֹּת עֹשֵׂה פֶלֶא:

Who is like unto Thee, O Lord, among the mighty? Who is like unto Thee, glorious in holiness, awe-inspiring, working wonders?

### Reader

Thy children acknowledged Thy sovereign power, and exclaimed:

### Choir

The Lord shall reign forever and ever.

### Reader

As Thou hast redeemed Israel and saved him from arms stronger than his own, so mayest Thou redeem all who are oppressed and persecuted. Praised be Thou, O Lord, Redeemer of Israel.

### Choir

The children of Israel shall keep the Sabbath, to observe the Sabbath throughout their generations, for a perpetual covenant. It is a sign between Me and the children of Israel forever.

Reader

מַלְכוּתְךָ רָאוּ בָנֶיךָ. זֶה אֵלִי עָנוּ וְאָמְרוּ:

Choir

יְיָ יִמְלֹךְ לְעֹלָם וָעֶד:

Reader

וְנֶאֱמַר כִּי־פָדָה יְהֹוָה אֶת־יַעֲקֹב וּגְאָלוֹ מִיַּד חָזָק
מִמֶּנּוּ. בָּרוּךְ אַתָּה יְיָ גָּאַל יִשְׂרָאֵל:

Choir

וְשָׁמְרוּ בְנֵי־יִשְׂרָאֵל אֶת־הַשַּׁבָּת לַעֲשׂוֹת אֶת־
הַשַּׁבָּת לְדֹרֹתָם בְּרִית עוֹלָם: בֵּינִי וּבֵין בְּנֵי יִשְׂרָאֵל
אוֹת הִוא לְעֹלָם:

### Congregation and Reader

Cause us, O Lord our God, to lie down each night in peace, and to awaken each morning to renewed life and strength. Spread over us the tabernacle of Thy peace. Help us to order our lives by Thy counsel, and lead us in the paths of righteousness. Be Thou a shield about us, protecting us from hate and war, from pestilence and sorrow. Curb Thou also within us the inclination to do evil, and shelter us beneath the shadow of Thy wings. Guard our going out and our coming in unto life and peace from this time forth and for evermore.

### Responsive Reading

Reader

Praised be Thou, O Lord, God of our fathers, God of Abraham, Isaac and Jacob, the ruler of heaven and earth.

Congregation

Thou shield of the fathers, protector of their children, revivest our drooping spirits.

The holy God, beyond compare, giveth rest to His people on His holy Sabbath Day.

We will serve Him with reverence, and offer thanks to His name continually.

To Him our thanks are due; He is the Lord of peace, who halloweth the Sabbath and blesseth it.

He sanctifieth our worship, and filleth our hearts with joy.

Congregation and Reader

הַשְׁכִּיבֵנוּ יְיָ אֱלֹהֵינוּ לְשָׁלוֹם. וְהַעֲמִידֵנוּ מַלְכֵּנוּ
לְחַיִּים. וּפְרוֹשׂ עָלֵינוּ סֻכַּת שְׁלוֹמֶךָ. וְתַקְּנֵנוּ בְּעֵצָה
טוֹבָה מִלְּפָנֶיךָ וְהוֹשִׁיעֵנוּ לְמַעַן שְׁמֶךָ. וְהָגֵן בַּעֲדֵנוּ
וְהָסֵר מֵעָלֵינוּ אוֹיֵב דֶּבֶר וְחֶרֶב וְרָעָב וְיָגוֹן וּבְצֵל
כְּנָפֶיךָ תַּסְתִּירֵנוּ. כִּי אֵל שׁוֹמְרֵנוּ וּמַצִּילֵנוּ אָתָּה. כִּי
אֵל מֶלֶךְ חַנּוּן וְרַחוּם אָתָּה. וּשְׁמוֹר צֵאתֵנוּ וּבוֹאֵנוּ
לְחַיִּים וּלְשָׁלוֹם מֵעַתָּה וְעַד עוֹלָם. וּפְרוֹשׂ עָלֵינוּ
סֻכַּת שְׁלוֹמֶךָ. בָּרוּךְ אַתָּה יְיָ שׁוֹמֵר עַמּוֹ יִשְׂרָאֵל
לָעַד:

Reader

בָּרוּךְ אַתָּה יְיָ אֱלֹהֵינוּ וֵאלֹהֵי אֲבוֹתֵינוּ אֱלֹהֵי
אַבְרָהָם אֱלֹהֵי יִצְחָק וֵאלֹהֵי יַעֲקֹב הָאֵל הַגָּדוֹל
הַגִּבּוֹר וְהַנּוֹרָא אֵל עֶלְיוֹן קֹנֵה שָׁמַיִם וָאָרֶץ:

מָגֵן אָבוֹת בִּדְבָרוֹ מְחַיֶּה הַכֹּל בְּמַאֲמָרוֹ. הָאֵל
הַקָּדוֹשׁ שֶׁאֵין כָּמוֹהוּ. הַמֵּנִיחַ לְעַמּוֹ בְּיוֹם שַׁבַּת קָדְשׁוֹ
כִּי בָם רָצָה לְהָנִיחַ לָהֶם. לְפָנָיו נַעֲבוֹד בְּיִרְאָה
וָפַחַד וְנוֹדֶה לִשְׁמוֹ בְּכָל־יוֹם תָּמִיד מֵעֵין הַבְּרָכוֹת.
אֵל הַהוֹדָאוֹת אֲדוֹן הַשָּׁלוֹם מְקַדֵּשׁ הַשַּׁבָּת וּמְבָרֵךְ
שְׁבִיעִי וּמֵנִיחַ בִּקְדֻשָּׁה לְעַם מְדֻשְּׁנֵי עֹנֶג זֵכֶר
לְמַעֲשֵׂה בְרֵאשִׁית:

### Reader

May the rest and quiet of this hour of worship refresh our inner life and renew in us the sense of Thy holy presence. Open our eyes that we behold truth and beauty in the words of the inspired teachers of Thy will. Animate our thoughts and endeavors with the power of Thy divine purposes, so that whatever our hand findeth to do, we may do with all our might. Fill our hearts with Sabbath peace and serenity, that we may hear the voice of Thy spirit and be moved to build our lives on the abiding foundations of Thy law.

### Congregation and Reader

Our God and God of our fathers, grant that our worship on this Sabbath be acceptable to Thee. Sanctify us through Thy commandments, and may we share in the blessings of Thy word. Teach us to be satisfied with the gifts of Thy goodness and gratefully to rejoice in all Thy mercies. Purify our hearts that we may serve Thee in truth. O help us to preserve the Sabbath as Israel's heritage from generation to generation, that it may bring rest and joy, peace and comfort to the dwellings of our brethren, and through it Thy name be hallowed in all the earth. Praised be Thou, O Lord, who sanctifiest the Sabbath.

### Silent Prayer

(or such other prayer as the heart may prompt)

In this glad hour of worship, I draw aside from toil and care, and lift my heart unto Thee for light and strength, for faith and courage. In the stress and turmoil of daily striving, I yield only too often to selfish ease and mean ambitions. I become so entangled in the things of earth that I lose the sense of life's simplicity and nobility. Fortify my spirit, enlighten my reason, and elevate my aims and desires, that I may devote all my powers of body and mind to Thy service. Thou hast implanted within me the yearning for the unseen and the infinite; instil Thou also within me fresh zeal and purpose, when my soul faints and my vision grows dim. O that my ideals would pervade all my thoughts and labors, that I might never lose sight of Thy supreme realities! I bow in reverence before Thee, Strength of my heart, my never-failing Light. Amen.

### (or the following Psalm)

#### (Psalm viii)

O Lord, our God, how glorious is Thy name in all the earth, Thy majesty is rehearsed above the heavens. Out of the mouth of babes and sucklings hast Thou founded strength, because of Thine adversaries; that Thou mightest still the enemy and the avenger. When I behold Thy heavens, the work of Thy fingers, the moon and the stars, which Thou hast established; what is man, that Thou art mindful of him and the son of man, that Thou thinkest of him? Yet Thou hast made him but little lower than the angels, and hast crowned him with glory and honor. Thou hast made him to have dominion over the works of Thy hands; Thou hast put all things under his feet: sheep and oxen, all of them, yea, and the beasts of the field; the fowl of the air, and the fish of the sea; whatsoever passeth through the paths of the seas.  O Lord, our God, how glorious is Thy name in all the earth!

## Choir

May the words of my mouth and the meditation of my heart be acceptable unto Thee, O Lord, my Rock and my Redeemer.  Amen.

(Those congregations which read the Torah, turn to page 94)

### READING FROM SCRIPTURE

(For ADORATION and KADDISH, turn to page 71)

## V

### Choir

(Psalm xcv, 1–7)

O come, let us sing unto the Lord; let us chant to the Rock of our salvation. Let us come before His presence with thanksgiving, let us shout for joy unto Him with psalms. For the Lord is a great God, and a great King above all gods; in whose hand are the depths of the earth; the heights of the mountains are His also. The sea is His, and He made it; and His hands formed the dry land. O come, let us bow down and bend the knee; let us kneel before the Lord our Maker; for He is our God, and we are the people of His pasture, and the flock of His hand.

לְכוּ נְרַנְּנָה לַיָי נָרִיעָה

לְצוּר יִשְׁעֵנוּ: נְקַדְּמָה פָנָיו

בְּתוֹדָה בִּזְמִרוֹת נָרִיעַ לוֹ:

כִּי אֵל גָּדוֹל יְיָ וּמֶלֶךְ גָּדוֹל

עַל־כָּל־אֱלֹהִים: אֲשֶׁר

בְּיָדוֹ מֶחְקְרֵי־אָרֶץ

וְתוֹעֲפוֹת הָרִים לוֹ: אֲשֶׁר־

לוֹ הַיָּם וְהוּא עָשֵׂהוּ וְיַבֶּשֶׁת

יָדָיו יָצָרוּ: בֹּאוּ נִשְׁתַּחֲוֶה

וְנִכְרָעָה נִבְרְכָה לִפְנֵי־יְיָ

עֹשֵׂנוּ: כִּי הוּא אֱלֹהֵינוּ

וַאֲנַחְנוּ עַם מַרְעִיתוֹ וְצֹאן

יָדוֹ הַיּוֹם אִם־בְּקֹלוֹ

תִשְׁמָעוּ:

### Silent Prayer

### Reader

Now that the daily task is laid aside and we are gathered in the house of God, the hush of solemnity comes over us, and we feel a refreshing rest in the holy quiet of the sanctuary. Softer than the twilight calm is the peace that comes to us here with healing on its wings. It restores our soul and we are refreshed out of the abundance of God's grace.

When the shades of night veil from our eyes the beauties of the earth, a world of holier splendor opens before the mind. At eventide, behold, there is light. The brightness of the fireside shines forth to tell that a divine spirit of love holds sway. How solemn does life, with its joys and its trials, appear in view of the duties and affections of home; how greatly all blessings are enriched, all cares and sorrows softened. At this hour, O God, Thy messenger of peace descends from on high to turn the hearts of the parents to the children and the hearts of the children to the parents, strengthening the bonds of devotion in the home and making it a sanctuary worthy of Thy presence.

We thank Thee, O God, for the holiness of this day which has ever fostered moderation, purity and fidelity in the souls of Israel. Like a beacon across a storm-tossed sea, the Sabbath sent its rays of comfort into Judah's tents when the darkness of persecution had enveloped them, and brought healing when the iron had entered the soul of the martyred people.

### Congregation and Reader

Let the day be no less welcome when our lot falls in brighter times and pleasanter places. May we ever prize and preserve Israel's heritage that it bring comfort and joy to us and to future generations. May the Sabbath cup be to us a cup of salvation, which we lift up calling upon the name of the Lord. And as this weekly day of rest and worship enjoined by Thy law has brought blessing to many nations, may it at last unite all men in a covenant of peace and holy fellowship. Amen.

## Responsive Reading

**Reader**

Behold, how good and how pleasant it is for brethren to dwell together in unity!

**Congregation**

*For therein hath the Lord ordained blessing, even life abundant.*

Except the Lord build the house, they labor in vain that build it.

*Except the Lord keep the city, the watchman waketh but in vain.*

Better is a dry morsel and quiet therewith, than a house full of feasting with strife.

*Better is little with the fear of the Lord than great treasure and turmoil therewith.*

I wait for the Lord, my soul doth wait, and in His word do I hope.

*O Israel, hope in the Lord; for with the Lord there is mercy, and with Him is plenteous redemption.*

I have set the Lord always before me; He is at my right hand, I shall not be moved.

*In His presence is fulness of joy, in His right hand bliss for evermore.*

(Congregation rises)

### Reader

Praise ye the Lord to whom all praise is due.

### Choir and Congregation

Praised be the Lord to whom all praise is due forever and ever.

(Congregation is seated)

### Reader

Praised be Thou, O Lord our God, ruler of the world, by whose law the shadows of evening fall and the gates of morn are opened. In wisdom Thou hast established the changes of time and seasons and ordered the ways of the stars in their heavenly courses. Creator of heaven and earth, O ever-living God, rule Thou over us forever. Praised be Thou, O Lord, for the day and its work and for the night and its rest.

### Congregation and Reader

Infinite as is Thy power even so is Thy love. Thou didst manifest it through Israel Thy people. By laws and commandments, by statutes and ordinances hast Thou led us in the way of righteousness and brought us to the light of truth. Therefore at our lying down and our rising up, we will meditate on Thy teachings and find in Thy laws true life and length of days. O that Thy love may never depart from our hearts. Praised be Thou, O Lord, who hast revealed Thy love through Israel.

(Congregation rises)

Reader

בָּרְכוּ אֶת־יְיָ הַמְבֹרָךְ:

Choir and Congregation

בָּרוּךְ יְיָ הַמְבֹרָךְ לְעוֹלָם וָעֶד:

(Congregation is seated)

Reader

בָּרוּךְ אַתָּה יְיָ אֱלֹהֵינוּ מֶלֶךְ הָעוֹלָם. אֲשֶׁר
בִּדְבָרוֹ מַעֲרִיב עֲרָבִים. בְּחָכְמָה פּוֹתֵחַ שְׁעָרִים.
וּבִתְבוּנָה מְשַׁנֶּה עִתִּים וּמַחֲלִיף אֶת־הַזְּמַנִּים.
וּמְסַדֵּר אֶת־הַכּוֹכָבִים בְּמִשְׁמְרוֹתֵיהֶם בָּרָקִיעַ
כִּרְצוֹנוֹ. בּוֹרֵא יוֹם וָלָיְלָה. יְיָ צְבָאוֹת שְׁמוֹ. אֵל
חַי וְקַיָּם תָּמִיד יִמְלֹךְ עָלֵינוּ לְעוֹלָם וָעֶד. בָּרוּךְ
אַתָּה יְיָ הַמַּעֲרִיב עֲרָבִים:

אַהֲבַת עוֹלָם בֵּית יִשְׂרָאֵל עַמְּךָ אָהָבְתָּ. תּוֹרָה
וּמִצְוֹת חֻקִּים וּמִשְׁפָּטִים אוֹתָנוּ לִמַּדְתָּ. עַל־כֵּן יְיָ
אֱלֹהֵינוּ בְּשָׁכְבֵּנוּ וּבְקוּמֵנוּ נָשִׂיחַ בְּחֻקֶּיךָ. וְנִשְׂמַח
בְּדִבְרֵי תוֹרָתֶךָ וּבְמִצְוֹתֶיךָ לְעוֹלָם וָעֶד. כִּי הֵם
חַיֵּינוּ וְאֹרֶךְ יָמֵינוּ. וּבָהֶם נֶהְגֶּה יוֹמָם וָלָיְלָה.
וְאַהֲבָתְךָ אַל־תָּסִיר מִמֶּנּוּ לְעוֹלָמִים. בָּרוּךְ אַתָּה
יְיָ אוֹהֵב עַמּוֹ יִשְׂרָאֵל:

(Congregation rises)

## Reader

Hear, O Israel: The Lord our God, the Lord is One.
Praised be His name whose glorious kingdom is forever and ever.

(Congregation is seated)

## Congregation and Reader

Thou shalt love the Lord, thy God, with all thy heart, with all thy soul, and with all thy might. And these words, which I command thee this day, shall be upon thy heart. Thou shalt teach them diligently unto thy children, and shalt speak of them when thou sittest in thy house, when thou walkest by the way, when thou liest down, and when thou risest up. Thou shalt bind them for a sign upon thy hand, and they shall be for frontlets between thine eyes. Thou shalt write them upon the doorposts of thy house and upon thy gates: That ye may remember and do all My commandments and be holy unto your God.

## Choir

The children of Israel shall keep the Sabbath, to observe the Sabbath throughout their generations, for a perpetual covenant. It is a sign between Me and the children of Israel forever.

(Congregation rises)

## Reader, then Choir and Congregation

שְׁמַע יִשְׂרָאֵל יְהֹוָה אֱלֹהֵינוּ יְהֹוָה אֶחָד:

בָּרוּךְ שֵׁם כְּבוֹד מַלְכוּתוֹ לְעוֹלָם וָעֶד:

(Congregation is seated)

## Reader

וְאָהַבְתָּ אֵת יְיָ אֱלֹהֶיךָ בְּכָל־לְבָבְךָ וּבְכָל־נַפְשְׁךָ

וּבְכָל־מְאֹדֶךָ: וְהָיוּ הַדְּבָרִים הָאֵלֶּה אֲשֶׁר אָנֹכִי

מְצַוְּךָ הַיּוֹם עַל לְבָבֶךָ: וְשִׁנַּנְתָּם לְבָנֶיךָ וְדִבַּרְתָּ

בָּם. בְּשִׁבְתְּךָ בְּבֵיתֶךָ וּבְלֶכְתְּךָ בַדֶּרֶךְ וּבְשָׁכְבְּךָ

וּבְקוּמֶךָ: וּקְשַׁרְתָּם לְאוֹת עַל יָדֶךָ. וְהָיוּ לְטֹטָפֹת

בֵּין עֵינֶיךָ: וּכְתַבְתָּם עַל מְזֻזוֹת בֵּיתֶךָ וּבִשְׁעָרֶיךָ:

לְמַעַן תִּזְכְּרוּ וַעֲשִׂיתֶם אֶת כָּל מִצְוֹתָי וִהְיִיתֶם

קְדֹשִׁים לֵאלֹהֵיכֶם: אֲנִי יְיָ אֱלֹהֵיכֶם:

## Choir

וְשָׁמְרוּ בְנֵי יִשְׂרָאֵל אֶת הַשַּׁבָּת לַעֲשׂוֹת אֶת־

הַשַּׁבָּת לְדֹרֹתָם בְּרִית עוֹלָם: בֵּינִי וּבֵין בְּנֵי יִשְׂרָאֵל

אוֹת הִוא לְעֹלָם:

## Congregation and Reader

Praised be the Lord by day and praised be He by night. Praised be He when we lie down and praised be He when we rise up. In His hands are the souls of all the living and the spirits of all flesh. In His hands, we entrust our spirit. Redeem Thou us, O God of truth. Heavenly Father, establish Thy kingdom and reign over us forever.

## Reader

O Lord our God, we turn to Thee in hope as did our fathers. May Thy mercy descend upon our people in all their habitations. Extend Thy protection and help unto our brothers who struggle in lands of darkness as victims of oppression and persecution. Fill the hearts of all men with a love of freedom and justice, that tyranny may vanish and the reign of righteousness be established everywhere on earth. Uphold also the hands of our brothers who toil to rebuild Zion. In their pilgrimage among the nations, Thy people have always turned in love to the land where Israel was born, where our prophets taught their imperishable message of justice and brotherhood and where our psalmists sang their deathless songs of love for Thee and of Thy love for us and all humanity. Ever enshrined in the hearts of Israel was the hope that Zion might be restored, not for their own pride or vainglory, but as a living witness to the truth of Thy word which shall lead the nations to the reign of peace. Grant us strength that with Thy help we may bring a new light to shine upon Zion. Imbue us who live in lands of freedom with a sense of Israel's spiritual unity that we may share joyously in the work of redemption so that from Zion shall go forth the law and the word of God from Jerusalem.

## Choir: Amen.

### Silent Prayer

(or such other prayer as the heart may prompt)

O Lord God, in Thine abundant mercy we have been preserved during the past week. Through the common days flow the refreshing waters of Thy lovingkindness, yet we forget the Source. May this hour awaken within us a sense of our dependence upon Thee. Create in us a clean heart and renew a right spirit within us that we may face our daily duty with a firm courage and a tranquil mind. May we learn to know that in loving and serving our fellowmen, we are loving and serving Thee. Do Thou guard us and our dear ones in the coming week. May we live together in love and unselfishness so that happiness and contentment may abide within our homes. May the spirit of the Sabbath fill our life with its blessed peace. Amen.

(or the following Psalm)

(Psalm lxvii)

God be gracious unto us, and bless us; may He cause His face to shine toward us; that Thy way may be known upon earth, Thy salvation among all nations. Let the peoples give thanks unto Thee, O God; let the peoples give thanks unto Thee, all of them. O let the nations be glad and sing for joy; for Thou wilt judge the peoples with equity, and lead the nations upon earth. Let the peoples give thanks unto Thee, O God; let the peoples give thanks unto Thee, all of them. The earth hath yielded her increase. May God bless us; and let all the ends of the earth fear Him.

## Choir

May the words of my mouth and the meditation of my heart be acceptable unto Thee, O Lord, my Rock and my Redeemer.

(Those congregations which read the Torah, turn to page 94)

## READING FROM SCRIPTURE

## ADORATION
(Congregation rises)

### Congregation and Reader

Let us adore the ever-living God, and render praise unto Him who spread out the heavens and established the earth, whose glory is revealed in the heavens above and whose greatness is manifest throughout the world. He is our God; there is none else.

We bow the head in reverence, and worship the King of kings, the Holy One, praised be He.

### Choir and Congregation

וַאֲנַחְנוּ כֹּרְעִים וּמִשְׁתַּחֲוִים וּמוֹדִים לִפְנֵי מֶלֶךְ
מַלְכֵי הַמְּלָכִים הַקָּדוֹשׁ בָּרוּךְ הוּא:

(Congregation is seated)

### Reader

May the time not be distant, O God, when Thy name shall be worshiped in all the earth, when unbelief shall disappear and error be no more. Fervently we pray that the day may come when all men shall invoke Thy name, when corruption and evil shall give way to purity and goodness, when superstition shall no longer enslave the mind, nor idolatry blind the eye, when all who dwell on earth shall know that to Thee alone every knee must bend and every tongue give homage. O may all, created in Thine image, recognize that they are brethren, so that, one in spirit and one in fellowship, they may be forever united before Thee.   Then

shall Thy kingdom be established on earth and the
word of Thine ancient seer be fulfilled: The Lord will
reign forever and ever.

## Congregation (or Choir)

On that day the Lord shall be One and His name shall
be One.

בַּיוֹם הַהוּא יִהְיֶה יְיָ אֶחָד וּשְׁמוֹ אֶחָד:

## I

## Reader

All you who mourn the loss of loved ones, and, at
this hour, remember the sweet companionship and the
cherished hopes that have passed away with them, give
ear to the word of comfort spoken in the name of God.
Only the body has died and has been laid in the dust.
The spirit lives in the shelter of God's love and mercy.
Our loved ones continue, also, in the remembrance of
those to whom they were precious. Their deeds of
lovingkindness, the true and beautiful words they spoke
are treasured up as incentives to conduct by which the
living honor the dead. And when we ask in our grief:
Whence shall come our help and our comfort? then in
the strength of faith let us answer with the Psalmist:
My help cometh from God. He will not forsake us
nor leave us in our grief. Upon Him we cast our burden and He will grant us strength according to the days

He has apportioned to us. All life comes from Him; all souls are in His keeping. Come then, and in the midst of sympathizing fellow-worshipers, rise and hallow the name of God.

(Turn to pages 76–77)

## II

### Reader

In nature's ebb and flow, God's eternal law abides. When tears dim our vision and grief clouds our understanding, we often lose sight of His eternal plan. Yet we know that growth and decay, life and death all reveal His purpose. He who is our support in the struggles of life is also our hope in death. We have set Him before us and shall not despair. In His hands are the souls of all the living and the spirits of all flesh. Under His protection we abide and by His love are we comforted. O Life of our life, Soul of our soul, cause Thy light to shine into our hearts, and fill our spirit with abiding trust in Thee.

(Turn to pages 76–77)

## III

### Reader

O Thou who givest life and ordainest death, we trust in Thee. Even when those we love enter into the shadow of death, our faith in Thee does not falter. For surely Thou wilt not abandon us to despair, nor those we love to the eternal midnight of the tomb. Thou hast placed man upon the earth, bestowed upon him a mind to seek truth, a heart to perceive love and beauty and Thou wilt not crush it all forever. Our life is more than a watch in the night, than yesterday when it is past, for Thou dost establish the work of Thy hands. Dust we are, and unto dust we return, but the spirit born of Thy spirit, breathed into the clay to animate and to ennoble, returns unto Thee, the Fountainhead of all spirits. Thou art in the setting as in the rising sun, in our bereavements as in our blessings, and Thine everlasting arms uphold us in the vicissitudes of life and in our lone journey through the valley of shadows.

Teach us then, O Father, to speak with all our hearts the words, hallowed by centuries of faith. Teach us to acknowledge Thy sovereignty and Thy wisdom with perfect trust that death is but the portal unto eternal life.

Let us, then, give praise unto God who is the source of our salvation and our abiding hope.

(Turn to pages 76–77)

## IV

### Reader

When cherished ties are broken and fond hopes shattered, only faith and confidence can lighten the heaviness of the heart. The pang of separation is hard to bear, but to brood over our sorrow is to embitter our grief.

The Psalmist said that in his affliction he learned the law of God. Indeed, not unavailing will be our grief, if it send us back to serve and bless the living. We learn how to counsel and comfort those who, like ourselves, are sorrow-stricken. Though absent, the departed still minister to our spirits, teaching us patience, faithfulness and devotion. Within the circle of daily association, we often failed to discern their worth and their loveliness. In the remembrance of their virtues and affections, the best and purest part of their nature lies eternally enshrined. Let us lift our head in hope, and summon our strength for duty. We dwell in the shelter of the Almighty, for He is our refuge and our fortress.

(Turn to pages 76–77)

## V

### Reader

The Lord giveth, the Lord taketh away, blessed be the name of the Lord. As we recall the beloved ones who have passed away, these words bring healing to the hurt that death has wrought. Our loved ones have answered the summons that sound for all men, for we are sojourners upon earth and our times are in His hands. We loose our hold upon life when our time is come, as the leaf falls from the bough when its day is done. The deeds of the righteous enrich the lives of men as the fallen leaf enriches the soil beneath. The dust returns to the earth, the spirit lives on with God's eternal years. Like the stars by day, our beloved dead are not seen with mortal eyes, but they shine on in the untroubled firmament of endless time. Let us be thankful for the companionship that continues in love that is stronger than death and spans the gulf of the grave. Cherishing their memory, let us, in the presence of the congregation, sanctify the name of God.

(Mourners rise)

### Reader

Extolled and hallowed be the name of God throughout the world which He has created according to His will. And may He speedily establish His kingdom of righteousness on earth. Amen.

### Congregation

Praised be His glorious name unto all eternity.

### Reader

Praised and glorified be the name of the Holy One, though He be above all the praises which we can utter. Our guide is He in life and our redeemer through all eternity.

### Congregation

Our help cometh from Him, the creator of heaven and earth.

### Reader

The departed whom we now remember have entered into the peace of life eternal. They still live on earth in the acts of goodness they performed and in the hearts of those who cherish their memory. May the beauty of their life abide among us as a loving benediction.

### Congregation: Amen.

### Reader

May the Father of peace send peace to all who mourn, and comfort all the bereaved among us.

### Congregation: Amen.

(Mourners are seated)

(Mourners rise)

Reader

יִתְגַּדַּל וְיִתְקַדַּשׁ שְׁמֵהּ רַבָּא. בְּעָלְמָא דִי בְרָא
כִרְעוּתֵהּ. וְיַמְלִיךְ מַלְכוּתֵהּ. בְּחַיֵּיכוֹן וּבְיוֹמֵיכוֹן
וּבְחַיֵּי דְכָל־בֵּית יִשְׂרָאֵל. בַּעֲגָלָא וּבִזְמַן קָרִיב.
וְאִמְרוּ אָמֵן:

Congregation

יְהֵא שְׁמֵהּ רַבָּא מְבָרַךְ לְעָלַם וּלְעָלְמֵי עָלְמַיָּא:

Reader

יִתְבָּרַךְ וְיִשְׁתַּבַּח וְיִתְפָּאַר וְיִתְרוֹמַם וְיִתְנַשֵּׂא
וְיִתְהַדָּר וְיִתְעַלֶּה וְיִתְהַלָּל שְׁמֵהּ דְּקֻדְשָׁא. בְּרִיךְ
הוּא. לְעֵלָּא מִן כָּל־בִּרְכָתָא וְשִׁירָתָא. תֻּשְׁבְּחָתָא
וְנֶחָמָתָא. דַּאֲמִירָן בְּעָלְמָא. וְאִמְרוּ אָמֵן:

עַל יִשְׂרָאֵל וְעַל צַדִּיקַיָּא. וְעַל־כָּל־מַן דְּאִתְפְּטַר
מִן עָלְמָא הָדֵין כִּרְעוּתֵהּ דֶּאֱלָהָא. יְהֵא לְהוֹן
שְׁלָמָא רַבָּא וְחִנָּא וְחִסְדָּא מִן־קֳדָם מָרֵא שְׁמַיָּא
וְאַרְעָא. וְאִמְרוּ אָמֵן:

יְהֵא שְׁלָמָא רַבָּא מִן־שְׁמַיָּא וְחַיִּים. עָלֵינוּ וְעַל־
כָּל־יִשְׂרָאֵל. וְאִמְרוּ אָמֵן:

עֹשֶׂה שָׁלוֹם בִּמְרוֹמָיו. הוּא יַעֲשֶׂה שָׁלוֹם עָלֵינוּ
וְעַל־כָּל־יִשְׂרָאֵל. וְאִמְרוּ אָמֵן:

(Mourners are seated)

## THE MOURNER'S KADDISH

### Reader

Yis-gad-dal v'yis-kad-dash sh'meh rab-bo, b'ol-mo di'v-ro kir'-u-seh v'yam-lich mal-chu-seh, b'cha-ye-chon u-v'yo-me-chon u-v'cha-yeh d'chol bes yis-ro-el, ba-a-go-lo u-viz-man ko-riv, v'im-ru O-men.

### Congregation

Y'heh sh'meh rab-bo m'vo-rach, l'o-lam ul'ol'meh ol-ma-yo:

### Reader

Yis-bo-rach v'yish-tab-bach, v'yis-po-ar, v'yis-ro-mam, v'yis-nas-seh, v'yis-had-dor, v'yis-al-leh, v'yis-hal-lol, sh'-meh d'kud'-sho, b'rich hu. L'e-lo min kol bir-cho-so v'shi-ro-so, tush-b'cho-so v'ne-cho-mo-so, da-a-mi-ron b'ol-mo, v'im-ru O-men:

Al yis-ro-el v'al tsa-de-ka-yo, v'al kol man d'isp'tar min ol-mo ho-dain kir-oo-seh de-e-lo-ho y'hai l'hon shlo-mo rab-bo v'chino v'chis-do min ko-dom mo-rai sh'ma-yo v'ar-o, v'im-ru O-men:

Y'heh sh'lo-mo rab-bo min sh'ma-yo v'cha-yim, o-le-nu v'al kol yis-ro-el, v'imru O-men:

O-seh sho-lom bim'-ro-mov, hu ya-a-seh sho-lom, o-le-nu v'al kol yis-ro-el, v'imru O-men.

## SPECIAL PRAYERS

### FOR SABBATH DURING PESACH

*Responsive Reading*

Reader

I love that the Lord should hear my voice and my supplications.

Congregation

*The cords of death encompassed me, I found trouble and sorrow.*

But I called upon the name of the Lord: I beseech Thee, O Lord, deliver my soul.

*Gracious is the Lord, and righteous; yea, our God is compassionate.*

The Lord preserveth the simple; I was brought low, and He saved me.

*Return, O my soul, unto thy rest; for the Lord hath dealt bountifully with thee.*

For Thou hast delivered my soul from death, mine eyes from tears, and my feet from stumbling.

*I shall walk before the Lord in the lands of the living.*

What can I render unto the Lord for all His benefits unto me?

*I will lift up the cup of salvation and call upon the name of the Lord.*

O praise the Lord all ye nations; laud Him, all ye peoples;

*For His mercy is great towards us; and the truth of the Lord endureth forever.   Hallelujah.*

## Reader

Lord of all generations, the past is Thy handiwork and the glories of the future Thy promise. On this festival of Passover, we are gathered in Thy house to recall Thy wonders of old. When we were slaves in Egypt and suffered under the lash of taskmasters, Thou didst send Thy servants, Moses and Aaron, to stand in the presence of Pharaoh and proclaim in Thy name: Let My people go that they may serve Me. The cruel heart of the tyrant and the might of his armies did not avail against Thy liberating word and Israel marched forth from Egypt with songs and rejoicing to find freedom in Thy service.

This was Thy will in ancient days and it is Thy law forever. Wherever the yoke of serfdom is broken, wherever tyrants are overthrown, wherever Thy children live as free men, there is Thy word fulfilled and Thy will triumphant. To every soul comes Thy command: Be servants unto Me alone and not slaves to man.

Teach us, O God, to accept and cherish Thy law of liberty. Guide us with Thy wisdom that we may grow in knowledge and in sympathy and keep our judgment free from passion or prejudice. May we strive for the redemption of our souls and thus become messengers of freedom to all Thy children.

In Thy power, O Lord, is the fate of nations. Thou who didst break Pharaoh's yoke and bid the slaves go free, be Thou our help in every time of peril. Let all men see that the might of armies and the power of tyrants must vanish like smoke before the force of Thy spirit.  May the coming year bring a new Passover of freedom to all Thy children in every land.  Amen.

(Continue on page 23)

### FOR SABBATH DURING SUCCOS

*Responsive Reading*

**Reader**

Thou crownest the year with Thy goodness and girdest the hills with joy.

**Congregation**

*The meadows are clothed with flocks, the valleys are covered with grain.*

God be gracious unto us and bless us.

*May He cause His face to shine upon us.*

Let Thy way be known upon earth, Thy salvation among all nations.

*Let the people give thanks unto Thee, O God, let the nations be glad.*

For Thou wilt judge the peoples with equity.

*Thou wilt lead the nations upon earth.*

The earth has yielded her increase; may the Lord, our God, bless us.

*Let all the ends of the earth revere Him.*

*Reader*

Lord of the universe, the stars in their courses and the changing seasons tell of Thine infinite might.  In these autumn days the waning summer and the falling leaves bring no melancholy into our hearts.  The season begins in joy with the bounteous gifts of Thine unfailing goodness. We behold the fruits of tree and vine and gather to celebrate the harvest, the joyous festival of Tabernacles.

The structures of stone and steel which our hands have wrought may make us boastful of human strength; but the fruits of field and orchard re-awaken our thoughts of Thee. When on this festival we bring into Thy house the products of soil and sunlight, our thoughts turn to the miracle of the seed, the mystery of growth, the refreshing rain and the ripening sun. We learn anew that it is Thou who blessest our toil wherever we labor. All that we have comes from Thee and we must devote it to purposes pleasing in Thy sight.

Thy bounty, O Lord, provides for all the needs of man if he be wise and understanding in the use of Thy blessings. Teach us then to employ Thy gifts for the happiness of all Thy children. Let there be no famine or scarcity in any household or in any land. As soil and rain and sun unite to do Thy will, so unify the hearts of Thy children to fulfil Thy command to live together in mutual blessing. Spread over us the tabernacle of peace and brotherhood, now and evermore. Amen.

(Continue on page 23)

### FOR SABBATH BEFORE PURIM

## Reader

On this Sabbath of Remembrance, when we recall Amalek, and all the foes who have ever threatened our existence, let us dwell on the power of faith and devotion which has preserved us to this hour. Many are the enemies that have risen against us, but trusting in Thee, O God, we have not been dismayed. Imbue us with the faith of former generations of Israel. Give us courage and steadfastness that, like Mordecai, we may bend the knee to Thee alone. Uphold us that, like Esther, we may walk undaunted in the path of loyalty. When adversity and sorrow come upon our people, may we face them manfully as trials of faith. Amid suffering and persecution may we continue to cling to Thee and perform our appointed tasks in confidence and fortitude. Strengthen us to combat prejudice, injustice and oppression when they strike not only against us but men of whatever race or belief. Let not divisions of blood and faith create distrust and strife. May we strive unceasingly for the triumph of truth and right over falsehood and wrong. Thus shall we be united in a true covenant of brotherhood and peace. Amen.

(Continue on page 23)

### FOR SABBATH OF REPENTANCE

#### Reader

O Lord our God, and God of our fathers, Thou hast placed us upon this earth and hast appointed us to do Thy will. But we follow too often our evil inclination and transgress Thy laws. In Thy gracious love, Thou hast given us the Sabbath, that we pause in our striving after worldly goods and seek the treasures of the spirit which consecrate life unto Thee. And this Sabbath of Repentance admonishes us to turn from the pursuit of life's vanities. It bids us consider well our earthly pilgrimage and measure the deeds of the past year in the light of what we might have accomplished, had we given ourselves wholly unto Thee. We are overcome with shame and self-reproach as we realize wherein we have fallen short. Truly, O God, we know our weakness, and feel humbled and chastened.

O God of mercy, we trust in Thee. In deep humility we approach Thy throne and lay our supplication before Thee. Strengthen our faith in Thee, that with wisdom and courage we may do Thy will. Help us to right the wrongs we have done to others and give us the grace to pardon those who offend against us. Enlighten our minds with Thy truth and touch our hearts with Thy mercy. May this day summon our energies to the fulfillment of the divine plan of our life, and may it bring to our souls that inner peace in which alone the voice of Thy spirit is heard. Be Thou with us, O God, and receive us in Thy boundless love for Thou art our hope and support. Amen.

(Continue on page 23)

## SERVICE FOR HANUKKAH

### Choir

(Psalm xxx)

| | |
|---|---|
| I will extol Thee, O Lord, for Thou hast raised me up, and hast not suffered mine enemies to rejoice over me. O Lord my God, I cried unto Thee, and Thou didst heal me; sing praise unto the Lord, O ye His godly ones, and give thanks to His holy name. For His anger is but for a moment, His favor is for a lifetime; weeping may tarry for the night, but joy cometh in the morning. Now I had said in my security: I shall never be moved. Thou hadst established, O Lord, in Thy favor my mountain as a stronghold —Thou didst hide Thy face; I was affrighted. Unto Thee, O Lord, did I call, and unto the Lord I made supplication: Shall the dust praise Thee? Shall it declare | מִזְמוֹר שִׁיר חֲנֻכַּת הַבַּיִת לְדָוִד: אֲרוֹמִמְךָ יְיָ כִּי דִלִּיתָנִי וְלֹא שִׂמַּחְתָּ אֹיְבַי לִי: יְיָ אֱלֹהָי שִׁוַּעְתִּי אֵלֶיךָ וַתִּרְפָּאֵנִי: יְיָ הֶעֱלִיתָ מִן שְׁאוֹל נַפְשִׁי חִיִּיתַנִי מִיָּרְדִי־בוֹר: זַמְּרוּ לַיְיָ חֲסִידָיו וְהוֹדוּ לְזֵכֶר קָדְשׁוֹ: כִּי רֶגַע בְּאַפּוֹ חַיִּים בִּרְצוֹנוֹ בָּעֶרֶב יָלִין בֶּכִי וְלַבֹּקֶר רִנָּה: וַאֲנִי אָמַרְתִּי בְשַׁלְוִי בַּל־אֶמּוֹט לְעוֹלָם: יְיָ בִּרְצוֹנְךָ הֶעֱמַדְתָּה לְהַרְרִי עֹז הִסְתַּרְתָּ פָנֶיךָ הָיִיתִי נִבְהָל: אֵלֶיךָ יְיָ אֶקְרָא וְאֶל־אֲדֹנָי אֶתְחַנָּן: מַה־ בֶּצַע בְּדָמִי בְּרִדְתִּי אֶל |

Thy truth? Hear, O Lord, and be gracious unto me; Lord, be Thou my helper. Thou didst turn for me my mourning into dancing; Thou didst loose my sackcloth, and gird me with gladness; so that my soul may sing praise to Thee, and not be silent; O Lord my God, I will give thanks unto Thee forever.

שַׁחַת הֲיוֹדְךָ עָפָר הֲיַגִּיד
אֲמִתֶּךָ: שְׁמַע־יְיָ וְחָנֵּנִי יְיָ
הֱיֵה עֹזֵר לִי: הָפַכְתָּ
מִסְפְּדִי לְמָחוֹל לִי פִּתַּחְתָּ
שַׂקִּי וַתְּאַזְּרֵנִי שִׂמְחָה:
לְמַעַן יְזַמֶּרְךָ כָבוֹד וְלֹא
יִדֹּם יְיָ אֱלֹהַי לְעוֹלָם
אוֹדֶךָּ:

## Responsive Reading

**Reader**

Marvelous things of the Lord, our God, have we heard, and our fathers have told us.

**Congregation**

They that trust in the Lord are as Mount Zion, which cannot be moved, but abideth forever.

Though they fall, they shall not be utterly cast down, for the Lord upholdeth them with His arm.

They shall not be afraid of evil tidings, for their times are in His hands.

Commit thy way unto the Lord, wait patiently for Him, and thou shalt never be forsaken.

He will draw thee out of the dark waters and show thee the path of life.

Lift up your eyes to the heavens and look upon the earth beneath;

For the heavens shall vanish away like smoke, and
   the earth shall wax old like a garment;
And they that dwell therein shall likewise cease to be;
   But My salvation shall be forever, and My favor unto
   all generations.

(Continue with Service IV from page 50 to page 57)

## Reader

### (From I. Maccabees)

It was on the fifteenth day of the month of Kislev,
that the messengers of King Antiochus set up an idol
on the altar of God, and had incense burnt in its honor.
And they gave orders that the people of Judea should
forsake the law and the covenant, profane the Sabbath
and pollute the sanctuary.  And many chose rather to
die than to forsake the holy covenant.  And the king's
officers came to the city of Modin, and said to Mattathias, the son of John, the son of Simon the Has-
monean, a priest of the sons of Joarib who dwelt in
Modin:  Thou art a great man and strengthened with
sons and brethren in this city.  Come, then, and fulfil
the king's command as all the heathen have done, and
the men of Judah and they that remained in Jerusalem.
And thou shalt be in the number of the king's friends.
But Mattathias answered and spake with a loud voice:
Though all the nations that are under the king's dominion obey him and fall away each one from the
religion of his fathers, yet will I and my sons and my
brethren walk in the covenant of our fathers.  God
forbid that we should forsake the Law to depart from
our faith either to the right hand or the left.  And

when in the sight of all one of the Jews came to sacrifice to the idol, Mattathias was inflamed with zeal, neither could he forbear to show his anger, and he slew him, and also the king's officer, and the altar he pulled down. And Mattathias cried throughout the city with a loud voice saying: Whosoever is zealous of the law and maintaineth the covenant, let him follow me. So he and his sons fled into the mountains, and they went about pulling down the heathen altars, and they rescued the law out of the hands of the Gentiles.

And the days of Mattathias drew near that he should die and he said to his sons: Be ye zealous for the law and give your lives for the covenant of your fathers. Remember what our fathers did in their generations. Was not Abraham found faithful in temptation, and it was accounted to him for righteousness? Phineas, our father, for that he was zealous exceedingly, obtained the covenant of an everlasting priesthood. David, for being faithful, inherited the throne of a kingdom forever and ever. Throughout all the ages none that put their trust in God were overcome. Therefore be strong, my sons, and show yourselves men in behalf of the law; for therein shall ye obtain glory. And he blessed them and was gathered to his fathers.

Then Judah, called Maccabee, rose up in his stead, and all his brethren aided him, and they fought with gladness the battle of Israel. He battled like a lion and the lawless shrunk for fear of him. He cheered Jacob by his mighty acts, and his memorial is blessed forever. And when all the people feared and trembled at the sight of the great number of the enemy, and said: What? Shall we be able, being a small company, to fight against so great and so strong a multitude? Judah answered: With the God of heaven it is all one to save by many or by few. And all the people shall know that there is One who redeemeth and saveth Israel. And Judah led them into battle, and behold the hosts of the enemy were discomfited before them. And Israel had a great deliverance. And they sang songs of thanksgiving, and praised the Lord of heaven for His goodness, because His mercy endureth forever.

And on the five and twentieth day of Kislev, the same day when three years before the altar of God had been profaned by the heathen, the sanctuary of God was dedicated anew with songs and music, and the people praised the God of heaven who had given them great victory, and they celebrated the Dedication of the Altar for eight days, and there was great rejoicing among the people. Moreover, Judah and his brethren with the whole congregation of Israel ordained that the days of the Dedication of the Altar should be celebrated, from year to year, for eight days in gladness and thanksgiving.

## Choir

The Lord is my strength and my song and He is become my salvation. I shall not die but live, and declare the works of the Lord.

## Reader

Rock of Israel, Father of all men! We are stirred by the sacred memories of Thy wondrous help unto our fathers in days of old. When violent men rose up against them to desecrate Thy sanctuary, to demolish its altar and to extinguish the light of the Torah, Thou didst reveal Thyself as their protector and deliverer. The weak faltered and knelt before the idols. But men of valor roused by Thy spirit fought for freedom of conscience and the right to worship God. Trusting in Thee, the weak triumphed over the strong, the few over the many, and the righteous over the wicked. The rod of the oppressor was broken. The temple rose from its desecration in greater glory than before. And the people that walked in darkness beheld a great light; they that dwelt in the shadow of death rejoiced in Thy salvation. And Israel emerged from the conflict strengthened and purified for his prophetic task.

Grant, O God, that the heroic example of the martyrs of old may ever inspire us with renewed devotion to our great heritage. Dangers still threaten our existence. Uphold us in our struggles for our preservation as a people of faith. Let not Thy holy spirit depart from us. Gird us for the battle against apathy, ignorance and intolerance which still threaten to extinguish Thy lamps and to destroy Thine altars. With the loyalty and zeal of the Maccabees, may we overcome the dark forces of tyranny, prejudice and hatred and spread the light of liberty, brotherhood and peace among men.

## Congregation and Reader

On this festival of Hanukkah, we rededicate ourselves to Thee and Thy service. As we kindle the Hanukkah lights in our homes and temples, may the light of Thy presence and Thy truth shine forth to dispel all darkness and lead all men unto Thee. Amen.

(Congregation standing)

## BLESSING OVER THE LIGHTS

Praised be Thou, O Lord our God, Ruler of the world, who hast sanctified us by Thy commandments, and bidden us kindle the Hanukkah lights.

בָּרוּךְ אַתָּה יְיָ אֱלֹהֵינוּ מֶלֶךְ הָעוֹלָם אֲשֶׁר קִדְּשָׁנוּ בְּמִצְוֹתָיו וְצִוָּנוּ לְהַדְלִיק נֵר שֶׁל חֲנֻכָּה:

Praised be Thou, O Lord our God, Ruler of the world, who didst wondrous things for our fathers, in days of old, at this season.

בָּרוּךְ אַתָּה יְיָ אֱלֹהֵינוּ מֶלֶךְ הָעוֹלָם שֶׁעָשָׂה נִסִּים לַאֲבוֹתֵינוּ בַּיָּמִים הָהֵם בַּזְּמַן הַזֶּה:

Praised be Thou, O Lord our God, Ruler of the world, who hast granted us life, sustained us, and permitted us to celebrate this joyous festival.

בָּרוּךְ אַתָּה יְיָ אֱלֹהֵינוּ מֶלֶךְ הָעוֹלָם שֶׁהֶחֱיָנוּ וְקִיְּמָנוּ וְהִגִּיעָנוּ לַזְּמַן הַזֶּה:

(Hanukkah Hymn)

(Congregation is seated)

(Those congregations which read the Torah, turn to page 94)

## SERMON

(For ADORATION and KADDISH, turn to page 71)

## CLOSING HYMN

## HANUKKAH HYMN

Rock of Ages, let our song
    Praise Thy saving power;
Thou, amidst the raging foes,
    Wast our shelt'ring tower.
Furious, they assailed us,
But Thine arm availed us,
            And Thy word
            Broke their sword
When our own strength failed us.


Kindling new the holy lamps,
    Priests approved in suffering,
Purified the nation's shrine,
    Brought to God their offering.
And His courts surrounding
Hear, in joy abounding,
            Happy throngs
            Singing songs
With a mighty sounding.


Children of the martyr-race,
    Whether free or fettered,
Wake the echoes of the songs
    Where ye may be scattered.
Yours the message cheering,
    That the time is nearing
            Which will see
            All men free,
Tyrants disappearing.

## KIDDUSH
## קדוש

*The Reader lifts the Kiddush cup and says:*

בָּרוּךְ אַתָּה יְיָ אֱלֹהֵינוּ מֶלֶךְ הָעוֹלָם אֲשֶׁר קִדְּשָׁנוּ
בְּמִצְוֹתָיו וְרָצָה בָנוּ. וְשַׁבַּת קָדְשׁוֹ בְּאַהֲבָה וּבְרָצוֹן
הִנְחִילָנוּ. זִכָּרוֹן לְמַעֲשֵׂה בְרֵאשִׁית. כִּי הוּא יוֹם
תְּחִלָּה לְמִקְרָאֵי־קֹדֶשׁ זֵכֶר לִיצִיאַת מִצְרָיִם. כִּי בָנוּ
בָחַרְתָּ וְאוֹתָנוּ קִדַּשְׁתָּ. וְשַׁבַּת קָדְשְׁךָ בְּאַהֲבָה
וּבְרָצוֹן הִנְחַלְתָּנוּ. בָּרוּךְ אַתָּה יְיָ. מְקַדֵּשׁ הַשַּׁבָּת:

Let us praise God with this symbol of joy, and thank
Him for the blessings of the past week, for life and
strength, for home and love and friendship, for the
discipline of our trials and temptations, for the happiness
that has come to us out of our labors. Thou hast
ennobled us, O God, by the blessings of work, and in
love hast sanctified us by Sabbath rest and worship as
ordained in the Torah: Six days shalt thou labor and
do all thy work, but the seventh day is the Sabbath to
be hallowed unto the Lord, thy God.

Praised be Thou, O Lord our God, King of the universe, who hast created the fruit of the vine.

בָּרוּךְ אַתָּה יְיָ אֱלֹהֵינוּ מֶלֶךְ הָעוֹלָם בּוֹרֵא פְּרִי הַגָּפֶן:

## TORAH SERVICE

### Reader
(Isaiah II, 1–4)

It shall come to pass, in the end of days, that the mountain of the Lord's house shall be exalted above the hills, and all nations shall flow unto it. And many peoples shall go and say: Come ye, and let us go up to the mountain of the Lord, to the house of the God of Jacob; that He may teach us of His ways, and we will walk in His paths. For out of Zion shall go forth the law, and the word of the Lord from Jerusalem.

### Choir

They shall not hurt nor destroy in all My holy mountain; for the earth shall be full of the knowledge of the Lord, as the waters cover the sea. And they shall sit every man under his vine and under his fig-tree; and none shall make them afraid.

לֹא־יָרֵעוּ וְלֹא יַשְׁחִיתוּ
בְּכָל־הַר קָדְשִׁי כִּי־מָלְאָה
הָאָרֶץ דֵּעָה אֶת־יְיָ כַּמַּיִם
לַיָּם מְכַסִּים: וְיָשְׁבוּ אִישׁ
תַּחַת גַּפְנוֹ וְתַחַת תְּאֵנָתוֹ
וְאֵין מַחֲרִיד:

(Congregation rises. Reader takes Scroll from Ark, and faces the Congregation:)

### Reader

This is the covenant which dedicates Israel to the One and Eternal God.

This is the Torah, the pillar of right and of truth.

This is the Law, that proclaims the Fatherhood of God and the Brotherhood of man.

### Congregation

May we never fail in gratitude to our fathers for this blessed heritage, and for the martyrdom they suffered in its defense.

### Reader

Let us acknowledge its truth, abide by its teachings and ever proclaim the watchword of our faith:

### Reader and Congregation, then Choir

שְׁמַע יִשְׂרָאֵל יְהֹוָה אֱלֹהֵינוּ יְהֹוָה אֶחָד׃

Hear, O Israel, the Lord our God, the Lord is One.

### Choir

True it is that the God of the universe is our King; throughout all generations He endureth; and His kingdom and faithfulness endure forever.

אֱמֶת אֱלֹהֵי עוֹלָם
מַלְכֵּנוּ: לְדוֹר וָדוֹר הוּא
קַיָּם, וּמַלְכוּתוֹ וֶאֱמוּנָתוֹ
לָעַד קַיֶּמֶת׃

(Congregation is seated)

Torah benedictions.  Torah is read.  Translation.  Haftarah.
(Special prayers, for Rosh Chodesh, etc.)

### Reader

Thou, O God, hast led Thy servants with unchanging love.  From the very beginning of our existence Thou hast destined us for a sacred task to toil for the speedy dawn of that day, when Thou wilt be revered and obeyed the whole world over, and all mankind will live in peace and unity.

Joyfully we consecrate ourselves anew this day to the work our fathers began. Ours, too, shall be the constant aim and effort to bring ever nearer that blessed age, when this shall be the faith of all mankind:

One God over all;

One brotherhood of all.

### Choir

Behold, how good and how pleasant it is for brethren to dwell together in unity!

הִנֵּה מַה־טּוֹב וּמַה־ נָּעִים שֶׁבֶת אַחִים גַּם־יָחַד:

(Congregation rises)

### Reader (lifts the Torah)

It hath been told thee, O man, what is good; and what the Lord doth require of thee: Only to do justly and to love mercy, and to walk humbly with Thy God.

### Choir

Light is sown for the righteous and joy for the upright in heart.

אוֹר זָרֻעַ לַצַּדִּיק וּלְיִשְׁרֵי־לֵב שִׂמְחָה:

(Torah is returned to the Ark)

## Reader

Behold, this is My covenant, saith the Lord; My spirit which is upon thee, and the words which I have put in thy mouth, shall not depart from thee, nor from thy children, nor from thy children's children, henceforth and forever.

וַאֲנִי זֹאת בְּרִיתִי אוֹתָם
אָמַר יְיָ, רוּחִי אֲשֶׁר עָלֶיךָ
וּדְבָרַי אֲשֶׁר־שַׂמְתִּי בְּפִיךָ
לֹא־יָמוּשׁוּ מִפִּיךָ וּמִפִּי
זַרְעֲךָ וּמִפִּי זֶרַע זַרְעֲךָ
אָמַר יְיָ מֵעַתָּה וְעַד־
עוֹלָם:

## Choir

The Lord will reign forever, thy God, O Zion, from generation to generation. Hallelujah!

יִמְלֹךְ יְיָ לְעוֹלָם
אֱלֹהַיִךְ צִיּוֹן לְדֹר וָדֹר
הַלְלוּיָהּ:

(Congregation is seated)

## CLOSING HYMN

The Lord of all did reign supreme
Ere yet this world was made and formed.
When all was finished by His will,
Then was His name as King proclaimed.

And should these forms no more exist,
He still will rule in majesty.
He was, He is, He shall remain;
His glory never shall decrease.

And one is He, and none there is
To be compared or joined to Him.
He ne'er began, and ne'er will end,
To Him belongs dominion's power.

He is my God, my living God;
To Him I flee when tried in grief;
My banner high, my refuge strong,
Who hears and answers when I call.

My spirit I commit to Him,
My body, too, and all I prize;
Both when I sleep and when I wake,
He is with me, I shall not fear.

**BENEDICTION**

## CLOSING HYMN

---

אֲדוֹן עוֹלָם אֲשֶׁר מָלַךְ. בְּטֶרֶם כָּל־יְצִיר נִבְרָא:

לְעֵת נַעֲשָׂה בְחֶפְצוֹ כֹּל. אֲזַי מֶלֶךְ שְׁמוֹ נִקְרָא:

וְאַחֲרֵי כִּכְלוֹת הַכֹּל. לְבַדּוֹ יִמְלֹךְ נוֹרָא:

וְהוּא הָיָה וְהוּא הֹוֶה. וְהוּא יִהְיֶה בְּתִפְאָרָה:

וְהוּא אֶחָד וְאֵין שֵׁנִי. לְהַמְשִׁיל לוֹ לְהַחְבִּירָה:

בְּלִי רֵאשִׁית בְּלִי תַכְלִית. וְלוֹ הָעֹז וְהַמִּשְׂרָה:

וְהוּא אֵלִי וְחַי גֹּאֲלִי. וְצוּר חֶבְלִי בְּעֵת צָרָה:

וְהוּא נִסִּי וּמָנוֹס לִי. מְנָת כּוֹסִי בְּיוֹם אֶקְרָא:

בְּיָדוֹ אַפְקִיד רוּחִי. בְּעֵת אִישַׁן וְאָעִירָה:

וְעִם רוּחִי גְּוִיָּתִי. יְיָ לִי וְלֹא אִירָא:

---

**BENEDICTION**

# Morning Service for
# the Sabbath

---

## I

### Choir

How goodly are thy tents, O Jacob, thy dwellings, O Israel! Through Thy great mercy, O God, I come to Thy house and bow down in Thy holy temple in the fear of Thee. O Lord, I love the place of Thy house and the abode in which Thy glory dwelleth. And so I bow down, and adore Thee, O God, my Maker. May my prayer be offered in an acceptable time; mayest Thou, in the greatness of Thy mercy, answer me according to Thy faithfulness.

מַה־טֹּבוּ אֹהָלֶיךָ יַעֲקֹב
מִשְׁכְּנֹתֶיךָ יִשְׂרָאֵל: וַאֲנִי
בְּרֹב חַסְדְּךָ אָבֹא בֵיתֶךָ
אֶשְׁתַּחֲוֶה אֶל־הֵיכַל
קָדְשְׁךָ בְּיִרְאָתֶךָ: יְיָ
אָהַבְתִּי מְעוֹן בֵּיתֶךָ וּמְקוֹם
מִשְׁכַּן כְּבוֹדֶךָ: וַאֲנִי
אֶשְׁתַּחֲוֶה וְאֶכְרָעָה
אֶבְרְכָה לִפְנֵי־יְיָ עֹשִׂי:
וַאֲנִי תְפִלָּתִי לְךָ יְיָ עֵת
רָצוֹן אֱלֹהִים בְּרָב־חַסְדֶּךָ
עֲנֵנִי בֶּאֱמֶת יִשְׁעֶךָ:

100

*Reader*

אלהי נשמה

The soul which Thou, O God, hast given unto me came pure from Thee. Thou hast created it, Thou hast formed it, Thou hast breathed it into me; Thou hast preserved it in this body and, at the appointed time, Thou wilt take it from this earth that it may enter upon life everlasting. While the breath of life is within me, I will worship Thee, Sovereign of the world and Lord of all souls. Praised be Thou, O God, in whose hands are the souls of all the living and the spirits of all flesh.

רבון כל העולמים

Lord of all worlds, not in reliance upon our own merit do we lay our supplications before Thee, but trusting in Thine infinite mercy alone. For what are we, what is our life, what our goodness, what our power? What can we say in Thy presence? Are not all the mighty men as naught before Thee and those of great renown as though they had never been; the wisest as if without knowledge, and men of understanding as if without discernment? Many of our works are vain, and our days pass away like a shadow. Our life would be altogether vanity, were it not for the soul which, fashioned in Thine own image, gives us assurance of our higher destiny and imparts to our fleeting days an abiding value.

Help us, O God, to banish from our hearts all vain-glory, pride of worldly possessions, and self-sufficient leaning upon our own reason. Fill us with the spirit of meekness and the grace of modesty that we may grow in wisdom and in reverence. May we never forget that all we have and prize is but lent to us, a trust for which we must render account to Thee. O heavenly Father, put into our hearts the love and awe of Thee, that we may consecrate our lives to Thy service and glorify Thy name in the eyes of all men.

### Congregation and Reader
#### יהי רצון

May it be Thy will, O Lord our God, to lead us in Thy ways, that Thy name may be honored and Israel be blessed by our actions. May we walk according to the precepts of Thy law, and, remaining firm in our devotion to Thee, may we never fall into temptation or shame. May our better nature always prompt us to discharge our duties faithfully and to do good with a willing heart. Gird us with strength to govern our inclinations in accordance with Thy will. Grant, O Father, that by our conduct we may win favor in Thine eyes and in the eyes of our fellowmen.

### Choir: Amen.

(Turn to page 118)

## II

### Choir

| | |
|---|---|
| Early will I seek Thee, God, my refuge strong; Late prepare to meet Thee With my evening song. | שַׁחַר אֲבַקֶּשְׁךָ צוּרִי וּמִשְׂגַּבִּי אֶעֱרוֹךְ לְפָנֶיךָ שַׁחְרִי וְגַם עַרְבִּי: |
| Though unto Thy greatness I with trembling soar,— Yet my inmost thinking Lies Thine eyes before. | לִפְנֵי גְדֻלָּתְךָ אֶעֱמֹד וְאֶבָּהֵל כִּי עֵינְךָ תִרְאֶה כָּל מַחְשְׁבוֹת לִבִּי: |
| What this frail heart dreameth And my tongue's poor speech, Can they even distant To Thy greatness reach? | מַה זֶּה אֲשֶׁר יוּכַל הַלֵּב וְהַלָּשׁוֹן לַעֲשׂוֹת וּמַה כֹּחַ רוּחִי בְּתוֹךְ קִרְבִּי: |
| Being great in mercy, Thou wilt not despise Praises which till death's hour From my soul shall rise. | הִנֵּה לְךָ תִּיטַב זִמְרַת אֱנוֹשׁ עַל כֵּן אוֹדְךָ בְּעוֹד תִּהְיֶה נִשְׁמַת אֱלוֹהַּ בִּי: |

### Reader

With spirits uplifted we enter Thy courts to dedicate

ourselves to Thy holy purposes. We seek to comprehend the wisdom of Thy ways and to perceive the goals which Thou hast set for us. We know that only by deeds of lovingkindness and the quest of truth and goodness may we draw nigh unto Thee. Cleanse Thou our hearts from falsehood and our hands from iniquity that we may be worthy to stand in Thy presence. In our darkness be Thou our light; in our confusion be Thou our guide; and in our weakness be Thou our strength. Amen.

## Responsive Reading

**Reader**

Rejoice in the Lord, ye righteous, for praise befitteth the upright.

**Congregation**

*The Lord loveth righteousness and justice, the earth is full of His kindness.*

The counsel of the Lord standeth forever

*And His purposes through all generations.*

He fashioneth the hearts of men

*He considereth all their deeds.*

A king is not saved by the multitude of his hosts

*Nor is a mighty man delivered by mere strength.*

Our soul waiteth for the Lord,

*He is our help and our shield.*

The Lord redeemeth the soul of His servants,

*None that take refuge in Him shall be forsaken.*

## Reader

נשמת כל חי

Every living soul shall praise Thee; the spirit of all flesh shall glorify Thy name. Thou art God from everlasting to everlasting and besides Thee there is no redeemer nor savior. Thou art the first and the last, the Lord of all generations. Thou rulest the world in kindness and all Thy creatures in mercy. Thou art our guardian who sleepest not and slumberest not. To Thee alone we give thanks. Yet though our lips overflow with song, and our tongues with joyous praise, we should still be unable to thank Thee even for a thousandth part of the bounties which Thou hast bestowed upon our fathers and upon us. Thou hast been our protector and our savior in every trial and peril. Thy mercy has watched over us, and Thy lovingkindness has never failed us.

## Congregation and Reader

Praised be Thy holy name. Thou hast made Thine eternal law our portion, and hast given us a goodly heritage. Open our eyes to the beauty of Thy truth and help us so to exemplify it in our lives that we may win all men for Thy law of righteousness. Gather all Thy children around the banner of Thy truth that Thy name may be hallowed through us in all the world and the entire human family be blessed with truth and peace. Amen.

(Turn to page 118)

## III

### Choir

מִזְמוֹר שִׁיר לְיוֹם הַשַּׁבָּת:

It is good to give thanks to the Lord and to sing praises to Thy name, O Most High; to declare Thy lovingkindness in the morning, and Thy faithfulness in the night seasons, with an instrument of ten strings and with the psaltery; with a solemn sound upon the harp. For Thou, Lord, hast made me glad through Thy works; I will exult in the works of Thy hands. How great are Thy works, O Lord! Thy thoughts are very deep. A brutish man knoweth not, neither doth a fool understand this. When the wicked spring up as

טוֹב לְהֹדוֹת לַיהוָה

וּלְזַמֵּר לְשִׁמְךָ עֶלְיוֹן:

לְהַגִּיד בַּבֹּקֶר חַסְדֶּךָ

וֶאֱמוּנָתְךָ בַּלֵּילוֹת: עֲלֵי־

עָשׂוֹר וַעֲלֵי־נָבֶל עֲלֵי

הִגָּיוֹן בְּכִנּוֹר: כִּי שִׂמַּחְתַּנִי

יְהוָה בְּפָעֳלֶךָ בְּמַעֲשֵׂי

יָדֶיךָ אֲרַנֵּן: מַה־גָּדְלוּ

מַעֲשֶׂיךָ יְהוָה מְאֹד עָמְקוּ

מַחְשְׁבֹתֶיךָ: אִישׁ־בַּעַר לֹא

יֵדָע וּכְסִיל לֹא יָבִין אֶת־

זֹאת: בִּפְרֹחַ רְשָׁעִים כְּמוֹ

עֵשֶׂב וַיָּצִיצוּ כָּל־פֹּעֲלֵי אָוֶן

the grass, and when all the workers of iniquity do flourish, it is that they may be destroyed forever. But Thou, O Lord, art exalted for evermore. For, lo, Thine enemies, O Lord, for lo, Thine enemies shall perish; all the workers of iniquity shall be scattered. The righteous shall blossom like the palmtree, and grow like the cedars in Lebanon. Rooted in the house of the Lord, they shall flower in the courts of our God. They shall be fruitful in old age, flourishing and verdant; to declare that the Lord is upright, my Rock, in whom there is no unrighteousness.

לְהִשָּׁמְדָם עֲדֵי־עַד: וְאַתָּה מָרוֹם לְעֹלָם יְהֹוָה. כִּי־הִנֵּה אֹיְבֶיךָ יְהֹוָה כִּי־הִנֵּה אֹיְבֶיךָ יֹאבֵדוּ יִתְפָּרְדוּ כָּל־פֹּעֲלֵי אָוֶן: וַתָּרֶם כִּרְאֵים קַרְנִי בַּלֹּתִי בְּשֶׁמֶן רַעֲנָן: וַתַּבֵּט עֵינִי בְּשׁוּרָי בַּקָּמִים עָלַי מְרֵעִים תִּשְׁמַעְנָה אָזְנָי: צַדִּיק כַּתָּמָר יִפְרָח כְּאֶרֶז בַּלְּבָנוֹן יִשְׂגֶּה: שְׁתוּלִים בְּבֵית יְהֹוָה. בְּחַצְרוֹת אֱלֹהֵינוּ יַפְרִיחוּ: עוֹד יְנוּבוּן בְּשֵׂיבָה. דְּשֵׁנִים וְרַעֲנַנִּים יִהְיוּ: לְהַגִּיד כִּי־יָשָׁר יְהֹוָה. צוּרִי וְלֹא־עַוְלָתָה בּוֹ:

### Reader

We come into Thy house, O Lord, to voice the longings of our hearts in prayer. In the pressure of daily living, we often forget Thee, and stifle the nobler impulses of our nature. On the Sabbath Day, in this hour of worship, we regain the feeling of our kinship with Thee. Help us, O Father, to keep alive this sense of our high lineage amid the labors and duties of our common life. When selfishness and greed prompt us to wrongdoing, may the sense of Thy nearness restrain our desires and save us from degradation. May the inspiration of this hour open our hearts that we may receive the helpless and despondent with sympathy and love. When summoned to give our strength to a noble cause, let the influence of our Sabbath worship fill us with eagerness and ardor that we may bring our offering with joy. May it be Thy will that our prayers be not barren of results; aid us to make them meaningful and fruitful. Hear Thou our supplication and bless us; for in Thee alone do we trust.

### Responsive Reading

Reader

Happy is the man whom God correcteth; therefore despise thou not the chastening of the Almighty.

Congregation

*For He maketh sore and bindeth up; He woundeth and His hands make whole.*

The sacrifices of God are a broken spirit; a broken and contrite heart, O God, Thou wilt not despise.

*Unto God would I commit my cause; who doeth great things and unsearchable.*

Why sayest thou, O Jacob, and speakest, O Israel: my
way is hid from the Lord, and my right is passed
over from my God?

*Hast thou not heard that the everlasting God fainteth
not, neither is weary?*

He giveth power to the faint, and to him that hath no
might He increaseth strength.

*Even the youths shall faint and be weary; and the
young men shall be powerless,*

But they that wait for the Lord shall renew their
strength.

*They shall mount up with wings as eagles; they shall
run, and not be weary; they shall walk, and not
be faint.*

### Reader

Thine everlasting arms, O Lord, uphold all creation.
Thou art our unfailing help. Darkness does not con-
ceal Thee from the eye of faith, nor do forces of destruction obscure Thy presence. Above the fury of
men and the raging of the tempests standest Thou.
Trusting in Thee we fear not the arrows of ill-fortune
that fly by day nor the pestilence that stalks by night.
When pain and sorrow try our souls, grant us courage
to meet them with hearts undismayed and with faith
that does not waver. We would not close our eyes to
the evils that beset our path, but struggle manfully

to turn them into stepping-stones leading upward unto Thee. Amid tears and tribulations may we behold the reassuring vision of Thy goodness. Amen.

## Congregation and Reader

### (Psalm xxiii)

The Lord is my shepherd, I shall not want. He maketh me to lie down in green pastures; He leadeth me beside the still waters. He restoreth my soul; He guideth me in straight paths for His name's sake. Yea, though I walk through the valley of the shadow of death, I will fear no evil, for Thou art with me; Thy rod and Thy staff, they comfort me. Thou preparest a table before me in the presence of mine enemies; Thou hast anointed my head with oil; my cup runneth over. Surely goodness and mercy shall follow me all the days of my life, and I shall dwell in the house of the Lord forever.

(Turn to page 118)

## IV

*Choir*

Sweet hymns and songs
will I recite
To sing of Thee, by day
and night.
Of Thee, who art my
soul's delight.

אַנְעִים זְמִירוֹת וְשִׁירִים
אֶאֱרוֹג
כִּי אֵלֶיךָ נַפְשִׁי תַעֲרוֹג:

How doth my soul within
me yearn
Beneath Thy shadow to
return,
Thy secret mysteries to
learn.

נַפְשִׁי חָמְדָה בְּצֵל יָדֶךָ
לָדַעַת כָּל־רָז סוֹדֶךָ:

And e'en while yet Thy
glory fires
My words, and hymns of
praise inspires,
Thy love it is my heart
desires.

מִדֵּי דַבְּרִי בִּכְבוֹדֶךָ
הוֹמֶה לִבִּי אֶל־דּוֹדֶיךָ:

יַעֲרַב־נָא שִׂיחִי עָלֶיךָ
כִּי נַפְשִׁי תַעֲרוֹג אֵלֶיךָ:

My meditation day and night,
May it be pleasant in Thy sight,
For Thou art all my soul's delight.

### Reader

Loving Father, hear us as we call unto Thee from the depths of our being. Dark is the world without Thee. Our ways are often confused; the good seems evil and the evil good. Material pursuits deaden us to the needs of the spirit. Swayed by the impulses of our senses, we frequently stifle the voice of conscience which speaks of Thee and of Thine eternal laws. We exchange our glory for things of naught. O God of truth and light, help us to find our way unto Thee. Open up within the desert of our souls the living fountain of Thy love that our lives may be brought to flower in the beauty of Thy goodness.

### Responsive Reading

**Reader**

Happy are they that are upright in the way, who walk in the law of the Lord.

**Congregation**

*Happy are they that keep His testimonies, that seek Him with a whole heart.*

Forever, O Lord, Thy word standeth fast; Thy faithfulness is unto all generations.

*Unless Thy law had been my delight, I should then have perished in mine affliction.*

Thy word is a lamp unto my feet, and a light unto my path.

*Open Thou mine eyes, that I may behold wondrous things out of Thy law.*

Who can discern errors?  Clear Thou me from hidden
faults.

Keep back Thy servant also from presumptuous sins,
that they may not have dominion over me;

The work of righteousness shall be peace; and the effect
of righteousness quietness and confidence forever.

Great peace have they that love Thy law, O God;
and there is no stumbling for them.

### Congregation and Reader

אתה אחד

Thou, O Lord, art one, and Thy name is one.  May
Thy truth unite all mankind into one holy bond of
brotherhood and may our love for one another be our
crown of glory and armor of strength.  Bless us, O God,
on this Sabbath, and grant that it be unto us a day of
rest and sanctification.  May it strengthen us in all noble purposes and holy resolves; may it encourage us to
seek truth from Thy fountain of truth, and inspire us
to become holy as Thou art holy.  To Thee and Thy
service we would consecrate this day, which in Thy love
Thou hast sanctified for us.  Amen.

(Turn to page 118)

## V

### *Choir*

(Psalm cxxii)

I rejoiced when they said unto me: Let us go unto the house of the Lord. Our feet are standing within thy gates, O Jerusalem; Jerusalem, that art builded as a city that is compact together; whither the tribes went up, even the tribes of the Lord, as a testimony unto Israel, to give thanks unto the name of the Lord. For there were set thrones for judgment, the thrones of the house of David. Pray for the peace of Jerusalem; may they prosper that love thee. Peace be within thy walls, and prosperity within thy palaces. For my brethren and companions' sakes, I will now say: Peace be within thee. For the sake of the house of the Lord our God, I will seek thy good.

שִׁיר הַמַּעֲלוֹת לְדָוִד
שָׂמַחְתִּי בְּאֹמְרִים לִי בֵּית
יְיָ נֵלֵךְ: עֹמְדוֹת הָיוּ
רַגְלֵינוּ בִּשְׁעָרַיִךְ יְרוּשָׁלָ͏ִם:
יְרוּשָׁלַ͏ִם הַבְּנוּיָה כְּעִיר
שֶׁחֻבְּרָה־לָּהּ יַחְדָּו: שֶׁשָּׁם
עָלוּ שְׁבָטִים שִׁבְטֵי־יָהּ
עֵדוּת לְיִשְׂרָאֵל לְהוֹדוֹת
לְשֵׁם יְיָ: כִּי שָׁמָּה יָשְׁבוּ
כִסְאוֹת לְמִשְׁפָּט כִּסְאוֹת
לְבֵית דָּוִד: שַׁאֲלוּ שְׁלוֹם
יְרוּשָׁלָ͏ִם יִשְׁלָיוּ אֹהֲבָיִךְ:
יְהִי־שָׁלוֹם בְּחֵילֵךְ שַׁלְוָה
בְּאַרְמְנוֹתָיִךְ: לְמַעַן־אַחַי
וְרֵעָי אֲדַבְּרָה־נָּא שָׁלוֹם
בָּךְ: לְמַעַן בֵּית־יְיָ אֱלֹהֵינוּ
אֲבַקְשָׁה טוֹב לָךְ:

## Reader

ברוך שאמר

Praised be He who by His creative word called the universe into being. Praised be He who sustains it by His might. Praised be He who orders it in His wisdom and establishes the world in righteousness.

## Congregation and Reader

Praised be Thou, O God, for Thy manifold mercies unto us, for our heritage of faith, for visions of truth and of duty and for the courage to remain true to our higher nature amid trials and temptations. Thy servants in all generations have found joy in worshiping Thee with pure hearts. With psalms and songs they glorified Thy name. We too would adore Thee with prayers of thanksgiving and with deeds of lovingkindness.

## Responsive Reading

Reader

Happy are they who dwell in Thy house, they are continually praising Thee.

Congregation

Happy are they who thus know Him; happy is the people whose God is the Lord.

I will extol Thee, my God, O King, and I will bless Thy name forever and ever.

Every day I will bless Thee, and I will praise Thy name forever and ever.

Great is the Lord and highly to be praised; and His greatness is beyond our finding out.

One generation shall praise Thy works to another, and shall declare Thy mighty acts.

I will speak of the splendor of Thy majesty and of Thy
wondrous works

And men shall tell of Thy mighty acts, and I will tell
of Thy greatness.

They shall herald Thy great goodness, and shall sing
of Thy righteousness.

The Lord is gracious and full of compassion, slow to
anger and of great mercy.

The Lord is good to all, and His tender mercies are over
all His works.

Thy kingdom is a kingdom for all ages, and Thy
dominion endureth throughout all generations.

The Lord upholdeth those who fall, and raiseth up
those who are bowed down.

The eyes of all wait upon Thee, and Thou givest them
their food in due season.

Thou openest Thy hand and satisfiest the desire of
every living being.

The Lord is righteous in all His ways, and gracious
in all His works.

The Lord is near unto all who call upon Him, to all
who call upon Him in truth.

My mouth shall utter the praise of the Lord; and let
all flesh bless His holy name forever and ever.

## Congregation and Reader

Thou, O Lord, hast endowed us with reason to dis-
tinguish between right and wrong and with freedom
to choose between good and evil. Though Thy greatness is beyond our understanding, Thou art near to the

hearts of the lowly who seek Thee and who strive to do Thy will. Teach us to be firm in our devotion to Thee in health and in sickness, in prosperity and adversity. May Thy law ever be a light unto us as we pursue our daily tasks. By Thy grace may we live in harmony with our dear ones, and work in peace and concord with all our neighbors. Amen.

*(Congregation rises)*

### Reader

Praise ye the Lord to whom all praise is due.

### Choir and Congregation

Praised be the Lord to whom all praise is due forever and ever.

*(Congregation is seated)*

### Reader

Praised be Thou, O Lord our God, Ruler of the world, who in Thy mercy makest light to shine over the earth and all its inhabitants, and renewest daily the work of creation. How manifold are Thy works, O Lord! In wisdom hast Thou made them all. The heavens declare Thy glory. The earth reveals Thy creative power. Thou formest light and darkness, ordainest good out of evil, bringest harmony into nature and peace to the heart of man.

Great has been Thy love for us and Thy compassion boundless. Our fathers put their trust in Thee and Thou didst teach them the law of life. Be gracious also unto us that we may understand and fulfil the teachings of Thy word. Enlighten our eyes in Thy law that we may cling unto Thy commandments. Unite our hearts to love and revere Thee. We trust in Thee

(Congregation rises)

### Reader

בָּרְכוּ אֶת־יְיָ הַמְבֹרָךְ:

### Choir and Congregation

בָּרוּךְ יְיָ הַמְבֹרָךְ לְעוֹלָם וָעֶד:

(Congregation is seated)

### Reader

בָּרוּךְ אַתָּה יְיָ אֱלֹהֵינוּ מֶלֶךְ הָעוֹלָם. יוֹצֵר אוֹר
וּבוֹרֵא חֹשֶׁךְ. עֹשֶׂה שָׁלוֹם וּבוֹרֵא אֶת־הַכֹּל:
הַמֵּאִיר לָאָרֶץ וְלַדָּרִים עָלֶיהָ בְּרַחֲמִים. וּבְטוּבוֹ
מְחַדֵּשׁ בְּכָל־יוֹם תָּמִיד מַעֲשֵׂה בְרֵאשִׁית: מָה
רַבּוּ מַעֲשֶׂיךָ יְיָ. כֻּלָּם בְּחָכְמָה עָשִׂיתָ. מָלְאָה
הָאָרֶץ קִנְיָנֶךָ: תִּתְבָּרַךְ יְיָ אֱלֹהֵינוּ עַל־שֶׁבַח מַעֲשֵׂה
יָדֶיךָ. וְעַל־מְאוֹרֵי־אוֹר שֶׁעָשִׂיתָ יְפָאֲרוּךָ סֶּלָה:
בָּרוּךְ אַתָּה יְיָ יוֹצֵר הַמְּאוֹרוֹת:
אַהֲבָה רַבָּה אֲהַבְתָּנוּ יְיָ אֱלֹהֵינוּ. חֶמְלָה גְדוֹלָה
וִיתֵרָה חָמַלְתָּ עָלֵינוּ: אָבִינוּ מַלְכֵּנוּ. בַּעֲבוּר
אֲבוֹתֵינוּ שֶׁבָּטְחוּ בְךָ וַתְּלַמְּדֵם חֻקֵּי חַיִּים. כֵּן
תְּחָנֵּנוּ וּתְלַמְּדֵנוּ: הָאֵר עֵינֵינוּ בְּתוֹרָתֶךָ. וְדַבֵּק לִבֵּנוּ
בְּמִצְוֹתֶיךָ. וְיַחֵד לְבָבֵנוּ לְאַהֲבָה וּלְיִרְאָה שְׁמֶךָ:

and rejoice in Thy saving power, for from Thee cometh
our help.  Thou hast called us and drawn us nigh unto
Thee to serve Thee in faithfulness.  Joyfully do we lift
up our voices and proclaim Thy unity.  Praised be
Thou, O God, who in Thy love hast called Thy people
Israel to serve Thee.

(Congregation rises)

## Reader

Hear, O Israel: The Lord our God, the Lord is One.

Praised be His name whose glorious kingdom is forever and ever.

(Congregation is seated)

## Congregation and Reader

Thou shalt love the Lord, thy God, with all thy
heart, with all thy soul, and with all thy might.  And
these words, which I command thee this day, shall be
upon thy heart.  Thou shalt teach them diligently unto
thy children, and shalt speak of them when thou sittest
in thy house, when thou walkest by the way, when
thou liest down, and when thou risest up.  Thou shalt
bind them for a sign upon thy hand and they shall be
for frontlets between thine eyes.  Thou shalt write them
upon the doorposts of thy house and upon thy gates:
That ye may remember and do all My commandments
and be holy unto your God.

## Responsive Reading

Reader

True and enduring is Thy word which Thou hast
spoken through Thy prophets.

כִּי בְשֵׁם קָדְשְׁךָ בָטָחְנוּ. נָגִילָה וְנִשְׂמְחָה בִּישׁוּעָתֶךָ.
כִּי אֵל פּוֹעֵל יְשׁוּעוֹת אָתָּה. וּבָנוּ בָחַרְתָּ וְקֵרַבְתָּנוּ
לְשִׁמְךָ הַגָּדוֹל סֶלָה בֶּאֱמֶת לְהוֹדוֹת לְךָ וּלְיַחֶדְךָ
בְּאַהֲבָה. בָּרוּךְ אַתָּה יְיָ הַבּוֹחֵר בְּעַמּוֹ יִשְׂרָאֵל
בְּאַהֲבָה:

(Congregation rises)

Reader, then Choir and Congregation

שְׁמַע יִשְׂרָאֵל יְהֹוָה אֱלֹהֵינוּ יְהֹוָה אֶחָד:
בָּרוּךְ שֵׁם כְּבוֹד מַלְכוּתוֹ לְעוֹלָם וָעֶד:

(Congregation is seated)

Reader

וְאָהַבְתָּ אֵת יְיָ אֱלֹהֶיךָ בְּכָל־לְבָבְךָ וּבְכָל־נַפְשְׁךָ
וּבְכָל־מְאֹדֶךָ: וְהָיוּ הַדְּבָרִים הָאֵלֶּה אֲשֶׁר אָנֹכִי
מְצַוְּךָ הַיּוֹם עַל־לְבָבֶךָ: וְשִׁנַּנְתָּם לְבָנֶיךָ וְדִבַּרְתָּ
בָּם. בְּשִׁבְתְּךָ בְּבֵיתֶךָ וּבְלֶכְתְּךָ בַדֶּרֶךְ וּבְשָׁכְבְּךָ
וּבְקוּמֶךָ: וּקְשַׁרְתָּם לְאוֹת עַל־יָדֶךָ. וְהָיוּ לְטֹטָפֹת
בֵּין עֵינֶיךָ: וּכְתַבְתָּם עַל־מְזֻזוֹת בֵּיתֶךָ וּבִשְׁעָרֶיךָ:
לְמַעַן תִּזְכְּרוּ וַעֲשִׂיתֶם אֶת־כָּל־מִצְוֹתָי וִהְיִיתֶם
קְדֹשִׁים לֵאלֹהֵיכֶם: אֲנִי יְיָ אֱלֹהֵיכֶם:

Responsive Reading

אֱמֶת. אֱלֹהֵי עוֹלָם מַלְכֵּנוּ. צוּר יַעֲקֹב מָגֵן יִשְׁעֵנוּ:

Congregation

Thou art the living God, Thy words bring life and light to the soul.

Thou art the strength of our life, the rock of our salvation; Thy kingdom and Thy truth abide forever.

Thou hast been the help of our fathers in time of trouble and art our refuge in all generations.

Thou art the first and the last, and besides Thee there is no redeemer nor helper.

As Thou hast saved Israel from Egyptian bondage, so mayest Thou send Thy help to all who are oppressed.

May Thy law rule in the hearts of all Thy children, and Thy truth unite them in bonds of fellowship.

May the righteous of all nations rejoice in Thy grace and triumph by Thy power.

O God, who art our refuge and our hope, we glorify Thy name now as did our fathers in ancient days:

## Choir

Who is like unto Thee, O Lord?  Who is like unto Thee, glorious in holiness, awe-inspiring, working wonders?

לְדוֹר וָדוֹר הוּא קַיָּם וּשְׁמוֹ קַיָּם. וּמַלְכוּתוֹ
וֶאֱמוּנָתוֹ לָעַד קַיֶּמֶת:

וּדְבָרָיו חַיִּים וְקַיָּמִים. נֶאֱמָנִים וְנֶחֱמָדִים לָעַד
וּלְעוֹלְמֵי עוֹלָמִים:

עֶזְרַת אֲבוֹתֵינוּ אַתָּה הוּא מֵעוֹלָם מָגֵן וּמוֹשִׁיעַ
לִבְנֵיהֶם אַחֲרֵיהֶם בְּכָל־דּוֹר וָדוֹר:

אַשְׁרֵי אִישׁ שֶׁיִּשְׁמַע לְמִצְוֹתֶיךָ וְתוֹרָתְךָ וּדְבָרְךָ
יָשִׂים עַל־לִבּוֹ:

אֱמֶת. שָׁאַתָּה הוּא יְיָ אֱלֹהֵינוּ. צוּר יְשׁוּעָתֵנוּ.
פּוֹדֵנוּ וּמַצִּילֵנוּ. מֵעוֹלָם שְׁמֶךָ. אֵין אֱלֹהִים זוּלָתֶךָ:

אַתָּה הוּא רִאשׁוֹן וְאַתָּה הוּא אַחֲרוֹן. וּמִבַּלְעָדֶיךָ
אֵין לָנוּ מֶלֶךְ גּוֹאֵל וּמוֹשִׁיעַ:

מִמִּצְרַיִם גְּאַלְתָּנוּ יְיָ אֱלֹהֵינוּ. וּמִבֵּית עֲבָדִים
פְּדִיתָנוּ:

עַל־זֹאת שִׁבְּחוּ אֲהוּבִים וְרוֹמְמוּ אֵל:

## Choir

מִי כָמֹכָה בָּאֵלִים יְיָ. מִי כָּמֹכָה נֶאְדָּר בַּקֹּדֶשׁ
נוֹרָא תְהִלֹּת עֹשֵׂה־פֶלֶא:

### Reader

A new song the redeemed sang unto Thy name. They proclaimed Thy sovereignty and said:

### Choir

The Lord shall reign forever and ever.

### Reader

O Rock of Israel, redeem those who are oppressed and deliver those who are persecuted. Praised be Thou, our Redeemer, the Holy One of Israel.

### Amen

### Reader

Praised be Thou, O Lord, God of our fathers, God of Abraham, Isaac and Jacob, great, mighty, and exalted. Thou bestowest lovingkindness upon all Thy children. Thou rememberest the devotion of the fathers. In Thy love Thou bringest redemption to their descendants for the sake of Thy name. Thou art our King and Helper, our Savior and Protector. Praised be Thou, O Lord, Shield of Abraham.

Eternal is Thy power, O Lord, Thou art mighty to save. In lovingkindness Thou sustainest the living; in the multitude of Thy mercies Thou preservest all. Thou upholdest the falling and healest the sick; freest the captives and keepest faith with Thy children in death as in life. Who is like unto Thee, Almighty God, Author of life and death, Source of salvation? Praised be Thou, O Lord, who hast implanted within us eternal life.

Reader

שִׁירָה חֲדָשָׁה שִׁבְּחוּ גְאוּלִים לְשִׁמְךָ עַל־שְׂפַת
הַיָּם יַחַד כֻּלָּם הוֹדוּ וְהִמְלִיכוּ וְאָמְרוּ:

Choir and Congregation

יְיָ יִמְלֹךְ לְעֹלָם וָעֶד:

Reader

צוּר יִשְׂרָאֵל. קוּמָה בְּעֶזְרַת יִשְׂרָאֵל. וּגְאַל לָנוּ יְיָ
צְבָאוֹת. שְׁמוֹ קְדוֹשׁ יִשְׂרָאֵל. בָּרוּךְ אַתָּה יְיָ גָּאַל
יִשְׂרָאֵל:

Choir: Amen.

Reader

בָּרוּךְ אַתָּה יְיָ אֱלֹהֵינוּ וֵאלֹהֵי אֲבוֹתֵינוּ. אֱלֹהֵי
אַבְרָהָם אֱלֹהֵי יִצְחָק וֵאלֹהֵי יַעֲקֹב. הָאֵל הַגָּדוֹל
הַגִּבּוֹר וְהַנּוֹרָא. אֵל עֶלְיוֹן. גּוֹמֵל חֲסָדִים טוֹבִים.
וְקֹנֵה הַכֹּל וְזוֹכֵר חַסְדֵי אָבוֹת. וּמֵבִיא גְאֻלָּה לִבְנֵי
בְנֵיהֶם לְמַעַן שְׁמוֹ בְּאַהֲבָה: מֶלֶךְ עוֹזֵר וּמוֹשִׁיעַ
וּמָגֵן. בָּרוּךְ אַתָּה יְיָ מָגֵן אַבְרָהָם:

אַתָּה גִבּוֹר לְעוֹלָם אֲדֹנָי. רַב לְהוֹשִׁיעַ. מְכַלְכֵּל
חַיִּים בְּחֶסֶד. מְחַיֵּה הַכֹּל בְּרַחֲמִים רַבִּים. סוֹמֵךְ
נוֹפְלִים וְרוֹפֵא חוֹלִים וּמַתִּיר אֲסוּרִים וּמְקַיֵּם
אֱמוּנָתוֹ לִישֵׁנֵי עָפָר. מִי כָמוֹךָ בַּעַל גְּבוּרוֹת. וּמִי
דּוֹמֶה לָּךְ. מֶלֶךְ מֵמִית וּמְחַיֶּה. וּמַצְמִיחַ יְשׁוּעָה:
בָּרוּךְ אַתָּה יְיָ נֹטֵעַ בְּתוֹכֵנוּ חַיֵּי עוֹלָם:

## SANCTIFICATION

(Congregation rises)

### Congregation and Reader

We sanctify Thy name on earth, as the heavens declare Thy glory; and in the words of the prophet we say:

Holy, holy, holy is the Lord of hosts; the whole earth is full of His glory.

### Reader

God our Strength, God our Lord, how excellent is Thy name in all the earth.

### Congregation and Reader

Praised be the glory of God in all the world.

### Reader

Our God is one; He is our Father, He is our King, He is our Helper and in His mercy He will answer our prayers in the sight of all the living.

### Congregation and Reader

The Lord will reign forever, thy God, O Zion, from generation to generation.   Hallelujah.

(Congregation is seated)

### Reader

From generation to generation we declare Thy greatness and throughout all ages proclaim Thy holiness; Thy praise shall never cease from our lips.   Praised be Thou, O Lord, the God of holiness.

## SANCTIFICATION
### (Congregation rises)

נְקַדֵּשׁ אֶת־שִׁמְךָ בָּעוֹלָם. כְּשֵׁם שֶׁמַּקְדִּישִׁים אוֹתוֹ
בִּשְׁמֵי מָרוֹם. כַּכָּתוּב עַל־יַד נְבִיאֶךָ. וְקָרָא זֶה אֶל־
זֶה וְאָמַר:

### Choir and Congregation

קָדוֹשׁ קָדוֹשׁ קָדוֹשׁ יְיָ צְבָאוֹת. מְלֹא כָל־הָאָרֶץ
כְּבוֹדוֹ:

### Reader

אַדִּיר אַדִּירֵנוּ יְיָ אֲדוֹנֵנוּ מָה־אַדִּיר שִׁמְךָ בְּכָל־
הָאָרֶץ:

### Choir and Congregation

בָּרוּךְ כְּבוֹד יְיָ מִמְּקוֹמוֹ:

### Reader

אֶחָד הוּא אֱלֹהֵינוּ. הוּא אָבִינוּ. הוּא מַלְכֵּנוּ. הוּא
מוֹשִׁיעֵנוּ. וְהוּא יַשְׁמִיעֵנוּ בְּרַחֲמָיו לְעֵינֵי כָּל־חָי:

### Choir and Congregation

יִמְלֹךְ יְיָ לְעוֹלָם אֱלֹהַיִךְ צִיּוֹן לְדֹר וָדֹר
הַלְלוּיָהּ:

### (Congregation is seated)

### Reader

לְדוֹר וָדוֹר נַגִּיד גָּדְלֶךָ. וּלְנֵצַח נְצָחִים קְדֻשָּׁתְךָ
נַקְדִּישׁ. וְשִׁבְחֲךָ אֱלֹהֵינוּ מִפִּינוּ לֹא יָמוּשׁ לְעוֹלָם
וָעֶד: בָּרוּךְ אַתָּה יְיָ הָאֵל הַקָּדוֹשׁ:

### Choir: Amen.

## I

### Reader

On this day, appointed for rest and spiritual quickening, we humbly approach Thee and thank Thee for so precious a gift. Each week this herald of peace comes to us with its message ever new, giving strength to the weary, relief to the burdened, and cheer to the faint of heart. It reminds us that Thy protecting hand is over us at all times, from the beginning even unto the end of our life; that it is Thou who blessest our work and helpest us to acquire the things we need for our sustenance.

Truly we feel Thy presence with us, O Father. As we see Thy hand in the world around us, even so do we know that Thou art near us in the working out of our destiny. Thou hast raised man high above all other creatures and hast crowned him with glory and honor, in that Thou gavest him the power to choose between good and evil.

Our souls thirst for Thee as does the hart after the refreshing waterbrook. When we would escape from the storms of earthly life, where can we find refuge but in Thee? As week swiftly follows week and man gives no heed, so pass the years away, and the end of our work draws nigh. Help us so to live that our souls may look upon these transient scenes with calmness and contentment, assured that at last we shall rest in the light of Thy countenance and rejoice in Thy goodness forever. Amen.

(Turn to page 138)

## II

*Reader*

Again has come the day which bids us lay aside the burden of care and the anxiety of the daily task. Thou hast commanded us to work, that we may free ourselves from that bondage of nature in which all other creatures on earth are held. But in the struggle for the mastery over things material, we often forget the divine purpose of our life. Driven by the desire for gain or the longing for pleasure, we become enslaved, fettered by new wants, oppressed by new burdens. Therefore hast Thou, O Father, in Thy love appointed for us a day of rest, that in Thy presence we may regain that freedom of the soul which comes through obedience to Thy commandments. Quickened by Thy spirit, may we learn how to ennoble the things of earth by sanctifying them to Thy service.

He who has worked faithfully during the week, and according to his strength has contributed to the larger work of mankind, will enjoy the delight of the Sabbath. In this spirit, O God, we would keep the day of rest Thou hast sanctified for our good. May its blessings gladden our hearts and inspire us to holier resolves and purer motives. Strengthen us, O God, and grant that new courage, new faith, new power may descend upon us and upon all who strive to do Thy will and to fulfil Thy benign purposes. Amen.

(Turn to page 138)

### III

#### Reader

Our Father in heaven, so establish this sanctuary, dedicated to Thy holy name, that the worship offered within its walls may be worthy of Thy greatness and Thy love; that every heart which seeks Thy presence here may find it, as did our fathers in the Temple on Zion; and that this house may be a house of prayer for all peoples.

#### Congregation

Our Father in heaven, hear our prayer and bless Thy servants.

#### Reader

Have compassion upon us and all our brethren of the house of Israel; preserve us from sickness, from war, from strife; keep us from hatred and uncharitableness toward our fellow-men; and grant that, dwelling in safety and walking in uprightness, we may enjoy the fruit of our labor in peace.

#### Congregation

May it please Thee, O Father, to hear our prayer.

#### Reader

Be with all men and women who spend themselves for the good of mankind and bear the burdens of others; who give bread to the hungry, clothe the naked and provide shelter for the homeless. Establish Thou, O God, the work of their hands and grant them an abundant harvest of the good seed they are sowing.

### Congregation

May it please Thee, O Father, to hear our prayer.

### Reader

Bless our children, O God, and help us so to fashion their souls by precept and example, that they may ever love the good, flee from sin, revere Thy word, and honor Thy name. Planted in the house of the Lord, may they flourish in the courts of our God; may they guard for future ages the truths revealed to our forefathers.

### Congregation

Our Father in heaven, hear our prayer and bless us. Amen.

(Turn to page 138)

## IV

### Reader

O God, who hast permitted us to see this new day and to greet its light in Thy house, we lift up our hearts in grateful praise of Thy goodness toward us. But how can we honor Thee worthily, how thank Thee as we ought, even for the least of Thy mercies? We know not what to render Thee for all Thy benefits. And yet must we not confess that often in the enjoyment of Thy gifts we forget the Giver, and because of the frequency and abundance of Thy blessings, we fail to appreciate the greatness of Thy bounty? Truly, we feel our ingratitude and are ashamed of it; the more so, since we are ready to murmur against Thee and to question Thy goodness, when our wishes are not fulfilled and days of trial are meted out unto us.

Help us, O God, to maintain within ourselves a constant spirit of gratitude toward Thee, to remember that not in words and songs alone should we express our thankfulness; our deeds should speak Thy praise; our willingness to share Thy blessings with others should testify to our gratitude. In prosperity may we not be tempted to say: My power and the might of my hand have gotten me this abundance; but may we remember that it is Thou, O God, who givest strength to acquire substance. And may we bear in mind that Thou who givest, canst also take away; and when Thou takest away, may we not have cause to reproach ourselves that we have not justly and wisely used Thy gifts.

O may our hearts never be so carried away by material success that we make idols of wealth, station or pleasure, and in striving after them become estranged from Thee. May every new blessing bring us nearer to Thee and make us more fervent in our devotion to Thy service, more faithful to our duties and more helpful to our fellowmen. Amen.

(Turn to page 138)

## V

### Reader

We thank Thee, O God, for the worship of this day and for the restoration of body and soul which comes to us through communion with Thee. We rejoice that Thou hast permitted us to be co-workers with Thee in the unfolding of Thy divine plan. Thou hast set Thy blessing upon labor, and hast enabled us to promote the well-being of all by the faithful work we do. Strengthen in us, O God, the spirit of service and sacrifice. May we never be tempted to profit by impoverishing and degrading the lives of others. Make us realize the wrong of letting others hunger while we are surfeited with the bounties of nature. Implant in our hearts, we pray Thee, a sense of responsibility and comradeship. Reveal to us the divine glory that abides in every soul, and the high dignity that invests all honest labor. Help us so to live that, by our own endeavors, we may hasten the day when all shall toil and serve side by side as brothers; when love and sympathy shall stir every heart, and greed and want no longer mar the beauty of Thy creation. Amen.

(Turn to page 138)

#### FOR THE SABBATH DURING PESACH

Lord our God and God of our fathers, Thou hast created the universe in wisdom and rulest all Thy creatures in love. At Thy bidding light dispels darkness and life springs forth from death. By Thy command, bleak winter has fled and gladsome spring has come. The earth has clothed herself in her garment of green; the voice of the turtle-dove is heard in the land. The plowman goes forth to his fields and the sower to his work. O let Thy gracious blessing of plenty and contentment reward our toil. Let neither want nor scarcity waste our land, but let all Thy children be satisfied of Thy boundless providence and Thine abundant grace.

As our fathers of old on this sacred festival rejoiced that Thou didst deliver them from the bondage of Egypt, so may we rejoice that Thou redeemest us from the deadening fetters of self-enslavement, and bringest us forth into the glorious freedom of service to Thee. Let Thy spirit breathe upon the house of Israel, so that, awakened to new life, we may consecrate ourselves to do Thy will and to promote the knowledge of Thee among men.

O hasten the day when Israel's hope shall be realized and Israel's mission fulfilled, when oppression and strife shall forever cease, and all men shall be bound together in an eternal covenant of brotherhood and love. Amen.

(Turn to page 138)

### FOR THE SABBATH DURING SUCCOS

We recall today with grateful hearts Thy loving providence which guided our fathers in their wanderings through the barren desert and the trackless wilderness. Under Thy protection the weary pilgrims found shelter and security. In famine Thou didst sustain them and from the flinty rock Thou didst slake their thirst.

We thank Thee that the same unfailing mercies have guided and sheltered us, their children, in all the years of our pilgrimage. Our hearts are filled with gratitude at the remembrance of Thy goodness. We pray Thee that the enjoyment of Thy blessings may awaken within us a spirit of contentment and fortitude, that we may neither grow proud through success nor become embittered by failure.

May we sympathize with those whose hopes have been disappointed and whose labors have been unfruitful. May our hands be outstretched to those who suffer, and our hearts be opened to those who are in need. Praised be Thou, O Lord, Giver of all good. Amen.

(Turn to page 138)

## FOR THE SABBATH DURING HANUKKAH

With grateful hearts we remember today Thy protection of old, when tyrants sought to destroy Thy people and to uproot the religion of Israel. We recall with joyful pride the steadfastness and valor of the Maccabees, their faith in Thee and their devotion to Thy law which inspired them to deeds of heroism. We thank Thee for the tender care with which Thou didst guard our fathers in those days and at all times. We commemorate the rededication of Thy sanctuary, the consecration of its altar unto Thy worship, and celebrate the rekindling of the perpetual lamp, whose rays shone forth out of the encircling darkness as the symbol of Thy presence and the beacon light of Thy truth for all mankind.

O be with us and our children today. Imbue us with perfect faith in Thee. Make us strong to do Thy will. Help us to understand and proclaim the truth, that not by might and not by power, but by Thy spirit alone can man prevail. Grant unto all men and nations the blessings of liberty, justice and peace. Let injustice and oppression everywhere cease, and hatred, cruelty and wrong pass away, so that all men may unite to worship Thee in love and devotion.

Bless, O God, the Hanukkah lights, that they may shed their radiance into our homes and our lives. May they kindle within us the flame of faith and zeal that, like the Maccabees of old, we battle bravely for Thy cause. Make us ever worthy of Thy love and Thy blessing, our Shield and our Protector. Amen.

(Turn to page 138)

### FOR THE SABBATH PRECEDING PURIM

Almighty God and Father, on this Sabbath of Remembrance, we come before Thee with words of praise and thanksgiving for the providential care and guidance under which Thy people Israel has ever lived, and for the manifold blessings which Thou hast vouchsafed unto us and all mankind.

We remember today the darkness and gloom which enveloped Israel's life in the past. Painful trials and bitter struggles, torment of body and agony of soul have been his portion through the dreary centuries of fiery hatred and bloody persecution. But sustained by the undying hope that in the end right will triumph over wrong, good over evil, and love over hate, he has held aloft the banner of Thy truth.

We today, loyal to the memory of those heroic martyrs, come to thank Thee for the blessed assurance that the living hope born in the prophetic soul of Israel will not remain unfulfilled. Before the mighty onrush of Thy light and love, we shall yet see the forces of darkness, cruel Amalek and vindictive Haman, succumb and vanish. And though many a bitter experience may await us before prejudice and hate shall have vanished, still do we trust, as did our fathers, that in the end all barriers to brotherhood shall be broken down.

Grant us, we beseech Thee, the vision to see and the courage to do Thy holy will. Imbue our hearts with the fidelity of Mordecai and the devotion of Esther, that we may never swerve from the path of duty and loyalty trod by our fathers. Endow us with patience and strength, with purity of heart and unity of purpose, that we may continue to proclaim Thy law of love and truth to the peoples of the earth, until all men shall have learned to call Thee Father and know one another as brothers.  Amen.

(Turn to page 138)

### FOR THE SABBATH OF REPENTANCE

On this Sabbath of Repentance, O our God, open our hearts to its solemn call to turn from the vanities of life and consider our destiny in the light of Thine eternal truth.  Help us to see whether we have indeed hearkened to Thy voice within us, and have done justly, loved mercy and walked humbly before Thee, or whether we have been negligent in the fulfilment of our duties and have strayed from the path of rectitude.

As we thus survey our life, we are filled with shame that we have fallen short of the purpose for which Thou didst send us hither, and have failed to use aright the manifold gifts which Thou didst bestow upon us.  Humbly we confess that our intentions and our deeds accuse us before the tribunal of our conscience and convict us in Thy sight, O righteous Judge of the world.

O God of holiness, Thou knowest that we are but flesh, and in our weakness often yield to selfish indulgence.  Create in us a pure heart, and a steadfast spirit renew Thou within us.  Strengthen us in our resolve to mend our ways.  Let our struggle with error and sin lead us to a clearer realization of the truth of Thy word and to a firmer adherence to Thy law of righteousness.  Help us to remove every misunderstanding between ourselves and our fellowmen.  O God, who art plenteous in mercy and forgiveness, do Thou establish peace and harmony within our souls, that we may be truly at one with Thee.  Amen.

*Congregation and Reader*

Our God and God of our fathers, grant that our worship on this Sabbath be acceptable to Thee. May we, sanctified through Thy commandments, become sharers in the blessings of Thy word. Teach us to be satisfied with the gifts of Thy goodness and gratefully to rejoice in all Thy mercies. Purify our hearts that we may serve Thee in truth. O help us to preserve the Sabbath as Israel's heritage from generation to generation, that it may ever bring rest and joy, peace and comfort to the dwellings of our brethren, and through it Thy name be hallowed in all the earth. Praised be Thou, O Lord, who sanctifiest the Sabbath.

### Choir: Amen

### Reader

Look with favor, O Lord, upon us, and may our service be acceptable unto Thee. Praised be Thou, O God, whom alone we serve in reverence.

*Congregation and Reader*

We gratefully acknowledge, O Lord our God, that Thou art our Creator and Preserver, the Rock of our life and the Shield of our help. We render thanks unto Thee for our lives which are in Thy hand, for our souls which are ever in Thy keeping, for Thy wondrous providence and for Thy continuous goodness, which Thou bestowest upon us day by day. Truly, Thy mercies never fail and Thy lovingkindness never ceases. Therefore do we forever put our trust in Thee.

Congregation and Reader

אֱלֹהֵינוּ וֵאלֹהֵי אֲבוֹתֵינוּ רְצֵה בִמְנוּחָתֵנוּ קַדְּשֵׁנוּ
בְּמִצְוֹתֶיךָ וְתֵן חֶלְקֵנוּ בְּתוֹרָתֶךָ שַׂבְּעֵנוּ מִטּוּבֶךָ
וְשַׂמְּחֵנוּ בִּישׁוּעָתֶךָ וְטַהֵר לִבֵּנוּ לְעָבְדְּךָ בֶּאֱמֶת
וְהַנְחִילֵנוּ יְיָ אֱלֹהֵינוּ בְּאַהֲבָה וּבְרָצוֹן שַׁבַּת קָדְשֶׁךָ
וְיָנוּחוּ בָהּ יִשְׂרָאֵל מְקַדְּשֵׁי שְׁמֶךָ. בָּרוּךְ אַתָּה יְיָ
מְקַדֵּשׁ הַשַּׁבָּת:

Reader

רְצֵה יְיָ אֱלֹהֵינוּ בְּעַמְּךָ יִשְׂרָאֵל וּתְפִלָּתָם בְּאַהֲבָה
תְקַבֵּל וּתְהִי לְרָצוֹן תָּמִיד עֲבֹדַת יִשְׂרָאֵל עַמֶּךָ:
בָּרוּךְ אַתָּה יְיָ שֶׁאוֹתְךָ לְבַדְּךָ בְּיִרְאָה נַעֲבוֹד:

Congregation and Reader

מוֹדִים אֲנַחְנוּ לָךְ שָׁאַתָּה הוּא יְיָ אֱלֹהֵינוּ וֵאלֹהֵי
אֲבוֹתֵינוּ לְעוֹלָם וָעֶד. צוּר חַיֵּינוּ מָגֵן יִשְׁעֵנוּ אַתָּה
הוּא לְדוֹר וָדוֹר נוֹדֶה לְּךָ וּנְסַפֵּר תְּהִלָּתֶךָ עַל־חַיֵּינוּ
הַמְּסוּרִים בְּיָדֶךָ וְעַל־נִשְׁמוֹתֵינוּ הַפְּקוּדוֹת לָךְ וְעַל־
נִסֶּיךָ שֶׁבְּכָל־יוֹם עִמָּנוּ וְעַל־נִפְלְאוֹתֶיךָ וְטוֹבוֹתֶיךָ
שֶׁבְּכָל־עֵת עֶרֶב וָבֹקֶר וְצָהֳרָיִם. הַטּוֹב כִּי־לֹא כָלוּ
רַחֲמֶיךָ וְהַמְרַחֵם כִּי־לֹא תַמּוּ חֲסָדֶיךָ מֵעוֹלָם קִוִּינוּ
לָךְ:

### Reader

Grant us peace, Thy most precious gift, O Thou eternal source of peace, and enable Israel to be its messenger unto the peoples of the earth. Bless our country that it may ever be a stronghold of peace, and its advocate in the council of nations. May contentment reign within its borders, health and happiness within its homes. Strengthen the bonds of friendship and fellowship among all the inhabitants of our land. Plant virtue in every soul, and may the love of Thy name hallow every home and every heart. Praised be Thou, O Lord, Giver of peace.

### Choir: Amen

### Silent Prayer

##### (or such other prayer as the heart may prompt)

O God, keep my tongue from evil and my lips from speaking guile. Be my support when grief silences my voice, and my comfort when woe bends my spirit. Implant humility in my soul, and strengthen my heart with perfect faith in Thee. Help me to be strong in temptation and trial and to be patient and forgiving when others wrong me. Guide me by the light of Thy counsel, that I may ever find strength in Thee, my Rock and my Redeemer. Amen.

### Choir

May the words of my mouth and the meditations of my heart be acceptable in Thy sight, O Lord, my Rock and my Redeemer.

## Reader

שִׂים שָׁלוֹם טוֹבָה וּבְרָכָה חֵן וָחֶסֶד וְרַחֲמִים
עָלֵינוּ וְעַל־כָּל־יִרְאֵי שְׁמֶךָ. בָּרְכֵנוּ אָבִינוּ כֻּלָּנוּ
כְּאֶחָד בְּאוֹר פָּנֶיךָ. כִּי בְאוֹר פָּנֶיךָ נָתַתָּ־לָּנוּ יְיָ
אֱלֹהֵינוּ תּוֹרַת חַיִּים וְאַהֲבַת חֶסֶד וּצְדָקָה וּבְרָכָה
וְרַחֲמִים וְחַיִּים וְשָׁלוֹם. וְטוֹב בְּעֵינֶיךָ לְבָרֵךְ אֶת־
עַמְּךָ יִשְׂרָאֵל וְאֶת־כָּל־הָעַמִּים בְּרֹב עֹז וְשָׁלוֹם:
בָּרוּךְ אַתָּה יְיָ עֹשֵׂה הַשָּׁלוֹם:

## Choir: Amen

## Silent Prayer

אֱלֹהַי נְצוֹר לְשׁוֹנִי מֵרָע וּשְׂפָתַי מִדַּבֵּר מִרְמָה:
וְלִמְקַלְלַי נַפְשִׁי תִדֹּם וְנַפְשִׁי כֶּעָפָר לַכֹּל תִּהְיֶה:
פְּתַח לִבִּי בְּתוֹרָתֶךָ וּבְמִצְוֹתֶיךָ תִּרְדּוֹף נַפְשִׁי: וְכֹל
הַחוֹשְׁבִים עָלַי רָעָה מְהֵרָה הָפֵר עֲצָתָם וְקַלְקֵל
מַחֲשַׁבְתָּם. לְמַעַן יֵחָלְצוּן יְדִידֶיךָ הוֹשִׁיעָה יְמִינְךָ
וַעֲנֵנִי: יִהְיוּ לְרָצוֹן אִמְרֵי פִי וְהֶגְיוֹן לִבִּי לְפָנֶיךָ יְיָ
צוּרִי וְגֹאֲלִי:

(To be read on Semi-holidays, Hanukkah and the New Moon)

### Reader and Choir

O give thanks unto the Lord, for He is good, for His mercy endureth forever. So let Israel now say, for His mercy endureth forever. So let the house of Aaron now say, for His mercy endureth forever. So let them that fear the Lord now say, for His mercy endureth forever.

הוֹדוּ לַיָי כִּי־טוֹב.

כִּי לְעוֹלָם חַסְדּוֹ:

יֹאמַר־נָא יִשְׂרָאֵל.

כִּי לְעוֹלָם חַסְדּוֹ:

יֹאמְרוּ־נָא בֵית־אַהֲרֹן.

כִּי לְעוֹלָם חַסְדּוֹ:

יֹאמְרוּ־נָא יִרְאֵי יְיָ.

כִּי לְעוֹלָם חַסְדּוֹ:

### Responsive Reading

**Reader**

In distress I called upon the Lord; He answered me with great deliverance.

**Congregation**

The Lord is for me; I will not fear: what can man do unto me?

It is better to take refuge in the Lord than to trust in man.

It is better to take refuge in the Lord than to trust in princes.

The Lord is my strength and song; and He is become my salvation.

The voice of rejoicing and salvation is in the tents of the righteous.

The right hand of the Lord doeth valiantly; the right hand of the Lord is exalted.

I shall not die, but live, and declare the works of the Lord.

The Lord hath chastened me grievously; but He hath not given me over to death.

Open to me the gates of righteousness; I will enter into them; I will give thanks unto the Lord.

This is the gate of the Lord; the righteous shall enter into it.

I will give thanks unto Thee, for Thou hast answered me, and art become my salvation.

The stone which the builders rejected is become the chief corner-stone.

This is the Lord's doing; it is marvelous in our eyes.

This is the day which the Lord hath made; we will rejoice and be glad in it.

We beseech Thee, O Lord, save now! We beseech Thee, O Lord, make us now to prosper!

Reader and Choir

אָנָּא יְיָ הַצְלִיחָה־נָּא: אָנָּא יְיָ הוֹשִׁיעָה־נָּא:

We beseech Thee, O Lord, save now!
We beseech Thee, O Lord, make us now to prosper

## READING OF SCRIPTURE
*Reader*
(Psalm xxiv)

The earth is the Lord's, and the fulness thereof; the world, and they that dwell therein. For He hath founded it upon the seas, and established it upon the flood. Who shall ascend the mountain of the Lord and who shall stand in His holy place? He that hath clean hands, and a pure heart; who hath not taken My name in vain, and hath not sworn deceitfully. He shall receive a blessing from the Lord, and justice from the God of his salvation. Such is the generation of them that seek Thee; that seek Thy presence, O God of Jacob.

*Choir*

| | |
|---|---|
| Lift up your heads, O ye gates, and be ye lifted up, ye everlasting doors, that the King of glory may come in. Who is the King of glory? The Lord of hosts; He is the King of glory. | שְׂאוּ שְׁעָרִים רָאשֵׁיכֶם. וּשְׂאוּ פִּתְחֵי עוֹלָם. וְיָבֹא מֶלֶךְ הַכָּבוֹד. מִי הוּא זֶה מֶלֶךְ הַכָּבוֹד. יְיָ צְבָאוֹת. הוּא מֶלֶךְ הַכָּבוֹד סֶלָה. |

TAKING THE SCROLL FROM THE ARK
(Congregation rises)

*Reader*

הָבוּ גֹדֶל לֵאלֹהֵינוּ וּתְנוּ כָבוֹד לַתּוֹרָה:

Let us declare the greatness of our God and render honor unto the Torah.

*Congregation then Choir*

בָּרוּךְ שֶׁנָּתַן תּוֹרָה לְעַמּוֹ יִשְׂרָאֵל בִּקְדֻשָׁתוֹ:

Praised be He who in His holiness has given the Torah unto Israel.

*Reader*

בֵּית יַעֲקֹב לְכוּ וְנֵלְכָה בְּאוֹר יְהֹוָה:

O house of Jacob, let us walk in the light of the Lord.

*Congregation and Reader, then Choir*

שְׁמַע יִשְׂרָאֵל יְהֹוָה אֱלֹהֵינוּ יְהֹוָה אֶחָד:

Hear, O Israel: The Lord, our God, the Lord is One.

(Congregation is seated)

*Choir*

Thine, O Lord, is the greatness, and the power, the glory, and the victory, and the majesty; for all that is in the heaven and in the earth is Thine; Thine is the kingdom, O Lord, and Thou art exalted as head above all.

לְךָ יְיָ הַגְּדֻלָּה וְהַגְּבוּרָה.

וְהַתִּפְאֶרֶת וְהַנֵּצַח וְהַהוֹד

כִּי כֹל בַּשָּׁמַיִם וּבָאָרֶץ.

לְךָ יְיָ הַמַּמְלָכָה וְהַמִּתְנַשֵּׂא

לְכֹל לְרֹאשׁ:

(Before reading from the Torah)

*Reader*

Praise ye the Lord to whom all praise is due.

Praised be the Lord to whom all praise is due forever and ever.

Praised be Thou, O Lord our God, Ruler of the world, who hast

בָּרְכוּ אֶת־יְיָ הַמְבֹרָךְ:

בָּרוּךְ יְיָ הַמְבֹרָךְ

לְעוֹלָם וָעֶד:

בָּרוּךְ אַתָּה יְיָ אֱלֹהֵינוּ

מֶלֶךְ הָעוֹלָם. אֲשֶׁר בָּחַר־

called us from among all peoples and hast given us Thy law. Praised be Thou, O Lord, Giver of the Law.

בָּנוּ מִכָּל־הָעַמִּים וְנָתַן לָנוּ אֶת־תּוֹרָתוֹ. בָּרוּךְ אַתָּה יְיָ נוֹתֵן הַתּוֹרָה:

### READING FROM THE TORAH
(After reading from the Torah)

Praised be Thou, O Lord our God, Ruler of the world, who hast given us the law of truth and hast implanted within us everlasting life. Praised be Thou, O Lord, Giver of the Law.

בָּרוּךְ אַתָּה יְיָ אֱלֹהֵינוּ מֶלֶךְ הָעוֹלָם. אֲשֶׁר נָתַן לָנוּ תּוֹרַת אֱמֶת וְחַיֵּי עוֹלָם נָטַע בְּתוֹכֵנוּ. בָּרוּךְ אַתָּה יְיָ נוֹתֵן הַתּוֹרָה:

(Before reading the Haftarah)

Praised be the Lord our God, for the law of truth and righteousness which He has revealed unto Israel, for the words of the prophets filled with His spirit and for the teachings of the sages whom He raised up aforetime and in these days.

בָּרוּךְ אַתָּה יְיָ אֱלֹהֵינוּ מֶלֶךְ הָעוֹלָם אֲשֶׁר בָּחַר בִּנְבִיאִים טוֹבִים וְרָצָה בְדִבְרֵיהֶם הַנֶּאֱמָרִים בֶּאֱמֶת. בָּרוּךְ אַתָּה יְיָ הַבּוֹחֵר בַּתּוֹרָה וּבְמֹשֶׁה עַבְדּוֹ וּבְיִשְׂרָאֵל עַמּוֹ וּבִנְבִיאֵי הָאֱמֶת וָצֶדֶק:

(Reading of the Haftarah)

*(After reading the Haftarah)*

For the Torah, for the privilege of worship, for the prophets, and for this Sabbath day, given us for sanctification and rest, for honor and for glory, let us thank and bless the Lord our God.

בָּרוּךְ אַתָּה יְיָ אֱלֹהֵינוּ מֶלֶךְ הָעוֹלָם צוּר כָּל־הָעוֹלָמִים צַדִּיק בְּכָל־הַדּוֹרוֹת הָאֵל הַנֶּאֱמָן הָאוֹמֵר וְעוֹשֶׂה הַמְדַבֵּר וּמְקַיֵּם שֶׁכָּל־דְּבָרָיו אֱמֶת וָצֶדֶק:

עַל־הַתּוֹרָה וְעַל־הָעֲבוֹדָה וְעַל־הַנְּבִיאִים וְעַל יוֹם הַשַּׁבָּת הַזֶּה שֶׁנָּתַתָּ לָנוּ יְיָ אֱלֹהֵינוּ אֲנַחְנוּ מוֹדִים לָךְ וּמְבָרְכִים אוֹתָךְ. יִתְבָּרַךְ שִׁמְךָ בְּפִי כָּל־חַי תָּמִיד לְעוֹלָם וָעֶד. בָּרוּךְ אַתָּה יְיָ מְקַדֵּשׁ הַשַּׁבָּת:

## PRAYERS FOR SPECIAL OCCASIONS

### Announcement of the New Moon

#### Reader

Almighty God, grant that the approaching month of ———— which begins ———— of the coming week, may be a messenger of good tidings to us all. Bestow upon us a life of health and peace, of sustenance and contentment. Help us to spend this month in the love of Thee and in the service of man, and so to order our way that it may be pleasing in Thy sight.

#### Choir: Amen

### PRAYER

Thou, who art the source of all blessings, be with this congregation and with all its members, their families and their households; prosper them in their various callings and occupations, help them in their needs, and guide them in their difficulties. Hear Thou the prayers of all who worship here this morning, comfort the sorrowing and cheer the silent sufferers. Bless those who guide and who serve this congregation, and those who contribute to its strength. Reward with the joy of goodness the charitable and the merciful who aid the poor, care for the sick, teach the ignorant, and extend a helping hand to those who have lost their way in the world.

Fervently we invoke Thy blessing upon our country and our nation. Guard them, O God, from calamity and injury; suffer not their adversaries to triumph over them, but let the glories of a just, righteous and God-fearing people increase from age to age. Enlighten with Thy wisdom and sustain with Thy power those whom the people have set in authority, the President, his counselors, and advisers, the judges, law-givers and executives, and all who are entrusted with our safety and with the guardianship of our rights and our liberties. May peace and good-will obtain among all the inhabitants of our land; may religion spread its blessings among us and exalt our nation in righteousness. Amen.

## RETURNING THE SCROLL TO THE ARK
(Congregation rises)

### Reader

O magnify the Lord with me and let us exalt His name together.

גַּדְּלוּ לַיָי אִתִּי. וּנְרוֹמְמָה שְׁמוֹ יַחְדָּו:

### Choir

His glory is in the earth and in the heavens. He is the strength of all His servants, the praise of them that truly love Him, the hope of Israel, the people He brought nigh to Himself. Hallelujah.

הוֹדוֹ עַל אֶרֶץ וְשָׁמָיִם: וַיָּרֶם קֶרֶן לְעַמּוֹ תְּהִלָּה לְכָל־חֲסִידָיו לִבְנֵי יִשְׂרָאֵל עַם קְרֹבוֹ הַלְלוּיָהּ:

### Reader

The law of the Lord is perfect, restoring the soul; the testimony of the Lord is sure, making wise the simple. The precepts of the Lord are right, rejoicing the heart; the judgments of the Lord are true; they are righteous altogether. Behold, a good doctrine has been given unto you; forsake it not.

תּוֹרַת יְיָ תְּמִימָה. מְשִׁיבַת נָפֶשׁ. עֵדוּת יְיָ נֶאֱמָנָה. מַחְכִּימַת פֶּתִי: פִּקּוּדֵי יְיָ יְשָׁרִים. מְשַׂמְּחֵי־לֵב. מִשְׁפְּטֵי יְיָ אֱמֶת. צָדְקוּ יַחְדָּו: כִּי לֶקַח טוֹב נָתַתִּי לָכֶם תּוֹרָתִי אַל־תַּעֲזֹבוּ:

(Congregation is seated)

### Choir

It is a tree of life to them that hold fast to it, and its supporters are happy. Its ways are ways of pleasantness, and all its paths are peace.

עֵץ חַיִּים הִיא לַמַּחֲזִיקִים בָּהּ וְתוֹמְכֶיהָ מְאֻשָּׁר: דְּרָכֶיהָ דַרְכֵי־נֹעַם וְכָל־נְתִיבוֹתֶיהָ שָׁלוֹם:

#### SERMON

#### ADORATION

(Congregation rises)

### Reader and Congregation

Let us adore the ever-living God, and render praise unto Him who spread out the heavens and established the earth, whose glory is revealed in the heavens above and whose greatness is manifest throughout the world. He is our God; there is none else.

We bow the head in reverence, and worship the King of kings, the Holy One, praised be He.

### Choir and Congregation

וַאֲנַחְנוּ כֹּרְעִים וּמִשְׁתַּחֲוִים וּמוֹדִים לִפְנֵי מֶלֶךְ מַלְכֵי הַמְּלָכִים הַקָּדוֹשׁ בָּרוּךְ הוּא:

(Congregation is seated)

### Reader

May the time not be distant, O God, when Thy name shall be worshiped in all the earth, when unbelief shall disappear and error be no more. We fervently pray that the day may come when all men shall invoke

Thy name, when corruption and evil shall give way to purity and goodness, when superstition shall no longer enslave the mind, nor idolatry blind the eye, when all who dwell on earth shall know that to Thee alone every knee must bend and every tongue give homage. O may all, created in Thine image, recognize that they are brethren, so that, one in spirit and one in fellowship, they may be forever united before Thee. Then shall Thy kingdom be established on earth and the word of Thine ancient seer be fulfilled: The Lord will reign forever and ever.

### Congregation (or Choir)

On that day the Lord shall be One and His name shall be One.

### Reader

And now ere we part, let us call to mind those who have finished their earthly course and have been gathered to the eternal home. Though vanished from bodily sight, they have not ceased to be; they abide in the shadow of the Most High. Let those who mourn for them be comforted. God will heal their aching hearts, for He is just and wise and merciful in all His doings, though no man can comprehend His ways. In the divine order of nature both life and death, joy and sorrow, serve beneficent ends, and in the fullness of time we shall know why we are tried, and why our love brings us sorrow as well as happiness. Wait patiently all ye that mourn, and be ye of good courage.

Rise, now, and in submission to God's inscrutable will, let us hallow His name:

(Mourners rise)

### Reader

Extolled and hallowed be the name of God throughout the world which He has created according to His will. And may he speedily establish His kingdom of righteousness on earth. Amen.

### Congregation

Praised be His glorious name unto all eternity.

### Reader

Praised and glorified be the name of the Holy One, though He be above all the praises which we can utter. Our guide is He in life and our redeemer through all eternity.

### Congregation

Our help cometh from Him, the creator of heaven and earth.

### Reader

The departed whom we now remember have entered into the peace of life eternal. They still live on earth in the acts of goodness they performed and in the hearts of those who cherish their memory. May the beauty of their life abide among us as a loving benediction.

### Congregation: Amen.

### Reader

May the Father of peace send peace to all who mourn, and comfort all the bereaved among us.

### Congregation: Amen.

(Mourners are seated)

(Mourners rise)

Reader

יִתְגַּדַּל וְיִתְקַדַּשׁ שְׁמֵהּ רַבָּא. בְּעָלְמָא דִּי־בְרָא
כִרְעוּתֵהּ. וְיַמְלִיךְ מַלְכוּתֵהּ. בְּחַיֵּיכוֹן וּבְיוֹמֵיכוֹן
וּבְחַיֵּי דְכָל־בֵּית יִשְׂרָאֵל. בַּעֲגָלָא וּבִזְמַן קָרִיב.
וְאִמְרוּ אָמֵן׃

Congregation

יְהֵא שְׁמֵהּ רַבָּא מְבָרַךְ לְעָלַם וּלְעָלְמֵי עָלְמַיָּא׃

Reader

יִתְבָּרַךְ וְיִשְׁתַּבַּח וְיִתְפָּאַר וְיִתְרוֹמַם וְיִתְנַשֵּׂא
וְיִתְהַדָּר וְיִתְעַלֶּה וְיִתְהַלָּל שְׁמֵהּ דְּקוּדְשָׁא. בְּרִיךְ
הוּא. לְעֵלָּא מִן כָּל־בִּרְכָתָא וְשִׁירָתָא. תֻּשְׁבְּחָתָא
וְנֶחָמָתָא. דַּאֲמִירָן בְּעָלְמָא. וְאִמְרוּ אָמֵן׃

עַל יִשְׂרָאֵל וְעַל צַדִּיקַיָּא. וְעַל־כָּל־מַן דְּאִתְפְּטַר
מִן עָלְמָא הָדֵין כִּרְעוּתֵהּ דֶּאֱלָהָא. יְהֵא לְהוֹן
שְׁלָמָא רַבָּא וְחִנָּא וְחִסְדָּא מִן־קֳדָם מָרֵא שְׁמַיָּא
וְאַרְעָא. וְאִמְרוּ אָמֵן׃

יְהֵא שְׁלָמָא רַבָּא מִן־שְׁמַיָּא וְחַיִּים. עָלֵינוּ וְעַל־
כָּל־יִשְׂרָאֵל. וְאִמְרוּ אָמֵן׃

עֹשֶׂה שָׁלוֹם בִּמְרוֹמָיו. הוּא יַעֲשֶׂה שָׁלוֹם עָלֵינוּ
וְעַל־כָּל־יִשְׂרָאֵל. וְאִמְרוּ אָמֵן׃

(Mourners are seated)

## CLOSING HYMN

Who is like Thee, O universal Lord?
Who dares Thy praise and glory share?
Who is in heaven, Most High, like Thee adored?
Who can on earth with Thee compare?
Thou art the one true God alone,
And firmly founded is Thy throne.

Thy tender love embraces all mankind,
As children all by Thee are blessed;
Repentant sinners with Thee mercy find,
Thy hand upholdeth the oppressed;
All worlds attest Thy power sublime,
Thy glory shines in every clime.

And to Thy might and love is joined in Thee
The highest wisdom's living spring;
Whate'er to us is deepest mystery,
Is clear to Thee, our Lord and King.
O God of wisdom, love and might,
We worship Thee, Eternal Light.

## BENEDICTION

## CLOSING HYMN

———

אֵין כַּאדוֹנֵנוּ.     אֵין כֵּאלֹהֵינוּ.
אֵין כְּמוֹשִׁיעֵנוּ:     אֵין כְּמַלְכֵּנוּ.

מִי כַּאדוֹנֵנוּ.     מִי כֵּאלֹהֵינוּ.
מִי כְמוֹשִׁיעֵנוּ:     מִי כְמַלְכֵּנוּ.

נוֹדֶה לַאדוֹנֵנוּ.     נוֹדֶה לֵאלֹהֵינוּ.
נוֹדֶה לְמוֹשִׁיעֵנוּ:     נוֹדֶה לְמַלְכֵּנוּ.

בָּרוּךְ אֲדוֹנֵנוּ.     בָּרוּךְ אֱלֹהֵינוּ.
בָּרוּךְ מוֹשִׁיעֵנוּ:     בָּרוּךְ מַלְכֵּנוּ.

אַתָּה הוּא אֲדוֹנֵנוּ.     אַתָּה הוּא אֱלֹהֵינוּ.
אַתָּה הוּא מוֹשִׁיעֵנוּ.     אַתָּה הוּא מַלְכֵּנוּ.

———

BENEDICTION

———

# Sabbath Afternoon Service

## Choir

Thy righteousness, O God, is an everlasting righteousness, and Thy law is truth; Thy righteousness is like the mighty mountains, Thy judgments are like the great deep; man and beast Thou preservest, O Lord. Blessed is the man that trusteth in the Lord, and whose trust the Lord is. Trust ye in the Lord for all time, for the Lord is God, an everlasting God. And they that know Thy name will put their trust in Thee, for Thou, Lord, dost not forsake them that seek Thee. Accept our prayers, O God, at this hour in the fulness of Thy grace. Hear us, O Lord, who art our stronghold and support.

צִדְקָתְךָ צֶדֶק לְעוֹלָם. וְתוֹרָתְךָ אֱמֶת. צִדְקָתְךָ כְּהַרְרֵי־אֵל. מִשְׁפָּטֶיךָ תְּהוֹם רַבָּה. אָדָם וּבְהֵמָה תוֹשִׁיעַ יְהוָֹה: בָּרוּךְ הַגֶּבֶר אֲשֶׁר יִבְטַח בַּיהוָֹה. וְהָיָה יְהוָֹה מִבְטַחוֹ: בִּטְחוּ בַיהוָֹה עֲדֵי־עַד. כִּי בְּיָהּ יְהוָֹה צוּר עוֹלָמִים: וְיִבְטְחוּ בְךָ יוֹדְעֵי שְׁמֶךָ. כִּי לֹא עָזַבְתָּ דוֹרְשֶׁיךָ יְהוָֹה: וַאֲנִי תְפִלָּתִי לְךָ יְיָ עֵת רָצוֹן אֱלֹהִים בְּרָב־ חַסְדֶּךָ עֲנֵנִי בֶּאֱמֶת יִשְׁעֶךָ:

157

## Responsive Reading
אשרי

**Reader**

Happy are they that dwell in Thy house, they are ever praising Thee.

**Congregation**

*Happy are they who thus know Him; happy is the people whose God is the Lord.*

I will extol Thee, my God, O King; and I will bless Thy name forever and ever.

*Every day will I bless Thee; and I will praise Thy name forever and ever.*

Great is the Lord, and highly to be praised; and His greatness is unsearchable.

*One generation shall laud Thy works to another, and shall declare Thy mighty acts.*

The glorious splendor of Thy majesty, and Thy wondrous works will I rehearse.

*And men shall speak of the might of Thy tremendous acts; and I will tell of Thy greatness.*

They shall utter the fame of Thy great goodness, and shall sing of Thy righteousness.

*The Lord is gracious, and full of compassion, slow to anger, and of great mercy.*

The Lord is good to all, and His tender mercies are over all His works.

*All Thy works shall praise Thee, O Lord, and Thy saints shall bless Thee.*

They shall speak of the glory of Thy kingdom, and talk of Thy might.

### Responsive Reading

אַשְׁרֵי יוֹשְׁבֵי בֵיתֶךָ. עוֹד יְהַלְלוּךָ סֶּלָה:

אַשְׁרֵי הָעָם שֶׁכָּכָה לּוֹ. אַשְׁרֵי הָעָם שֶׁיְיָ אֱלֹהָיו:

אֲרוֹמִמְךָ אֱלוֹהַי הַמֶּלֶךְ. וַאֲבָרְכָה שִׁמְךָ לְעוֹלָם וָעֶד:

בְּכָל-יוֹם אֲבָרְכֶךָ. וַאֲהַלְלָה שִׁמְךָ לְעוֹלָם וָעֶד:

גָּדוֹל יְיָ וּמְהֻלָּל מְאֹד. וְלִגְדֻלָּתוֹ אֵין חֵקֶר:

דּוֹר לְדוֹר יְשַׁבַּח מַעֲשֶׂיךָ. וּגְבוּרֹתֶיךָ יַגִּידוּ:

הֲדַר כְּבוֹד הוֹדֶךָ. וְדִבְרֵי נִפְלְאֹתֶיךָ אָשִׂיחָה:

וֶעֱזוּז נוֹרְאֹתֶיךָ יֹאמֵרוּ. וּגְדֻלָּתְךָ אֲסַפְּרֶנָּה:

זֵכֶר רַב-טוּבְךָ יַבִּיעוּ. וְצִדְקָתְךָ יְרַנֵּנוּ:

חַנּוּן וְרַחוּם יְיָ. אֶרֶךְ אַפַּיִם וּגְדָל-חָסֶד:

טוֹב-יְיָ לַכֹּל. וְרַחֲמָיו עַל-כָּל-מַעֲשָׂיו:

יוֹדוּךָ יְיָ כָּל-מַעֲשֶׂיךָ. וַחֲסִידֶיךָ יְבָרְכוּכָה:

כְּבוֹד מַלְכוּתְךָ יֹאמֵרוּ. וּגְבוּרָתְךָ יְדַבֵּרוּ:

לְהוֹדִיעַ לִבְנֵי הָאָדָם גְּבוּרֹתָיו. וּכְבוֹד הֲדַר מַלְכוּתוֹ:

*To make known to the sons of men His mighty acts,
and the glory of the majesty of His kingdom.*

Thy kingdom is a kingdom for all ages, and Thy dominion endureth throughout all generations.

*The Lord upholdeth all that fall, and raiseth up all
those that are bowed down.*

The eyes of all wait for Thee, and Thou givest them
their food in due season.

*Thou openest Thy hand and satisfiest every living
thing with favor.*

The Lord is righteous in all His ways, and gracious in all
His works.

*The Lord is nigh unto all them that call upon Him,
to all that call upon Him in truth.*

He will fulfil the desire of them that hear Him; He also
will hear their cry and will save them.

*The Lord preserveth all them that love Him, but all
the wicked will He destroy.*

My mouth shall speak the praise of the Lord; and let all
flesh bless His holy name forever and ever.

*Let us praise the Lord henceforth and forever.*

### Choir

Thus saith the Lord: This is My covenant with thee;
My spirit that is upon thee and My word which I
have put in thy mouth shall not depart from thee,
nor from thy children, nor from thy children's children forever, saith the Lord.

(Turn to page 124)

מַלְכוּתְךָ מַלְכוּת כָּל־עֹלָמִים. וּמֶמְשַׁלְתְּךָ בְּכָל־דּוֹר וָדֹר:

סוֹמֵךְ יְיָ לְכָל־הַנֹּפְלִים. וְזוֹקֵף לְכָל־הַכְּפוּפִים:

עֵינֵי כֹל אֵלֶיךָ יְשַׂבֵּרוּ. וְאַתָּה נוֹתֵן־לָהֶם אֶת־אָכְלָם בְּעִתּוֹ:

פּוֹתֵחַ אֶת־יָדֶךָ. וּמַשְׂבִּיעַ לְכָל־חַי רָצוֹן:

צַדִּיק יְיָ בְּכָל־דְּרָכָיו. וְחָסִיד בְּכָל־מַעֲשָׂיו:

קָרוֹב יְיָ לְכָל־קֹרְאָיו. לְכֹל אֲשֶׁר יִקְרָאֻהוּ בֶאֱמֶת:

רְצוֹן־יְרֵאָיו יַעֲשֶׂה. וְאֶת־שַׁוְעָתָם יִשְׁמַע וְיוֹשִׁיעֵם:

שׁוֹמֵר יְיָ אֶת־כָּל־אֹהֲבָיו. וְאֵת כָּל־הָרְשָׁעִים יַשְׁמִיד:

תְּהִלַּת יְיָ יְדַבֶּר־פִּי. וִיבָרֵךְ כָּל־בָּשָׂר שֵׁם קָדְשׁוֹ לְעוֹלָם וָעֶד:

וַאֲנַחְנוּ נְבָרֵךְ יָהּ מֵעַתָּה וְעַד־עוֹלָם הַלְלוּיָהּ:

### Choir

וַאֲנִי זֹאת בְּרִיתִי אוֹתָם אָמַר יְהֹוָה. רוּחִי אֲשֶׁר עָלֶיךָ. וּדְבָרַי אֲשֶׁר שַׂמְתִּי בְּפִיךָ. לֹא יָמוּשׁוּ מִפִּיךָ וּמִפִּי זַרְעֲךָ וּמִפִּי זֶרַע זַרְעֲךָ אָמַר יְהֹוָה מֵעַתָּה וְעַד עוֹלָם:

(Turn to page 125)

*Reader and Congregation*

Heavenly Father, Thou art One, and Thy name is One; may Thy truth unite all mankind into one holy bond of brotherhood, and may our love for one another be our crown of glory and armor of strength. Bless us, O God, on this Sabbath, and grant that it be unto us a day of perfect rest and sanctification. May it strengthen us in all noble purposes and holy resolves; may it encourage us to seek truth from Thy fountain of truth, and inspire us to become holy as Thou art holy. To Thee and Thy service we would consecrate this day, which in Thy love Thou hast sanctified for us. Amen.

---

*Reader and Congregation*

אַתָּה אֶחָד וְשִׁמְךָ אֶחָד. וּמִי כְּעַמְּךָ יִשְׂרָאֵל גּוֹי אֶחָד בָּאָרֶץ: תִּפְאֶרֶת גְּדֻלָּה. וַעֲטֶרֶת יְשׁוּעָה. יוֹם מְנוּחָה וּקְדֻשָּׁה לְעַמְּךָ נָתָתָּ: מְנוּחַת אַהֲבָה וּנְדָבָה. מְנוּחַת אֱמֶת וֶאֱמוּנָה. מְנוּחַת שָׁלוֹם וְשַׁלְוָה וְהַשְׁקֵט וָבֶטַח. מְנוּחָה שְׁלֵמָה שָׁאַתָּה רוֹצֶה בָּהּ. יַכִּירוּ בָנֶיךָ וְיֵדְעוּ כִּי מֵאִתְּךָ הִיא מְנוּחָתָם וְעַל־מְנוּחָתָם יַקְדִּישׁוּ אֶת־שְׁמֶךָ:

Choir: Amen

(For Taking Out of Scroll, see p. 144)

## Responsive Reading

(Psalm civ)

Reader

Bless the Lord, O my soul.  O Lord my God, Thou art very great; Thou art clothed with glory and majesty.

Congregation

*Who coverest Thyself with light as with a garment, who stretchest out the heavens like a curtain;*

Who makest winds Thy messengers, the flaming fire Thy ministers.

*Who didst establish the earth upon its foundations, that it should not be moved forever and ever.*

Thou didst cover it with the deep as with a vesture; the waters stood above the mountains.

*At Thy rebuke they fled, at the voice of Thy thunder they hasted away.*

The mountains rose, the valleys sank down unto the place which Thou hadst founded for them.

*Thou didst set a bound which they should not pass over.*

Who sendest forth springs into the valleys; they run between the mountains;

*Beside them dwell the fowl of the heaven, from among the branches they sing.*

Who waterest the mountains from Thine upper chambers; the earth is full of the fruit of Thy works.

*Who causest the grass to spring up for the cattle, and herb for the service of man; to bring forth bread out of the earth.*

Who appointest the moon for seasons; the sun knoweth
his going down.

Thou makest darkness, and it is night, wherein all
the beasts of the forest do creep forth.

The sun ariseth, they slink away, and couch in their
dens.

Man goeth forth unto his work, and to his labor
until the evening.

How manifold are Thy works, O Lord! in wisdom hast
Thou made them all; the earth is full of Thy
creatures.

Yonder sea, great and wide, therein are creeping
things innumerable, living creatures, both small
and great.

All of them wait for Thee, that Thou mayest give them
their food in due season.

Thou givest it unto them, they gather it; Thou openest Thy hand, they are satisfied with good.

May the glory of the Lord endure forever; let the Lord
rejoice in His works!

I will sing unto the Lord as long as I live, I will sing
praise to my God while I have any being.

Let my musing be sweet unto Him; as for me, I will
rejoice in the Lord.

Let sinners cease out of the earth, and let the wicked
be no more.

Bless the Lord, O my soul.   Hallelujah!

(For Adoration and Kaddish, turn to p. 150)

## SAYINGS OF THE FATHERS

פרקי אבות

*One of the following chapters is read on each Sabbath from the Sabbath after Passover until the Sabbath before the Feast of Weeks.*

### I

Moses received the Torah on Sinai and handed it down to Joshua; Joshua gave it to the elders; the elders to the prophets; and the prophets handed it down to the men of the Great Assembly. They said three things: Be deliberate in judgment; raise up many disciples; and build a fence around the Torah.

Simon the Just who was one of the last survivors of the Great Assembly, used to say: The world rests upon three things: upon the Torah, upon worship, and upon acts of kindness.

Antigonos of Socho who received the Torah from Simon the Just, used to say: Be not like servants who serve their master for the sake of receiving a reward; be rather like servants who serve their master without thinking of a reward; let the fear of Heaven be upon you.

Jose ben Joezer, of Zeredah, and Jose ben Jochanan, of Jerusalem, received the tradition from the preceding masters. The former said: Let thy house be a meeting-place for the wise; sit gladly at their feet, and drink in their words with eagerness. The latter said: Let thy house be wide open, and the poor be regarded as members of thy household.

Joshua ben Perachyah and Nittai, the Arbelite, received the tradition from them. The former said:

Provide for thyself a teacher, and get thee a companion, and judge all men by their merits. The latter said: Keep thee far from a bad neighbor, and do not associate with the wicked, and abandon not the belief in divine retribution.

Judah ben Tabbai and Simeon ben Shatach received the tradition from them. The former said: (As judge), act not the counsel's part; while the litigants are standing before thee, let them be regarded by thee as guilty; but when they are departed from thy presence, regard them as innocent, both having acquiesced in the verdict. The latter said: Be thorough in the examination of witnesses, and be heedful of thy words, lest through them the witnesses be led to testify falsely.

Shemayah and Abtalyon received the tradition from them. The former said: Love work, hate domination, and seek no undue intimacy with the ruling power. The latter said: Ye sages, be heedful of your words, lest your disciples be misled and the name of Heaven be profaned.

Hillel and Shammai received the tradition from them. Hillel said: Be of the disciples of Aaron, loving peace and pursuing it, loving all fellow-creatures, thus bringing them nigh unto the Torah. He also used to say: He who aggrandizes his name, loses his name; he who does not increase his knowledge, decreases it; he who does not seek to acquire wisdom, forfeits his life; and he who makes unworthy use of the crown of learning is wasting his powers. He also used to say: If I am not for myself, who will be for me? Yet if I am for myself only, what am I? And if not now, when?

Shammai said: Set a fixed time for thy study of the Torah; say little and do much; and receive all men with a cheerful countenance.

Rabban Simeon ben Gamaliel said: All the days of my life have been passed in the company of the wise, and I have found naught of better service than silence; not learning but doing is the chief thing; and whoso multiplies words causes sin. He also said: The world is founded upon three things: upon truth, justice, and peace; as is implied in the biblical command, Execute the judgment of truth and peace in your gates.

Rabbi Chananya ben Akashya said: The Holy One, blessed be He, was pleased to confer merit upon Israel, and therefore He gave them a Torah of great volume and many commandments, as it is written, It pleased the Lord, for His righteousness' sake, to magnify the Torah and make it honorable.

## II

Rabbi Judah said: Which is the right course that a man should choose for himself?—That which honors him in his own eyes and in the eyes of his fellowman. Be as scrupulous about a light precept as about a grave one, for thou knowest not the measure of reward allotted for those precepts. Balance the material loss involved in the observance of a precept against the spiritual gain, and the material gain accruing from transgression against the spiritual loss. Reflect upon three things, and thou wilt not fall into sin: Know what is above thee, a seeing eye, a hearing ear, and all thy deeds recorded in a book.

Rabban Gamaliel, the son of Rabbi Judah, said: Excellent is the study of the Torah when combined with a worldly occupation, for the effort demanded by both makes sin to be forgotten. All study of the Torah which is not supplemented by work must prove futile in the end, and may lead to iniquity. All who occupy themselves with communal affairs shall do so in the service of God.

Hillel said: Separate not thyself from the congregation; trust not in thyself until the day of thy death; pass not judgment upon thy neighbor until thou art come into his place; and do not say, When I have leisure I will study; thou mayest never have the leisure. He also used to say: A man void of intelligence cannot be sensitive to sin, nor can an ignorant person be pious, nor is the shamefaced apt to learn, nor can a passionate man teach, nor can one who is excessively engaged in business grow wise. In a place where there are no men, strive thou to be a man. He also used to say: The more flesh, the more worms; the more wealth, the more anxiety; the more Torah, the more life; the more study, the more wisdom; the more counsel, the more understanding; the more righteousness, the more peace. He who has acquired a good name, has enriched his manhood; he who has acquired knowledge of the Torah, has attained unto life eternal.

Rabbi Jochanan ben Zakkai used to say: If thou hast learned much Torah, do not arrogate to thyself moral excellence, for thereunto wast thou created. He also said once to his disciples: Go forth and see which is the good a man shall cherish most. Rabbi Eliezer said: A generous eye; Rabbi Joshua said: A loyal friend;

Rabbi Jose said: A good neighbor; Rabbi Simeon said: The gift of foresight; Rabbi Elazar said: A good heart. Thereupon Rabbi Jochanan said: I prefer the answer of Rabbi Elazar ben Arach to those of the rest of you, for in his words yours are included.

Rabbi Eliezer said: Let the honor of thy neighbor be as dear to thee as thine own; suffer not thyself to be easily angered; and repent one day before thy death.

Rabbi Joshua said: An envious eye, an evil mind, and hatred of fellow-creatures lead man to destruction.

Rabbi Jose said: Let the property of thy neighbor be as dear to thee as thine own; qualify thyself for the study of the Torah, since it cannot be transmitted to thee like a heritage; and let all thy actions be in the service of God.

Rabbi Simeon said: When thou prayest, do not make thy prayer a form of routine; let it rather be an appeal to God for mercy and grace.

Rabbi Elazar said: Be diligent in the study of the Torah, and know how to refute the unbeliever; know, too, in whose service thou toilest, and who is thy Employer that will pay thee the reward of thy labor.

Rabbi Tarphon said: The day is short, the work is much, the laborers are slothful, the reward is much and the Master is urgent. He also used to say: It is not incumbent upon thee to complete the work, but neither art thou free to desist from it altogether.

## III

Akabya ben Mahalalel said: Reflect upon three things, and thou wilt not fall into sin: Know whence thou camest, and whither thou art going, and before whom thou art destined to give a full account.

Rabbi Chanina, an assistant of the high-priest, said: Pray for the welfare of the government, since but for the fear thereof men would swallow each other alive.

Rabbi Chalafta ben Dosa, of the village of Chananya, said: When ten people sit together occupying themselves with the Torah, God's presence dwells in their midst.

Rabbi Eliezer of Bartotha said: Render unto God what belongs to Him, for thou and all thou hast are His; as David said: For all things come of Thee, and of Thine own have we given Thee.

Rabbi Chanina ben Dosa said: He in whom fear of sin takes precedence of wisdom, his wisdom will endure; but he in whom wisdom takes precedence of fear of sin, his wisdom will not endure. He also used to say: He whose works exceed his wisdom, his wisdom will endure; but he whose wisdom exceeds his works, his wisdom will not endure. He also used to say: He who has earned man's esteem, will also receive favor of God; but he who is not worthy of such esteem, cannot expect to find favor with Him.

Rabbi Dosa ben Horkinas said: Sleeping away the morning, carousing at noonday, childish babbling and the company of the vulgar, waste a man's life.

Rabbi Ishmael said: Be submissive to an elder, courteous to the young, and receive all men with cheerfulness.

Rabbi Akiba said: Mockery and frivolity are conducive to lewdness. Tradition is a safeguard of the

Torah, tithes are a safeguard of wealth, vows are a safeguard of abstinence, and a safeguard of wisdom is silence. He also used to say: Everything is foreseen, yet free will is given; the world is judged by grace, yet all is according to the greatness of the work. He also used to say: Everything is given on trust, and a net is spread for all the living; the store-house is open and the dealer sells on credit; the ledger lies open and the hand makes the entry; whoever wishes may come and borrow; but the collectors make their regular daily rounds, and exact payment from man with or without his consent; they have a firm basis for their claim, and the judgment is founded on truth.

Rabbi Elazar ben Azaryah said: Where there is no Torah, there are no manners, and without manners there is no Torah; where there is no wisdom, there is no piety, and without piety, there can be no wisdom; where there is no knowledge, there is no understanding, and without understanding there can be no knowledge; where there is want of food, there is no Torah, and without Torah there can be no sufficiency. He also used to say: With what is he to be compared whose wisdom exceeds his works?—with a tree whose branches are many, but whose roots are few; there comes a storm, plucks it up and fells it to the ground, as Scripture has it: For he shall be like a tamarisk in the desert, and shall not see when good cometh; but shall inhabit the parched places in the wilderness, a salt land and not inhabited. But what does he resemble whose works exceed his wisdom?—a tree whose branches are few, but whose roots are many: the stormiest winds may bear down and rage upon it, but they cannot stir it from its place; as Scripture has it: And he shall be like a tree planted by waters and that spreadeth out its roots by the river; and shall not see when heat cometh, but its foliage shall be luxuriant; and shall not be anxious in the year of drought, neither shall cease from yielding fruit.

## IV

Ben Zoma said: Who is a wise man? He who learns from everybody, as it is written: From all my teachers I have gotten understanding. Who is a hero? He who controls his passions; as it is written: He that is slow to anger is better than the mighty, and he that ruleth his spirit than he that taketh a city. Who is a rich man? He who rejoiceth in his lot; as it is written: When thou eatest the labor of thy hands happy art thou and it shall be well with thee. Who is honored? He who honors his fellowmen; as it is written: For them that honor Me I will honor, and they that despise Me shall be lightly esteemed.

Ben Azzai said: Hasten to do even a slight precept, and flee from transgression; for one virtue brings another in its train, and one sin entails another; for the reward of virtue is virtue itself, and sin is requited with sin. He also used to say: Despise no man, and consider nothing as too far-removed to come to pass; for there is no man but has his day, and no thing but has its place.

Rabbi Ishmael said: He who learns in order to teach, will be afforded the opportunity to learn and to teach, but he who learns in order to practise will be afforded the opportunity to learn and to teach, to observe and to practise.

Rabbi Zadok said: Make not of the Torah a crown wherewith to exalt thyself, nor use it as a spade to dig therewith.

Rabbi Jose said: He who honors the Torah will himself be honored by mankind, but he who dishonors the Torah will himself be dishonored by mankind.

Rabbi Meir said: Curtail thy business, and engage in the study of the Torah; practise humility before all men.

Rabbi Jochanan, the sandal-maker, said: Every assembly which is in the service of God is destined to endure, but that which is not in the service of God is not destined to endure.

Rabbi Simeon said: There are three crowns, the crown of the Torah, the crown of the priesthood, and the crown of royalty; but the crown of a good name excels them all.

Rabbi Mattithyah ben Cheresh said: Give every man a friendly greeting; be rather a tail to lions than a head to foxes.

Rabbi Jacob said: This world is, as it were, the antechamber of the world to come; prepare thyself in the antechamber that thou mayest be admitted into the reception hall. He also used to say: One hour of repentance and good deeds in this world is better than the whole life of the world to come.

Rabbi Simeon ben Elazar said: Seek not to appease thy neighbor in the hour of his wrath, nor to comfort him while his dead still lies before him; in the hour when his vow is made, pester him not with your questions, and strive not to see him in the hour of his disgrace.

Rabbi Jose bar Judah, from the village of Babli, said:

With whom is he to be compared who learns from the young? With him who eats unripe grapes and drinks wine fresh from the wine-press; and with whom is he to be compared who learns from the old? With him who eats ripe grapes and drinks old wine.

Rabbi Meir said: Look not at the pitcher but at what it contains; many a new pitcher is full of old wine, and many an old one does not even hold new wine.

Rabbi Elazar Hakkappar said: Envy, sensuality, and ambition destroy man's life. He also said: They that are born are destined to die; and the dead, to be brought to life again; and the living, to be judged, to know, to make known, and to be made conscious that He is God, He the Fashioner, He the Creator, He the Discerner, He the Judge, He the Witness, He the Accuser; He it is that will judge, praised be He, and with Him there is no injustice, no oversight, no partiality, no bribery. Know that everything is according to the reckoning; and let not thy imagination betray thee into the hope that the grave will be a place of refuge for thee. For without thy consent wast thou created, and born into the world without thy choice; thou art now living without thy volition, and wilt have to die without thy approval; so likewise without thy consent wilt thou have to render account before the supreme King, the holy One, blessed be He.

## V

There are seven things that mark the uncultured, and seven that mark the wise. The wise man does not speak before one who is greater in wisdom than he; he does not interrupt another in his speech; he is not hasty to answer; he asks pertinent questions, and answers to the point; he speaks first upon the matter first in order, and last upon the last; when he does not understand the matter under discussion, he confesses: I do not understand it; and when the truth is presented, he readily acknowledges it. The reverse of these things marks the uncultured man.

The sword comes into the world because of justice being delayed, because of justice being perverted, and because of those who render wrong decisions.

There are four types of men: He who says, What is mine is mine and what is thine is thine—the common type, or, as some have it, the Sodom type; he who says, What is mine is thine and what is thine is mine—typical of the boor; he who says, What is mine is thine and what is thine is thine—characteristic of the saint; and he who says, What is thine is mine and what is mine is mine—typical of the wicked.

There are four kinds of tempers: That which is easily provoked and easily pacified, the disadvantage counterbalanced by the advantage; that which is hard to provoke and hard to appease, the advantage neutralized by the disadvantage; that which is hard to provoke and easy to pacify, the temper of the saint; and that which is easy to provoke and hard to pacify, the temper of the wicked.

There are four kinds of pupils: he who readily understands and quickly forgets, his advantage disappearing in his disadvantage; he who grasps with difficulty and forgets with difficulty, his disadvantage being offset by his advantage; he who is quick to understand and slow to forget, a lot most happy; and he who is slow to understand and quick to forget, a lot most unfortunate.

Four qualities, represented by a sponge, a funnel, a strainer and a sieve, differentiate those that sit at the feet of the wise: a sponge which absorbs everything; a funnel, which lets in at one end and out at the other; a strainer which lets the wine pass out and retains the dregs; a sieve which removes the bran and gathers the fine flour.

Every controversy waged in the service of God must in the end lead to a permanent result; but if not waged in the service of God, it cannot lead to a permanent result.

Whoever possesses these three attributes is of the disciples of Abraham, our father, but whoever possesses the other three attributes is of the disciples of Balaam, the wicked: a generous eye, a humble mind, and a lowly spirit mark one as a disciple of Abraham, our father; an envious eye, a haughty mind, and a proud spirit characterize a disciple of Balaam the wicked.

Juda ben Tema said: Be bold as a leopard, swift as an eagle, fleet as a hart, and strong as a lion to do the will of thy Father who is in heaven.

Ben Bag Bag said: Turn it (the Torah), and turn it again, for every thing is in it; contemplate it, and grow grey and old over it; stir not from it, for thou canst have no better rule than this.

Ben He He said: According to the effort is the reward.

## VI

Rabbi Meir said: Whoever labors in the Torah for its own sake is worthy of many things; moreover, the whole world is indebted to him. He is called beloved friend, lover of God, lover of mankind. It clothes him with meekness and reverence. It fits him to become just, pious, upright, and faithful. It keeps him far from sin, and brings him near to virtue. Through him the world enjoys counsel and sound knowledge, understanding and strength; as it is said: Counsel is mine and knowledge; I am understanding; I have strength. It gives him sovereignty and dominion and discerning judgment. To him the secrets of the Torah are revealed. He is made like a never-failing spring and like a river that flows on with ever-increasing vigor. He becomes modest, long suffering, and forgiving of insults. It magnifies and exalts him above all things.

He who learns from his neighbor a single chapter, a single rule, a single verse, a single expression, or even a single letter, ought to pay him honor.

This is the mode of living the study of the Torah entails: a morsel of bread and salt thou must eat, and water by measure thou must drink; upon the ground thou must sleep, and a life of trouble thou must live, whilst thou toilest in the Torah.

Seek not greatness for thyself, and covet not honor; let thy works exceed thy learning; and hanker not after the table of kings, for thy table is greater than theirs, and thy crown is greater than theirs; thy Employer can be trusted to pay thee the reward of thy work.

Whoever reports a thing in the name of him that said it, brings deliverance into the world, as it is said: And Esther told the king in the name of Mordecai.

Rabbi Simeon ben Judah, in the name of Rabbi

Simeon ben Jochai, said: Beauty, strength, riches, honor, wisdom, old age, a hoary head, and children are comely to the righteous and comely to the world.

Rabbi Jose ben Kisma said: I was once traveling on the road when a man met me and saluted me, and I returned the salutation. He said to me, Rabbi, from what place art thou? I said to him, I come from a great city of sages and scribes. He said to me, If thou art willing to dwell with us in our place, I will give thee a thousand thousand golden dinars and precious stones and pearls. I said to him, Wert thou to give me all the silver and gold and precious stones and pearls in the world, I would not dwell anywhere but in a home of the Torah; and thus it is written in the book of Psalms by the hands of David, King of Israel: The law of Thy mouth is better unto me than thousands of gold and silver. Moreover, in the hour of a man's departure neither silver nor gold nor precious stones nor pearls accompany him, but only Torah and good works, as it is said: When thou walkest it shall lead thee; when thou liest down it shall watch over thee; and when thou awakest it shall talk to thee.

Five possessions the Holy One, praised be He, acquired unto Himself in this world, and these are: the Torah, heaven and earth, Abraham, Israel and the sanctuary.

Whatever the Holy One, praised be He, created in this world, He created but for His glory, as it is said: Everything that is called by My name, it is for My glory, I have created it; I have formed it, yea, I have made it.

סכות     שבועות     פסח

# Services for the Three Festivals

———

Passover
Weeks
Tabernacles

# Evening Service for Pesach, Shavuos and Succos

*Choir*

HYMN

---

**FOR THE FIRST DAY OF PESACH**

*Reader*

O Lord our God, and God of our fathers, we greet this festival of freedom with joyous hearts, and come into Thy house to seek Thy presence. As Thou didst redeem our fathers from the slavery of Egypt and didst lead them to the land of their inheritance, so hast Thou been our Savior and Guardian through all the centuries. Thy providence has guided us by day and by night.

We thank Thee, O God, our Redeemer, that our lot has fallen in this blessed land, dedicated to liberty and peace. May we be imbued with a deep sense of our duty as free men; and, when we gather in our homes in happy family reunion, may we be mindful of those who still dwell in the house of bondage and eat the bread of affliction. O that the good tidings of redemption may soon be heard in every land. May those who hunger after freedom and justice be satisfied, and may all mankind be blessed with the joys of brotherhood and peace.

Praised be Thou, O Lord our God, Ruler of the

world, who hast granted us life, sustained us, and permitted us to celebrate this joyous festival.

בָּרוּךְ אַתָּה יְיָ אֱלֹהֵינוּ מֶלֶךְ הָעוֹלָם שֶׁהֶחֱיָנוּ
וְקִיְּמָנוּ וְהִגִּיעָנוּ לַזְּמַן הַזֶּה:

(Turn to page 186)

### FOR THE SEVENTH DAY OF PESACH

## Reader

O Lord our God, on this closing eve of the feast of our freedom, we gather to thank Thee for the blessings which it has bestowed and for the message it has brought. Delivered by Thy hand from the tyrant's might, Israel sang a song of praise unto Thee by the shore of the Red Sea. Many times since hast Thou saved us from the fury of men and from the floods of destruction. In peril and in need hast Thou been our tower of strength. O continue to redeem us and all Thy children from danger and oppression. Wherever men groan under the yoke of servitude, hasten to deliver them. Cleanse the hearts of men and their rulers of the passions of hate and strife, of greed and lust for power, and fill them with good will and the love of justice. Speed the Passover of the future, when tyranny and slavery shall cease, when sword and spear shall be broken, and freedom and peace shall reign forever. On that day, all men shall come to know that they are brothers and with gladness and song proclaim Thee their God and Redeemer. Amen.

(Turn to page 186)

## FOR SHAVUOS

### Reader

O everliving God, Thou art our unfailing Guide; Thy word is the law of our life. On this festival of Shavuos we commemorate the sacred day when Israel entered into covenant with Thee. Freed from Pharaoh's bondage our fathers journeyed through the wilderness till at last they stood in reverence at the foot of Sinai and heard the unforgettable words: I am the Lord thy God.

Wherever our fathers wandered they carried the memory of Thy revelation. Written upon the tablets of their heart was Thy behest that they dedicate their lives to Thee and merit the dignity of priesthood in Thy service. In Thy Name they strove to break the yoke of the oppressed, and to bring freedom to the captive. They gave bread to the hungry and shelter to the homeless. They sought an ever deeper knowledge of Thee and Thy will, that they might open the eyes of the blind and lead all men to the light of Thy presence.

On this day of Israel's dedication, we pray for renewed awareness of Thy revelation. When the world is filled with sorrow and confusion and the path is hidden from our gaze, help us to see Thine eternal purpose. Strengthen our confidence in the triumph of justice among men and nations. Confirm our faith in Thy covenant that we may continue to carry Thy message of brotherhood and peace among all the children of men.

(Turn to page 186)

## FOR SUCCOS

### Reader

Creator of the universe, we come before Thee on this eve of our harvest festival to extol Thy greatness and goodness. Thou art revealed to us in the glorious promise of spring, in the mysterious power of summer's growth, and in the rich fulfillment of autumn's harvest.

In this season of the year, when our fathers had gathered the fruits of the field, they made joyous pilgrimage to Thy sanctuary to voice their gratitude for Thy loving care. To us today, as to our fathers of old, Thou art the fountain from which all blessings flow. In all the experiences of life, we recognize that Thy guiding hand establishes our work and that Thy love lifts our lives to nobler effort.

May the inspiration of this day strengthen our faith in Thee. Purify our spirits that in our daily tasks we may be conscious of Thy presence. As when we plant so when we reap, may we turn our thoughts to Thee and to Thy plan for the children of men. Help us to see that no work truly prospers unless it bring blessing to other lives, and no gain truly enriches if it add not to the happiness of others. Grant that we may never seek to dispossess others of what they have planted, nor build our joy on the misfortune of our fellowmen. Help us so to live that when we shall have gathered our final harvest, many shall rise up and call us blessed.

(Turn to page 186)

## FOR SHEMINI ATZERES

### Reader

Into Thy gates, O Father and King, do we enter with thanksgiving, and into Thy courts with praise. We bless Thy name who art from everlasting to everlasting. Out of chaos didst Thou call the world into being and set upon it the seal of Thy law. Thou didst endow creation with purpose and beauty. In our hearts too Thou hast kindled Thy light that we may rejoice in the beauty of Thy world and the majesty of Thy ways.

On this day, O Father, we conclude the holy season in reverence and joy. The mighty accents of the Shofar, calling us to repentance and to atonement, have stirred our hearts. From the world within we turn to the world without and lift grateful hearts to Thee for Thine unfailing bounty, for the harvest of fruit and grain with which Thou hast blessed us. Continue to bestow Thy benediction upon us. Teach us to seek Thee ever more within the sanctuary of our souls, within the tabernacle of Thy world, and in the congregation of Thy worshipers.

(Congregation rises)

### Reader

Praise ye the Lord, to whom all praise is due.

### Choir and Congregation

Praised be the Lord to whom all praise is due forever and ever.

(Congregation is seated)

### Reader

Praised be Thou, O Lord our God, ruler of the world, by whose law the shadows of evening fall and the gates of morn are opened. Thy wisdom established the changes of times and seasons and ordered the ways of the stars in their heavenly courses. Creator of heaven and earth, O ever-living God, rule Thou over us forever. Praised be Thou, O Lord, for the day and its work and for the night and its rest.

### Congregation and Reader

Infinite as is Thy power so is Thy love. Thou didst manifest it through Israel Thy servant. By laws and commandments, by statutes and ordinances hast Thou led us in the way of righteousness and brought us to the light of truth. Therefore at our lying down and our rising up, let us meditate on Thy teachings and find in Thy laws true life and length of days. O that Thy love may never depart from our hearts. Praised be Thou, O Lord, who hast revealed Thy love through Israel.

(Congregation rises)

### Reader

בָּרְכוּ אֶת־יְיָ הַמְבֹרָךְ:

### Choir and Congregation

בָּרוּךְ יְיָ הַמְבֹרָךְ לְעוֹלָם וָעֶד:

(Congregation is seated)

### Reader

בָּרוּךְ אַתָּה יְיָ אֱלֹהֵינוּ מֶלֶךְ הָעוֹלָם. אֲשֶׁר בִּדְבָרוֹ מַעֲרִיב עֲרָבִים. בְּחָכְמָה פּוֹתֵחַ שְׁעָרִים. וּבִתְבוּנָה מְשַׁנֶּה עִתִּים וּמַחֲלִיף אֶת־הַזְּמַנִּים. וּמְסַדֵּר אֶת־הַכּוֹכָבִים בְּמִשְׁמְרוֹתֵיהֶם בָּרָקִיעַ כִּרְצוֹנוֹ. בּוֹרֵא יוֹם וָלָיְלָה. יְיָ צְבָאוֹת שְׁמוֹ. אֵל חַי וְקַיָּם תָּמִיד יִמְלֹךְ עָלֵינוּ לְעוֹלָם וָעֶד. בָּרוּךְ אַתָּה יְיָ הַמַּעֲרִיב עֲרָבִים:

אַהֲבַת עוֹלָם בֵּית יִשְׂרָאֵל עַמְּךָ אָהָבְתָּ. תּוֹרָה וּמִצְוֹת חֻקִּים וּמִשְׁפָּטִים אוֹתָנוּ לִמַּדְתָּ. עַל־כֵּן יְיָ אֱלֹהֵינוּ בְּשָׁכְבֵּנוּ וּבְקוּמֵנוּ נָשִׂיחַ בְּחֻקֶּיךָ. וְנִשְׂמַח בְּדִבְרֵי תוֹרָתֶךָ וּבְמִצְוֹתֶיךָ לְעוֹלָם וָעֶד. כִּי הֵם חַיֵּינוּ וְאֹרֶךְ יָמֵינוּ. וּבָהֶם נֶהְגֶּה יוֹמָם וָלָיְלָה. וְאַהֲבָתְךָ אַל־תָּסִיר מִמֶּנּוּ לְעוֹלָמִים. בָּרוּךְ אַתָּה יְיָ אוֹהֵב עַמּוֹ יִשְׂרָאֵל:

(Congregation rises)

### Reader

Hear, O Israel: The Lord our God, the Lord is One.

Praised be His name whose glorious kingdom is forever and ever.

(Congregation is seated)

### Congregation and Reader

Thou shalt love the Lord, thy God, with all thy heart, with all thy soul, and with all thy might. And these words, which I command thee this day, shall be upon thy heart. Thou shalt teach them diligently unto thy children, and shalt speak of them when thou sittest in thy house, when thou walkest by the way, when thou liest down, and when thou risest up. Thou shalt bind them for a sign upon thy hand, and they shall be for frontlets between thine eyes. Thou shalt write them upon the doorposts of thy house and upon thy gates: That ye may remember and do all My commandments and be holy unto your God.

### Responsive Reading

Reader

Eternal truth it is that Thou alone art God, and there is none else.

Congregation

And through Thy power alone has Israel been redeemed from the hand of oppressors.

Great deeds hast Thou wrought in our behalf and wonders without number.

Thou hast kept us in life; our footsteps have not faltered.

(Congregation rises)
Reader, then Choir and Congregation

שְׁמַע יִשְׂרָאֵל יְהֹוָה אֱלֹהֵינוּ יְהֹוָה אֶחָד:

בָּרוּךְ שֵׁם כְּבוֹד מַלְכוּתוֹ לְעוֹלָם וָעֶד:

(Congregation is seated)
Reader

וְאָהַבְתָּ אֵת יְיָ אֱלֹהֶיךָ בְּכָל־לְבָבְךָ וּבְכָל־נַפְשְׁךָ
וּבְכָל־מְאֹדֶךָ: וְהָיוּ הַדְּבָרִים הָאֵלֶּה אֲשֶׁר אָנֹכִי
מְצַוְּךָ הַיּוֹם עַל־לְבָבֶךָ: וְשִׁנַּנְתָּם לְבָנֶיךָ וְדִבַּרְתָּ
בָּם. בְּשִׁבְתְּךָ בְּבֵיתֶךָ וּבְלֶכְתְּךָ בַדֶּרֶךְ וּבְשָׁכְבְּךָ
וּבְקוּמֶךָ: וּקְשַׁרְתָּם לְאוֹת עַל־יָדֶךָ. וְהָיוּ לְטֹטָפֹת
בֵּין עֵינֶיךָ: וּכְתַבְתָּם עַל־מְזֻזוֹת בֵּיתֶךָ וּבִשְׁעָרֶיךָ:
לְמַעַן תִּזְכְּרוּ וַעֲשִׂיתֶם אֶת־כָּל־מִצְוֹתָי וִהְיִיתֶם
קְדֹשִׁים לֵאלֹהֵיכֶם: אֲנִי יְיָ אֱלֹהֵיכֶם:

Responsive Reading

אֱמֶת וֶאֱמוּנָה כָּל־זֹאת וְקַיָּם עָלֵינוּ. כִּי הוּא יְיָ
אֱלֹהֵינוּ וְאֵין זוּלָתוֹ. וַאֲנַחְנוּ יִשְׂרָאֵל עַמּוֹ:

הַפּוֹדֵנוּ מִיַּד מְלָכִים. מַלְכֵּנוּ הַגּוֹאֲלֵנוּ מִכַּף כָּל־
הֶעָרִיצִים:

הָעֹשֶׂה גְדֹלוֹת עַד־אֵין חֵקֶר. וְנִפְלָאוֹת עַד־אֵין
מִסְפָּר:

הַשָּׂם נַפְשֵׁנוּ בַּחַיִּים. וְלֹא נָתַן לַמּוֹט רַגְלֵנוּ:

Thy love has watched over us in the night of oppression;

*Thy mercy has sustained us in the hour of trial.*

And now that we live in a land of freedom may we continue to be faithful to Thee and Thy word.

*May Thy law rule the life of all Thy children and Thy truth unite their hearts in fellowship.*

O God, our refuge and our hope, we glorify Thy name now as did our fathers in ancient days:

### Choir

Who is like unto Thee, O Lord? Who is like unto Thee, glorious in holiness, revered in worship, wondrous in works?

### Reader

Thy children acknowledged Thy sovereign power, and exclaimed:

### Choir

The Lord shall reign forever and ever.

### Reader

As Thou hast redeemed Israel and saved him from arms stronger than his own, so mayest Thou redeem all who are oppressed and persecuted. Praised be Thou, O Lord, Redeemer of Israel.

### Choir

And Moses declared unto the children of Israel the appointed seasons of the Lord.

הָעָשָׂה לָנוּ נִסִּים בְּמִצְרָיִם. אוֹתוֹת וּמוֹפְתִים
בְּאַדְמַת בְּנֵי־חָם:

וַיּוֹצֵא אֶת־עַמּוֹ יִשְׂרָאֵל מִתּוֹכָם לְחֵירוּת עוֹלָם.
וְרָאוּ בָנָיו גְּבוּרָתוֹ. שִׁבְּחוּ וְהוֹדוּ לִשְׁמוֹ:

וּמַלְכוּתוֹ בְּרָצוֹן קִבְּלוּ עֲלֵיהֶם מֹשֶׁה וּבְנֵי
יִשְׂרָאֵל:

לְךָ עָנוּ שִׁירָה בְּשִׂמְחָה רַבָּה וְאָמְרוּ כֻלָּם:

Choir

מִי־כָמֹכָה בָּאֵלִים יְיָ. מִי כָּמֹכָה נֶאְדָּר בַּקֹּדֶשׁ
נוֹרָא תְהִלֹּת עֹשֵׂה פֶלֶא:

Reader

מַלְכוּתְךָ רָאוּ בָנֶיךָ. זֶה אֵלִי עָנוּ וְאָמְרוּ:

Choir

יְיָ יִמְלֹךְ לְעֹלָם וָעֶד:

Reader

וְנֶאֱמַר כִּי־פָדָה יְהֹוָה אֶת־יַעֲקֹב וּגְאָלוֹ מִיַּד חָזָק
מִמֶּנּוּ. בָּרוּךְ אַתָּה יְיָ גָּאַל יִשְׂרָאֵל:

Choir

וַיְדַבֵּר מֹשֶׁה אֶת־מוֹעֲדֵי יְהֹוָה אֶל־בְּנֵי יִשְׂרָאֵל:

*Reader*

Praised be Thou, O Lord, God of our fathers, God of Abraham, Isaac and Jacob, great, mighty, and exalted. Thou bestowest lovingkindness upon all Thy children. Thou rememberest the devotion of the fathers, and, in love, bringest redemption to their descendants for the sake of Thy name. Thou art our King and Helper, Savior and Protector. Praised be Thou, O Lord, Shield of Abraham.

Eternal is Thy power, O Lord, Thou art mighty to save. In lovingkindness Thou sustainest the living; in the multitude of Thy mercies, Thou preservest all. Thou upholdest the falling, healest the sick; bringest freedom to the captives and keepest faith with Thy children in death as in life. Who is like unto Thee, Almighty God, Author of life and death, Source of salvation? Praised be Thou, O Lord, who hast implanted within us immortal life.

Thou art holy, Thy name is holy and Thy worshipers proclaim Thy holiness. Praised be Thou, O Lord, the holy God.

*Congregation and Reader*

We render thanks unto Thee that Thou hast called us from among all nations, and hast consecrated us to Thy service. Thou hast sanctified us through Thy commandments, that through Israel Thy great and holy name may become known in all the earth. Thou hast

Reader

בָּרוּךְ אַתָּה יְיָ אֱלֹהֵינוּ וֵאלֹהֵי אֲבוֹתֵינוּ. אֱלֹהֵי
אַבְרָהָם אֱלֹהֵי יִצְחָק וֵאלֹהֵי יַעֲקֹב. הָאֵל הַגָּדוֹל
הַגִּבּוֹר וְהַנּוֹרָא. אֵל עֶלְיוֹן. גּוֹמֵל חֲסָדִים טוֹבִים.
וְקֹנֵה הַכֹּל וְזוֹכֵר חַסְדֵי אָבוֹת. וּמֵבִיא גְאֻלָּה לִבְנֵי
בְנֵיהֶם. לְמַעַן שְׁמוֹ בְּאַהֲבָה: מֶלֶךְ עוֹזֵר וּמוֹשִׁיעַ
וּמָגֵן. בָּרוּךְ אַתָּה יְיָ מָגֵן אַבְרָהָם:

אַתָּה גִבּוֹר לְעוֹלָם אֲדֹנָי. רַב לְהוֹשִׁיעַ. מְכַלְכֵּל
חַיִּים בְּחֶסֶד. מְחַיֶּה הַכֹּל בְּרַחֲמִים רַבִּים. סוֹמֵךְ
נוֹפְלִים וְרוֹפֵא חוֹלִים וּמַתִּיר אֲסוּרִים. וּמְקַיֵּם
אֱמוּנָתוֹ לִישֵׁנֵי עָפָר. מִי כָמוֹךָ בַּעַל גְּבוּרוֹת. וּמִי
דוֹמֶה-לָּךְ. מֶלֶךְ מֵמִית וּמְחַיֶּה. וּמַצְמִיחַ יְשׁוּעָה:
בָּרוּךְ אַתָּה יְיָ נֹטֵעַ בְּתוֹכֵנוּ חַיֵּי עוֹלָם:

אַתָּה קָדוֹשׁ וְשִׁמְךָ קָדוֹשׁ וּקְדוֹשִׁים בְּכָל-יוֹם
יְהַלְלוּךָ סֶּלָה. בָּרוּךְ אַתָּה יְיָ הָאֵל הַקָּדוֹשׁ:

Choir: Amen.

Congregation and Reader

אַתָּה בְחַרְתָּנוּ מִכָּל-הָעַמִּים לִהְיוֹת לְךָ לְעַם
סְגֻלָּה. וְקִדַּשְׁתָּנוּ בְּמִצְוֹתֶיךָ. וְקֵרַבְתָּנוּ מַלְכֵּנוּ
לַעֲבוֹדָתֶךָ. וְשִׁמְךָ הַגָּדוֹל וְהַקָּדוֹשׁ עָלֵינוּ קָרָאתָ:

ordained for us feasts of joy, and seasons of gladness: this Feast of

(*Passover*—the season of our deliverance from Egypt.)
(*Weeks*—the time of the giving of the Law.)
(*Tabernacles*—the season of the harvest.)
(*Conclusion*—the season of our gladness.)

Bestow upon all who worship here the blessing of Thy holy festivals; and may we so celebrate them as to be worthy of Thy benediction. Praised be Thou, O Lord, who sanctifiest (the Sabbath) Israel and the festivals.

וַתִּתֶּן־לָנוּ יְיָ אֱלֹהֵינוּ מוֹעֲדִים לְשִׂמְחָה. חַגִּים
וּזְמַנִּים לְשָׂשׂוֹן אֶת־יוֹם (הַשַּׁבָּת הַזֶּה וְאֶת־יוֹם)

| הַשְּׁמִינִי חַג הָעֲצֶרֶת | חַג הַסֻּכּוֹת הַזֶּה. | חַג הַשָּׁבֻעוֹת הַזֶּה. | חַג הַמַּצּוֹת הַזֶּה. |
|---|---|---|---|
| הַזֶּה. זְמַן שִׂמְחָתֵנוּ | זְמַן שִׂמְחָתֵנוּ | זְמַן מַתַּן תּוֹרָתֵנוּ | זְמַן חֵרוּתֵנוּ |

(בְּאַהֲבָה) מִקְרָא קֹדֶשׁ זֵכֶר לִיצִיאַת מִצְרָיִם:

וְהִשִּׂיאֵנוּ יְיָ אֱלֹהֵינוּ אֶת־בִּרְכַּת מוֹעֲדֵי קָדְשֶׁךָ.
כַּאֲשֶׁר רָצִיתָ וְאָמַרְתָּ לְבָרְכֵנוּ. בָּרוּךְ אַתָּה יְיָ
מְקַדֵּשׁ (הַשַּׁבָּת) יִשְׂרָאֵל וְהַזְּמַנִּים:

Choir: Amen.

## FOR THE FIRST DAY OF PESACH

### Reader

O God of the universe, Thou dost manifest Thy creative power in the world about us. The springtime brings back the beauty of sunshine and song, of color and fragrance. The bondage of winter is broken.

We are bidden to observe this season when Thou didst redeem our fathers from the slavery of Egypt, that they might go forth to serve Thee in freedom. Help us to cast off the chains that bind our spirits, and to free ourselves from the selfishness and indifference that keep us from Thee. May there be a springtime of release within our souls, a reawakening of love for Thee.

Grant, O God, that Thy people Israel may be freed from the tyranny that sorely besets them, and from the sorrow and despair that burden their hearts.

Redeem us, O God, from the serfdom of ignorance and irreverence that we may continue to fulfil our historic task as Thy servants and witnesses. Strengthen our hearts with unswerving faith and serene trust in Thy providence. Thus shall we become champions of justice upon earth.

Fervently we pray for the universal springtide in the life of mankind when the long winter of intolerance and hatred shall have passed, the vision of the prophets fulfilled and the glory of Thy kingdom acknowledged of all men.

(Turn to page 201)

## FOR THE SEVENTH DAY OF PESACH

### Reader

With grateful hearts and joyous songs, we stand before Thee, O God, stirred anew by the revived memories of Thy wondrous redemption in days of yore. Marvelous have been Thy works at all times to the children of men. Thou satisfiest the longing soul and the hungry Thou fillest with good. They that sit in darkness and in the shadow of death cry unto Thee and are delivered from their affliction.

God of freedom, Thy children still groan under the burden of cruel taskmasters. Slavery debases their bodies and minds, and robs them of the enjoyment of Thy bounties. The fear of cruelty and the peril of death blight the souls of men. O break Thou the irons that bind them. Teach men to understand that by forging chains for others they forge chains for themselves, that as long as some are in fetters no one is truly free. Help them to see that liberty is the very breath of life and that only in the atmosphere of freedom can truth, prosperity and peace flourish. Imbue us with courage to guard our heritage of freedom above all material goods and to preserve it for others so that all men shall dwell together in safety and none shall make them afraid. Amen.

(Turn to page 201)

## FOR SHAVUOS

### Reader

God and Father, our hearts are filled with joy and thankfulness to Thee on this sacred festival. Unfailingly, year by year, Thou dost clothe the earth in radiant beauty and bid it bring forth its bounteous blessings. In humble acknowledgement of Thy boundless providence, our fathers brought to Thine altars on this holy day the first fruits of their harvest. They chanted songs of gratitude to Thee for the many gifts of garden and field and for the ripening of the fruit of the spirit. Thus did they celebrate the season when Thou didst reveal Thy law unto Israel and didst enter into a covenant with Thy people, a covenant sealed with the pledge: All that the Lord hath spoken we will do and we will heed.

Each year on this holy festival this vow is renewed, when our sons and daughters stand before Thee to enter into Israel's eternal covenant. In the same words which their fathers spoke, they vow to do and to heed and with the same devotion they pledge themselves unto Thee. Be Thou with them, O God, as Thou wast with our fathers. Sanctify us all for Thy service. Grant that the good seed we sow may ripen into a harvest of righteousness and truth. Amen.

(Turn to page 201)

## FOR SUCCOS

### Reader

O Living God, we thank Thee that Thou hast not left us to grope after Thee in the dark; that Thy law has been a lamp unto our feet, and a light unto our path. In this harvest season, when Thy people had gathered in their crops, Thy law did enjoin upon them to leave their homes and make their abode in frail booths. Thus didst Thou remind them of the transient nature of earthly possessions, of the insecurity of a life stayed on prosperity without faith in Thee.

Vouchsafe unto us, too, O Father, an understanding of this truth, so that no arrogance may tarnish the joy of success, no self-exaltation debase the love of achievement. Teach us to be humble. Keep far from us the pride of possession and the despair of want. In poverty save us, O God, from bitterness; in abundance rescue us from self-indulgence. Incline our hearts unto Thee and keep us from covetousness. Kindle within us a passion for a better world. Enlarge our sympathies, make us eager to ease the sorrow and distress of men and thus learn to know the joy of service. Lift up our eyes that, like our fathers, we too may see, through the leafy booth, the light of sun and star so that our souls may soar to Thee.

(Turn to page 201)

## FOR SHEMINI ATZERES

### Reader

Almighty God, who didst lead our fathers through the wilderness and bring them to the Promised Land, we give thanks unto Thee for Thy providential care from of old and to this day. Thou didst cause our fathers to dwell within the sheltering booth of Thy peace and didst guide them with a pillar of cloud by day and a pillar of fire by night. Thus didst Thou lead them from darkness to the light of Thy worship. As Thou didst pour out upon them the gifts of Thy bounty, so didst Thou bestow upon them the blessing of Thy law, that they should seek after truth and strive to do justice, to love mercy and to walk humbly with Thee.

We beseech Thee to teach us also to emulate Thine own grace and mercy. Thou givest us our food in due season; may we learn to share with the needy, and to shelter the stranger. May Thy truth be graven upon our heart.

Send unto us each year a deeper understanding of Thy word. Cause Thy truth to fall upon our hearts like seed upon fertile ground. As we read it again and again, may the faith of the patriarchs, the vision of the lawgiver, and the fervor of the prophets be renewed within us. Grant, O Father, that we may learn to love Thy law ever more deeply and to find in it the beauty of holiness. Make this a day of sacred joy unto us, so that from our hearts and from the hearts of all men may rise the song: This is the day which the Lord hath made; let us be glad and rejoice in it. Amen.

### Reader

Look with favor, O Lord, upon us, and may our service be acceptable unto Thee. Praised be Thou, O God, whom alone we serve in reverence.

### Congregatión and Reader

We gratefully acknowledge, O Lord, our God, that Thou art our Creator and Preserver, the Rock of our life and the Shield of our help. We render thanks unto Thee for our lives which are in Thy hand, for our souls which are ever in Thy keeping, for Thy wondrous providence and for Thy continuous goodness, which Thou bestowest upon us day by day. Truly Thy mercies never fail and Thy lovingkindness never ceases. Therefore do we forever put our trust in Thee.

### Reader

Grant us peace, Thy most precious gift, O Thou eternal source of peace, and enable Israel to be its messenger unto the peoples of the earth. Bless our country that it may ever be a stronghold of peace, and its advocate in the council of nations. May contentment reign within its borders, health and happiness within its homes. Strengthen the bonds of friendship and fellowship among all the inhabitants of our land. Plant virtue in every soul, and may the love of Thy name hallow every home and every heart. Praised be Thou, O Lord, Giver of peace.

### Choir: Amen.

**HYMN**

**SERMON**

**HYMN**

## ADORATION

---

(Congregation rises)

### Congregation and Reader

Let us adore the ever-living God, and render praise unto Him who spread out the heavens and established the earth, whose glory is revealed in the heavens above and whose greatness is manifest throughout the world. He is our God; there is none else.

We bow the head in reverence, and worship the King of kings, the Holy One, praised be He.

### Choir and Congregation

וַאֲנַחְנוּ כֹּרְעִים וּמִשְׁתַּחֲוִים וּמוֹדִים לִפְנֵי מֶלֶךְ
מַלְכֵי הַמְּלָכִים הַקָּדוֹשׁ בָּרוּךְ הוּא:

(Congregation is seated)

### Reader

May the time not be distant, O God, when Thy name shall be worshiped in all the earth, when unbelief shall disappear and error be no more. We fervently pray that the day may come when all men shall invoke Thy name, when corruption and evil shall give way to purity and goodness, when superstition shall no longer enslave the mind, nor idolatry blind the eye, when all who dwell on earth shall know that to Thee alone every knee must bend and every tongue give homage. O may all, created in Thine image, recognize that they are brethren, so that, one in spirit and one in fellowship, they may be forever united before Thee. Then shall Thy kingdom be established on earth and the word of Thine ancient seer be fulfilled: The Lord will reign forever and ever.

### Congregation (or Choir)

On that day the Lord shall be One and His name shall be One.

### Reader

Thou, O heavenly Father, bestowest the blessing of life and recallest the soul to Thyself in Thine own good time. We thank Thee for the sweet memory of our loved ones whose earthly life has ended. May their hallowed influence continue to be a joy and source of strength and comfort to us. May they inspire us to a more useful life, to higher hopes and greater contentment of spirit.

Send Thy consolation, we pray Thee, to those who today remember the loss of their beloved. Speak peace to hearts that are wounded by recent bereavement. Comfort them with the thought of Thy fatherly love, vouchsafed unto Thy trusting children.

In filial submission to Thy will and in joyous hope of life everlasting, we praise Thee in whose hands are the souls of all the living and the spirits of all flesh.

*(Mourners rise)*

### Reader

Extolled and hallowed be the name of God throughout the world which He has created according to His will. And may He speedily establish His kingdom of righteousness on earth. Amen.

### Congregation

Praised be His glorious name unto all eternity.

### Reader

Praised and glorified be the name of the Holy One, though He be above all the praises which we can utter. Our guide is He in life and our redeemer through all eternity.

### Congregation

Our help cometh from Him, the creator of heaven and earth.

### Reader

The departed whom we now remember have entered into the peace of life eternal. They still live on earth in the acts of goodness they performed and in the hearts of those who cherish their memory. May the beauty of their life abide among us as a loving benediction.

### Congregation: Amen.

### Reader

May the Father of peace send peace to all who mourn, and comfort all the bereaved among us.

### Congregation: Amen.

*(Mourners are seated)*

(Mourners rise)

Reader

יִתְגַּדַּל וְיִתְקַדַּשׁ שְׁמֵהּ רַבָּא. בְּעָלְמָא דִי־בְרָא
כִרְעוּתֵהּ. וְיַמְלִיךְ מַלְכוּתֵהּ. בְּחַיֵּיכוֹן וּבְיוֹמֵיכוֹן
וּבְחַיֵּי דְכָל־בֵּית יִשְׂרָאֵל. בַּעֲגָלָא וּבִזְמַן קָרִיב.
וְאִמְרוּ אָמֵן:

Congregation

יְהֵא שְׁמֵהּ רַבָּא מְבָרַךְ לְעָלַם וּלְעָלְמֵי עָלְמַיָּא:

Reader

יִתְבָּרַךְ וְיִשְׁתַּבַּח וְיִתְפָּאַר וְיִתְרוֹמַם וְיִתְנַשֵּׂא
וְיִתְהַדָּר וְיִתְעַלֶּה וְיִתְהַלָּל שְׁמֵהּ דְּקוּדְשָׁא. בְּרִיךְ
הוּא. לְעֵלָּא מִן כָּל־בִּרְכָתָא וְשִׁירָתָא. תֻּשְׁבְּחָתָא
וְנֶחֱמָתָא. דַּאֲמִירָן בְּעָלְמָא. וְאִמְרוּ אָמֵן:

עַל יִשְׂרָאֵל וְעַל צַדִּיקַיָּא. וְעַל־כָּל־מַן דְּאִתְפְּטַר
מִן עָלְמָא הָדֵין כִּרְעוּתֵהּ דֶּאֱלָהָא. יְהֵא לְהוֹן
שְׁלָמָא רַבָּא וְחִנָּא וְחִסְדָּא מִן־קֳדָם מָרֵא שְׁמַיָּא
וְאַרְעָא. וְאִמְרוּ אָמֵן:

יְהֵא שְׁלָמָא רַבָּא מִן־שְׁמַיָּא וְחַיִּים. עָלֵינוּ וְעַל־
כָּל־יִשְׂרָאֵל. וְאִמְרוּ אָמֵן:

עֹשֶׂה שָׁלוֹם בִּמְרוֹמָיו. הוּא יַעֲשֶׂה שָׁלוֹם עָלֵינוּ
וְעַל־כָּל־יִשְׂרָאֵל. וְאִמְרוּ אָמֵן:

(Mourners are seated)

## KIDDUSH

### On Sabbath Eve:

We praise Thee, O God, and thank Thee for all the blessings of the week that is gone; for life, health and strength; for home, love and friendship; for the discipline of our trials and temptations; for the happiness of our success and prosperity. Thou hast commanded us: Six days shalt thou labor and do all thy work, but the seventh day is a Sabbath unto the Lord thy God. Thou hast ennobled us, O God, by the blessings of work, and in love and grace sanctified us by the blessings of rest.

### On Week Days:

With song and praise, (and with the symbols of our feast,) let us renew the memories of our past.

Praised art Thou, O Lord our God, King of the universe, who hast sanctified us with Thy commandments. In love hast Thou given us, O Lord our God, solemn days of joy and seasons of gladness: this Feast of

(*Passover*—the season of our deliverance from Egypt.)

(*Weeks*—the time of the giving of the Law.)

(*Tabernacles*—the season of the harvest.)

(*Conclusion*—the season of our gladness.)

Thou hast called us to Thy service and hast made us share in the blessings of Thy holy festivals. Praised art Thou, O Lord, who sanctifiest Israel and the festive seasons.

Praised be Thou, O Lord our God, Ruler of the world, who hast created the fruit of the vine.

# סדר קידוש לרגלים

## SANCTIFICATION FOR THE FESTIVALS

סכות and שבועות ,פסח

When the festival occurs on שבת begin here:

וַיְהִי עֶרֶב וַיְהִי בֹקֶר

יוֹם הַשִּׁשִּׁי: וַיְכֻלּוּ הַשָּׁמַיִם וְהָאָרֶץ וְכָל־צְבָאָם:
וַיְכַל אֱלֹהִים בַּיּוֹם הַשְּׁבִיעִי מְלַאכְתּוֹ אֲשֶׁר עָשָׂה
וַיִּשְׁבֹּת בַּיּוֹם הַשְּׁבִיעִי מִכָּל־מְלַאכְתּוֹ אֲשֶׁר עָשָׂה:
וַיְבָרֶךְ אֱלֹהִים אֶת־יוֹם הַשְּׁבִיעִי וַיְקַדֵּשׁ אֹתוֹ כִּי בוֹ
שָׁבַת מִכָּל־מְלַאכְתּוֹ אֲשֶׁר־בָּרָא אֱלֹהִים לַעֲשׂוֹת:

When the festival occurs on week-days, begin here:

סַבְרִי מָרָנָן וְרַבָּנָן וְרַבּוֹתַי

בָּרוּךְ אַתָּה יְיָ אֱלֹהֵינוּ מֶלֶךְ הָעוֹלָם בּוֹרֵא פְּרִי הַגָּפֶן:

On שבת add the words in small characters.

בָּרוּךְ אַתָּה יְיָ אֱלֹהֵינוּ מֶלֶךְ הָעוֹלָם אֲשֶׁר בָּחַר־
בָּנוּ מִכָּל־עָם וְרוֹמְמָנוּ מִכָּל־לָשׁוֹן וְקִדְּשָׁנוּ בְּמִצְוֹתָיו.
וַתִּתֶּן־לָנוּ יְיָ אֱלֹהֵינוּ בְּאַהֲבָה שבתות למנוחה ּ מוֹעֲדִים
לְשִׂמְחָה חַגִּים וּזְמַנִּים לְשָׂשׂוֹן. אֶת־יוֹם השבת הזה ואת יום

(On Succos when Kiddush is recited in the Succah, add the following benediction:)

Praised art Thou, O Lord our God, King of the universe, who hast sanctified us through Thy commandments and ordained that we shall dwell in booths.

Praised be Thou, O Lord our God, Ruler of the world, who hast granted us life, sustained us, and permitted us to celebrate this joyous festival.

| שמיני עצרת On<br>שמחת תורה | סכות On | שבועות On | פסח On |
|---|---|---|---|
| הַשְּׁמִינִי חַג<br>הָעֲצֶרֶת הַזֶּה.<br>זְמַן שִׂמְחָתֵנוּ | חַג הַסֻּכּוֹת<br>הַזֶּה. זְמַן<br>שִׂמְחָתֵנוּ | חַג הַשָּׁבֻעוֹת<br>הַזֶּה זְמַן<br>מַתַּן תּוֹרָתֵנוּ | חַג הַמַּצּוֹת<br>הַזֶּה. זְמַן<br>חֵרוּתֵנוּ |

בְּאַהֲבָה מִקְרָא קֹדֶשׁ זֵכֶר לִיצִיאַת מִצְרָיִם. כִּי בָנוּ

בָחַרְתָּ וְאוֹתָנוּ קִדַּשְׁתָּ מִכָּל־הָעַמִּים וְשַׁבָּת וּמוֹעֲדֵי

קָדְשֶׁךָ בְּאַהֲבָה וּבְרָצוֹן בְּשִׂמְחָה וּבְשָׂשׂוֹן הִנְחַלְתָּנוּ.

בָּרוּךְ אַתָּה יְיָ מְקַדֵּשׁ הַשַּׁבָּת וְ יִשְׂרָאֵל וְהַזְּמַנִּים:

(On Succos when Kiddush is recited in the Succah add the following benediction:)

בָּרוּךְ אַתָּה יְיָ אֱלֹהֵינוּ מֶלֶךְ הָעוֹלָם אֲשֶׁר קִדְּשָׁנוּ

בְּמִצְוֹתָיו וְצִוָּנוּ לֵישֵׁב בַּסֻּכָּה:

בָּרוּךְ אַתָּה יְיָ אֱלֹהֵינוּ מֶלֶךְ הָעוֹלָם שֶׁהֶחֱיָנוּ

וְקִיְּמָנוּ וְהִגִּיעָנוּ לַזְּמַן הַזֶּה:

# Morning Service for Pesach, Shavuos and Succos

## Choir

### (Psalm c)

Shout unto the Lord, all the earth; serve the Lord with gladness; come before His presence with singing. Know ye that the Lord He is God; it is He that hath made us, and we are His, His people, and the flock of His pasture. Enter into His gates with thanksgiving, and into His courts with praise; give thanks unto Him, and bless His name. For the Lord is good; His mercy endureth forever; and His faithfulness unto all generations.

הָרִיעוּ לַיָי כָּל־הָאָרֶץ: עִבְדוּ אֶת־יְיָ בְּשִׂמְחָה. בֹּאוּ לְפָנָיו בִּרְנָנָה: דְּעוּ כִּי־יְיָ הוּא אֱלֹהִים. הוּא עָשָׂנוּ. וְלוֹ אֲנַחְנוּ. עַמּוֹ וְצֹאן מַרְעִיתוֹ: בֹּאוּ שְׁעָרָיו בְּתוֹדָה. חֲצֵרֹתָיו בִּתְהִלָּה. הוֹדוּ לוֹ בָּרְכוּ שְׁמוֹ: כִּי טוֹב יְיָ. לְעוֹלָם חַסְדּוֹ. וְעַד־דּוֹר וָדֹר אֱמוּנָתוֹ:

## FOR THE FIRST DAY OF PESACH

### Reader

How lovely are Thy dwelling-places, O Lord; better is a day in Thy courts than a thousand elsewhere; happy

216

are they who dwell in Thy house, they are continually praising Thee. Incline Thine ear, answer us, be gracious unto us, O God, and cause us to rejoice, for unto Thee we lift up our souls. Teach us Thy way that we may walk firmly in Thy truth. Show us Thy kindness, grant us Thy salvation. Be with us on this day of the feast of our freedom and at all times, O Thou, our God and our Father, our Rock and our Support. Amen.

(Turn to page 215)

### FOR THE SEVENTH DAY OF PESACH

#### Reader

Our God and Father! As the festal week of Passover draws to its close, we come into Thy house in the knowledge that where Thou art, there are unending life and hope, liberty and peace. Thou dost revive the spirit of the downcast and lift up from the very gates of death. Bestow Thy blessing upon us and grant renewal of courage to hearts that have grown weary in the battle for justice. Strengthen their faith in the ultimate triumph of the right. Let Thy light shine into our spirits and liberate us and all the children of men from fear and anguish. May the hope of springtime and the promise of freedom find speedy fulfillment in a glorious harvest of life enriched and redeemed. Amen.

(Turn to page 215)

### FOR SHAVUOS

#### Reader

Thou, O Lord, art the source of knowledge and truth. Thy laws and commandments enlighten our mind and show us the path of righteousness. On this Festival of Shavuos we recall the day when, at the mountain of revelation, our fathers vowed to govern their will by Thine and to accept those ordinances by which man may nobly live.

In all the centuries that followed, Thy law was never forgotten in Israel. Our fathers meditated on it day and night. The meaning of Thy commandments grew ever clearer to them as the generations passed. The Torah became the treasured inheritance of the congregation of Jacob.

We, their children, love Thy law, O God. Our fathers taught it diligently so that each generation might understand it and observe it in joy. On this day which commemorates Thy revelation, we bring our children unto Thine altar to declare their allegiance to Thee and Thy commandments. Be Thou with them on this sacred day. Grant that Thy word proclaimed of old become a living message to every soul. Now and throughout their lives may they come with clean hands and pure heart to ascend Thy holy mountain. Amen.

(Turn to page 215)

### FOR SUCCOS

#### Reader

With deep gratitude and joy, O our God, we come into Thy courts to offer unto Thee prayers of praise and thanksgiving. All that we are, we owe to Thee; all that we have is a gift from Thy hand. Earth and sky, rain and sunshine, flower and fruit, all the beauty and bounty of nature, attune our souls to thoughts of Thy beneficence. In all things we feel Thy nearness and behold the tender care with which Thou dost watch over the children of men.

On this day, we pray Thee, O Father, that we may learn to labor in Thy spirit and to live in harmony with Thy law. When tempted to hoard Thy blessings, to impoverish others that we might prosper, open Thou our eyes to the wrong and privation we would thus inflict on our own brothers. When, goaded by selfishness and greed, we would ignore the rights of the weak and forget the common kinship of all men, reveal Thou unto us, we beseech Thee, the divine pattern of life shown to the seers of old. The earth is Thine and the fulness thereof; help us to realize that the blessings we enjoy are but tokens of Thy love, and that when we use Thy gifts in the service of our fellowmen we offer thanksgiving unto Thee. Turn Thou our strength to tasks of justice, mercy and peace, so that, in our labors for the common good, we may find the joy and exaltation of the righteous life. We live in the shelter of Thy protection; teach us to serve Thee in truth, in humility, and in love.

Grant, O God, that this festival may bring gladness to our homes. May we share our blessings with the needy and lift the burden of care from the heavy-laden, that all may celebrate this day in joy before Thee. Amen.

(Turn to page 215)

## FOR SHEMINI ATZERES

### Reader

O Thou who dost reveal Thyself in endless ways, deepen within us the sense of Thy presence in the world and in the sanctuary of our hearts. As on this holy season our fathers came to worship Thee, so do we bow down before Thee in thanksgiving. Thou, O Lord, hast made us glad through Thy deeds, and we will exult in the works of Thy hands.

We thank Thee also for Thy law, which has hallowed our lives. We rejoice in it as did our fathers. Make this our day of rededication to Thy law. May it resound in our hearts with the sanctity of the past and with the promise of days to come. Renew its message for us with each passing year. As we read it again and again may we find in it enrichment of life.

Help us, O Father, to gather all the prayers we have uttered throughout this sacred season and to bind them into the resolve to consecrate our lives anew unto Thee and Thy service. Thou art holy and biddest us seek holiness. Thou art the Maker of the world, the source of its beauty, its majesty and its meaning. Thou art the giver of law, the light that makes radiant the heart of man and draws it toward Thee. We praise Thee, O Father, for the manifold paths that lead to Thee, and we beseech Thee to set our feet upon Thy ways. Amen.

*Congregation and Reader*

Almighty and merciful God, who hast called our fathers to Thy service, and hast opened their eyes to behold Thy wondrous works and to proclaim Thy law unto all nations, Thou art the same today even as Thou wast at the beginning; Thou art our God in this life, and Thou art our hope and refuge in the life to come. Creator of heaven and earth, of the sea and all that is therein, Thine alone is the power in the heaven above and on the earth below, and none can say unto Thee: What doest Thou? Our heavenly Father, help us that by our lives we may sanctify Thy name before men, and testify of Thee and of Thy holy law. Praised be Thou, O Lord, who hast revealed to us Thy law of truth.

## Reader

Every living soul shall praise Thee; the spirit of all flesh shall glorify Thy name. Thou art God from everlasting to everlasting and besides Thee there is no redeemer nor savior. Thou art the first and the last, the Lord of all generations. Thou rulest the world in kindness and all Thy creatures in mercy. Thou art our guardian who sleepeth not and slumbereth not. To Thee alone we give thanks. Yet, though our lips should overflow with song, and our tongues with joyous praise, we should still be unable to thank Thee even for a thousandth part of the bounties which Thou hast bestowed upon our fathers and upon us. Thou hast been our protector and our savior in every trial and peril. Thy mercy has watched over us, and Thy lovingkindness has never failed us.

## Congregation and Reader

Praised be Thy holy name. Thou hast made Thine eternal law our portion, and hast given us a goodly heritage. Open our eyes to the beauty of Thy truth and help us so to exemplify it in our lives that we may win all men for Thy law of righteousness. Gather all Thy children around Thy banner of truth that Thy name may be hallowed through us in all the world and the entire human family may be blessed with truth and peace. Amen.

Reader

נִשְׁמַת כָּל־חַי תְּבָרֵךְ אֶת־שִׁמְךָ יְיָ אֱלֹהֵינוּ. וְרוּחַ
כָּל־בָּשָׂר תְּפָאֵר וּתְרוֹמֵם זִכְרְךָ מַלְכֵּנוּ תָּמִיד: מִן
הָעוֹלָם וְעַד־הָעוֹלָם אַתָּה אֵל. וּמִבַּלְעָדֶיךָ אֵין
לָנוּ מֶלֶךְ גּוֹאֵל וּמוֹשִׁיעַ פּוֹדֶה וּמַצִּיל. וּמְפַרְנֵס
וּמְרַחֵם. בְּכָל־עֵת צָרָה וְצוּקָה. אֵין לָנוּ מֶלֶךְ אֶלָּא
אַתָּה: אֱלֹהֵי הָרִאשׁוֹנִים וְהָאַחֲרוֹנִים. הַמְּנַהֵג עוֹלָמוֹ
בְּחֶסֶד וּבְרִיּוֹתָיו בְּרַחֲמִים. לְךָ לְבַדְּךָ אֲנַחְנוּ
מוֹדִים: אִלּוּ פִינוּ מָלֵא שִׁירָה כַּיָּם וּלְשׁוֹנֵנוּ רִנָּה
כַּהֲמוֹן גַּלָּיו. וְשִׂפְתוֹתֵינוּ שֶׁבַח כְּמֶרְחֲבֵי רָקִיעַ. אֵין
אֲנַחְנוּ מַסְפִּיקִים לְהוֹדוֹת לְךָ יְיָ אֱלֹהֵינוּ וֵאלֹהֵי
אֲבוֹתֵינוּ. עַל־כָּל־הַטּוֹבוֹת שֶׁעָשִׂיתָ עִם־אֲבוֹתֵינוּ
וְעִמָּנוּ: מִמִּצְרַיִם גְּאַלְתָּנוּ יְיָ אֱלֹהֵינוּ וּמִבֵּית עֲבָדִים
פְּדִיתָנוּ. בְּרָעָב זַנְתָּנוּ. וּבְשָׂבָע כִּלְכַּלְתָּנוּ: מֵחֶרֶב
הִצַּלְתָּנוּ וּמִדֶּבֶר מִלַּטְתָּנוּ. וּמֵחֳלָיִם רָעִים וְנֶאֱמָנִים
דִּלִּיתָנוּ: עַד־הֵנָּה עֲזָרוּנוּ רַחֲמֶיךָ. וְלֹא־עֲזָבוּנוּ
חֲסָדֶיךָ. וְאַל־תִּטְּשֵׁנוּ יְיָ אֱלֹהֵינוּ לָנֶצַח: עַל־כֵּן
נְהַלֶּלְךָ וּנְשַׁבֵּחֲךָ וּנְפָאֶרְךָ וּנְבָרֵךְ אֶת־שֵׁם קָדְשֶׁךָ:
בָּרוּךְ אַתָּה יְיָ. אֵל מֶלֶךְ גָּדוֹל בַּתִּשְׁבָּחוֹת. אֵל
הַהוֹדָאוֹת. אֲדוֹן הַנִּפְלָאוֹת. הַבּוֹחֵר בְּשִׁירֵי זִמְרָה.
מֶלֶךְ אֵל חֵי הָעוֹלָמִים:

(Congregation rises)

### Reader

Praise ye the Lord to whom all praise is due.

### Choir and Congregation

Praised be the Lord to whom all praise is due forever and ever.

(Congregation is seated)

### Reader

Praised be Thou, O Lord our God, Ruler of the world, who in Thy mercy makest light to shine over the earth and all its inhabitants, and renewest daily the work of creation. How manifold are Thy works, O Lord! In wisdom hast Thou made them all. The heavens declare Thy glory. The earth reveals Thy creative power. Thou formest light and darkness, ordainest good out of evil, bringest harmony into nature and peace to the heart of man.

Great has been Thy love unto us and boundless Thy compassion. Our fathers put their trust in Thee and Thou didst teach them the law of life. Be gracious also unto us that we may understand and fulfil the teachings of Thy word. Enlighten our eyes in Thy law that we may cling unto Thy commandments. Unite our hearts to love and revere Thee. We trust in

(Congregation rises)

Reader

בָּרְכוּ אֶת־יְיָ הַמְבֹרָךְ:

Choir and Congregation

בָּרוּךְ יְיָ הַמְבֹרָךְ לְעוֹלָם וָעֶד:

(Congregation is seated)

Reader

בָּרוּךְ אַתָּה יְיָ אֱלֹהֵינוּ מֶלֶךְ הָעוֹלָם. יוֹצֵר אוֹר
וּבוֹרֵא חֹשֶׁךְ. עֹשֶׂה שָׁלוֹם וּבוֹרֵא אֶת־הַכֹּל:
הַמֵּאִיר לָאָרֶץ וְלַדָּרִים עָלֶיהָ בְּרַחֲמִים. וּבְטוּבוֹ
מְחַדֵּשׁ בְּכָל־יוֹם תָּמִיד מַעֲשֵׂה־בְרֵאשִׁית: מָה רַבּוּ
מַעֲשֶׂיךָ יְיָ. כֻּלָּם בְּחָכְמָה עָשִׂיתָ. מָלְאָה הָאָרֶץ
קִנְיָנֶךָ: תִּתְבָּרַךְ יְיָ אֱלֹהֵינוּ עַל־שֶׁבַח מַעֲשֵׂה יָדֶיךָ.
וְעַל־מְאוֹרֵי־אוֹר שֶׁעָשִׂיתָ יְפָאֲרוּךָ סֶּלָה: בָּרוּךְ אַתָּה
יְיָ יוֹצֵר הַמְּאוֹרוֹת:

אַהֲבָה רַבָּה אֲהַבְתָּנוּ יְיָ אֱלֹהֵינוּ. חֶמְלָה גְדוֹלָה
וִיתֵרָה חָמַלְתָּ עָלֵינוּ: אָבִינוּ מַלְכֵּנוּ. בַּעֲבוּר
אֲבוֹתֵינוּ שֶׁבָּטְחוּ בְךָ וַתְּלַמְּדֵם חֻקֵּי חַיִּים. כֵּן תְּחָנֵּנוּ
וּתְלַמְּדֵנוּ: הָאֵר עֵינֵינוּ בְּתוֹרָתֶךָ. וְדַבֵּק

Thee and rejoice in Thy saving power, for from Thee cometh our help. Thou hast called us and drawn us nigh unto Thee to serve Thee in faithfulness. Joyfully do we lift up our voices and proclaim Thy unity. Praised be Thou, O God, who in Thy love hast called Thy people Israel to serve Thee.

(Congregation rises)

### Reader

Hear, O Israel: The Lord our God, the Lord is One. Praised be His name whose glorious kingdom is forever and ever.

(Congregation is seated)

### Congregation and Reader

Thou shalt love the Lord, thy God, with all thy heart, with all thy soul, and with all thy might. And these words, which I command thee this day, shall be upon thy heart. Thou shalt teach them diligently unto thy children, and shalt speak of them when thou sittest in thy house, when thou walkest by the way, when thou liest down, and when thou risest up. Thou shalt bind them for a sign upon thy hand, and they shall be for frontlets between thine eyes. Thou shalt write them upon the doorposts of thy house and upon thy gates: That ye may remember and do all My commandments and be holy unto your God.

לִבֵּנוּ בְּמִצְוֹתֶיךָ. וְיַחֵד לְבָבֵנוּ לְאַהֲבָה וּלְיִרְאָה
שְׁמֶךָ: כִּי בְשֵׁם קָדְשְׁךָ בָּטֶחְנוּ. נָגִילָה וְנִשְׂמְחָה
בִּישׁוּעָתֶךָ. כִּי אֵל פּוֹעֵל יְשׁוּעוֹת אָתָּה. וּבָנוּ בָחַרְתָּ
וְקֵרַבְתֵּנוּ לְשִׁמְךָ הַגָּדוֹל סֶלָה בֶּאֱמֶת. לְהוֹדוֹת לְךָ
וּלְיַחֶדְךָ בְּאַהֲבָה. בָּרוּךְ אַתָּה יְיָ הַבּוֹחֵר בְּעַמּוֹ
יִשְׂרָאֵל בְּאַהֲבָה:

*(Congregation rises)*

### Reader and Congregation

שְׁמַע יִשְׂרָאֵל יְהֹוָה אֱלֹהֵינוּ יְהֹוָה אֶחָד:
בָּרוּךְ שֵׁם כְּבוֹד מַלְכוּתוֹ לְעוֹלָם וָעֶד:

*(Congregation is seated)*

### Reader

וְאָהַבְתָּ אֵת יְיָ אֱלֹהֶיךָ בְּכָל־לְבָבְךָ וּבְכָל־נַפְשְׁךָ
וּבְכָל־מְאֹדֶךָ: וְהָיוּ הַדְּבָרִים הָאֵלֶּה אֲשֶׁר אָנֹכִי
מְצַוְּךָ הַיּוֹם עַל־לְבָבֶךָ: וְשִׁנַּנְתָּם לְבָנֶיךָ וְדִבַּרְתָּ
בָּם. בְּשִׁבְתְּךָ בְּבֵיתֶךָ וּבְלֶכְתְּךָ בַדֶּרֶךְ וּבְשָׁכְבְּךָ
וּבְקוּמֶךָ: וּקְשַׁרְתָּם לְאוֹת עַל־יָדֶךָ. וְהָיוּ לְטֹטָפֹת
בֵּין עֵינֶיךָ: וּכְתַבְתָּם עַל־מְזוּזוֹת בֵּיתֶךָ וּבִשְׁעָרֶיךָ:
לְמַעַן תִּזְכְּרוּ וַעֲשִׂיתֶם אֶת־כָּל־מִצְוֹתָי וִהְיִיתֶם
קְדֹשִׁים לֵאלֹהֵיכֶם: אֲנִי יְיָ אֱלֹהֵיכֶם:

## Responsive Reading

**Reader**

True and enduring is Thy word which Thou hast spoken through Thy prophets.

**Congregation**

Thou art the living God, Thy words bring life and light to the soul.

Thou art the strength of our life, the rock of our salvation; Thy kingdom and Thy truth abide forever.

Thou hast been the help of our fathers in time of trouble and art our refuge in all generations.

Thou art the first and the last, and besides Thee there is no redeemer nor helper.

As Thou hast saved Israel from Egyptian bondage, so mayest Thou send Thy help to all who are oppressed.

May Thy law rule in the hearts of all Thy children, and Thy truth unite them in bonds of fellowship.

May the righteous of all nations triumph by Thy power and rejoice in Thy grace.

O God, who art our refuge and our hope, we glorify Thy name now as did our fathers in ancient days:

## Choir

Who is like unto Thee, O Lord? Who is like unto Thee, glorious in holiness, revered in worship, wondrous in works?

*Responsive Reading*

אֱמֶת. אֱלֹהֵי עוֹלָם מַלְכֵּנוּ. צוּר יַעֲקֹב מָגֵן יִשְׁעֵנוּ:

לְדוֹר וָדוֹר הוּא קַיָּם וּשְׁמוֹ קַיָּם. וּמַלְכוּתוֹ

וֶאֱמוּנָתוֹ לָעַד קַיֶּמֶת:

וּדְבָרָיו חַיִּים וְקַיָּמִים. נֶאֱמָנִים וְנֶחֱמָדִים לָעַד

וּלְעוֹלְמֵי עוֹלָמִים:

עֶזְרַת אֲבוֹתֵינוּ אַתָּה הוּא מֵעוֹלָם מָגֵן וּמוֹשִׁיעַ

לִבְנֵיהֶם אַחֲרֵיהֶם בְּכָל־דּוֹר וָדוֹר:

אַשְׁרֵי אִישׁ שֶׁיִּשְׁמַע לְמִצְוֹתֶיךָ וְתוֹרָתְךָ וּדְבָרְךָ

יָשִׂים עַל־לִבּוֹ:

אֱמֶת. שָׁאַתָּה הוּא יְיָ אֱלֹהֵינוּ. צוּר יְשׁוּעָתֵנוּ.

פּוֹדֵנוּ וּמַצִּילֵנוּ. מֵעוֹלָם שְׁמֶךָ. אֵין אֱלֹהִים זוּלָתֶךָ:

אַתָּה הוּא רִאשׁוֹן וְאַתָּה הוּא אַחֲרוֹן. וּמִבַּלְעָדֶיךָ

אֵין לָנוּ מֶלֶךְ גּוֹאֵל וּמוֹשִׁיעַ:

מִמִּצְרַיִם גְּאַלְתָּנוּ יְיָ אֱלֹהֵינוּ. וּמִבֵּית עֲבָדִים

פְּדִיתָנוּ:

עַל־זֹאת שִׁבְּחוּ אֲהוּבִים וְרוֹמְמוּ אֵל:

*Choir*

מִי־כָמֹכָה בָּאֵלִים יְיָ. מִי כָּמֹכָה נֶאְדָּר בַּקֹּדֶשׁ

נוֹרָא תְהִלֹּת עֹשֵׂה פֶּלֶא:

### Reader

A new song the redeemed sang unto Thy name. They proclaimed Thy sovereignty and said:

### Choir

The Lord shall reign forever and ever.

### Reader

O Rock of Israel, redeem those who are oppressed and deliver those who are persecuted. Praised be Thou, our Redeemer, the Holy One of Israel.

### Choir: Amen

### Reader

Praised be Thou, O Lord, God of our fathers, God of Abraham, Isaac and Jacob, great, mighty, and exalted. Thou bestowest lovingkindness upon all Thy children. Thou rememberest the devotion of the fathers, and, in love, bringest redemption to their descendants for the sake of Thy name. Thou art our King and Helper, Savior and Protector. Praised be Thou, O Lord, Shield of Abraham.

Eternal is Thy power, O Lord, Thou art mighty to save. In lovingkindness Thou sustainest the living; in the multitude of Thy mercies, Thou preservest all. Thou upholdest the falling, healest the sick; bringest freedom to the captives and keepest faith with Thy children in death as in life. Who is like unto Thee, Almighty God, Author of life and death, Source of salvation? Praised be Thou, O Lord, who hast implanted within us immortal life.

Reader

שִׁירָה חֲדָשָׁה שִׁבְּחוּ גְאוּלִים לְשִׁמְךָ עַל־שְׂפַת
הַיָּם יַחַד כֻּלָּם הוֹדוּ וְהִמְלִיכוּ וְאָמְרוּ:

Choir

יְיָ יִמְלֹךְ לְעֹלָם וָעֶד:

Reader

צוּר יִשְׂרָאֵל. קוּמָה בְּעֶזְרַת יִשְׂרָאֵל. וּגְאָלֵנוּ יְיָ
צְבָאוֹת שְׁמוֹ. קְדוֹשׁ יִשְׂרָאֵל. בָּרוּךְ אַתָּה יְיָ גָּאַל
יִשְׂרָאֵל:

Choir: Amen.
Reader

בָּרוּךְ אַתָּה יְיָ אֱלֹהֵינוּ וֵאלֹהֵי אֲבוֹתֵינוּ. אֱלֹהֵי
אַבְרָהָם אֱלֹהֵי יִצְחָק וֵאלֹהֵי יַעֲקֹב. הָאֵל הַגָּדוֹל
הַגִּבּוֹר וְהַנּוֹרָא. אֵל עֶלְיוֹן. גּוֹמֵל חֲסָדִים טוֹבִים.
וְקֹנֵה הַכֹּל וְזוֹכֵר חַסְדֵי אָבוֹת. וּמֵבִיא גְאֻלָּה לִבְנֵי
בְנֵיהֶם. לְמַעַן שְׁמוֹ בְּאַהֲבָה: מֶלֶךְ עוֹזֵר וּמוֹשִׁיעַ
וּמָגֵן. בָּרוּךְ אַתָּה יְיָ מָגֵן אַבְרָהָם:

אַתָּה גִּבּוֹר לְעוֹלָם אֲדֹנָי. רַב לְהוֹשִׁיעַ. מְכַלְכֵּל
חַיִּים בְּחֶסֶד. מְחַיֶּה הַכֹּל בְּרַחֲמִים רַבִּים. סוֹמֵךְ
נוֹפְלִים וְרוֹפֵא חוֹלִים וּמַתִּיר אֲסוּרִים. וּמְקַיֵּם
אֱמוּנָתוֹ לִישֵׁנֵי עָפָר. מִי כָמוֹךָ בַּעַל גְּבוּרוֹת. וּמִי

Thou art holy, Thy name is holy and Thy worshipers proclaim Thy holiness. Praised be Thou, O Lord, the holy God.

### SANCTIFICATION

(Congregation rises)

## Congregation and Reader

We sanctify Thy name on earth, as the heavens glorify Thee on high; and in the words of the prophet we say:

Holy, holy, holy is the Lord of hosts; the whole earth is full of His glory.

## Reader

God our Strength, God our Lord, how excellent is Thy name in all the earth.

## Congregation and Reader

Praised be the glory of God throughout the world.

## Reader

Our God is one; He is our Father, He is our King, He is our Helper and in His mercy He will answer our prayers in the sight of all the living.

## Congregation and Reader

The Lord will reign forever, thy God, O Zion, from generation to generation.

(Congregation is seated)

דּוֹמֶה-לָּךְ. מֶלֶךְ מֵמִית וּמְחַיֶּה. וּמַצְמִיחַ יְשׁוּעָה:
בָּרוּךְ אַתָּה יְיָ נֹטֵעַ בְּתוֹכֵנוּ חַיֵּי עוֹלָם:
אַתָּה קָדוֹשׁ וְשִׁמְךָ קָדוֹשׁ וּקְדוֹשִׁים בְּכָל-יוֹם
יְהַלְלוּךָ סֶּלָה. בָּרוּךְ אַתָּה יְיָ הָאֵל הַקָּדוֹשׁ:

### SANCTIFICATION
(Congregation rises)

נְקַדֵּשׁ אֶת שִׁמְךָ בָּעוֹלָם. כְּשֵׁם שֶׁמַּקְדִּישִׁים אוֹתוֹ
בִּשְׁמֵי מָרוֹם. כַּכָּתוּב עַל-יַד נְבִיאֶךָ. וְקָרָא זֶה אֶל-
זֶה וְאָמַר:

Choir and Congregation

קָדוֹשׁ קָדוֹשׁ קָדוֹשׁ יְיָ צְבָאוֹת. מְלֹא כָל-הָאָרֶץ
כְּבוֹדוֹ:

Reader

אַדִּיר אַדִּירֵנוּ יְיָ אֲדוֹנֵנוּ מָה-אַדִּיר שִׁמְךָ בְּכָל-
הָאָרֶץ:

Congregation and Choir

בָּרוּךְ כְּבוֹד יְיָ מִמְּקוֹמוֹ:

Reader

אֶחָד הוּא אֱלֹהֵינוּ. הוּא אָבִינוּ. הוּא מַלְכֵּנוּ.
הוּא מוֹשִׁיעֵנוּ: וְהוּא יַשְׁמִיעֵנוּ בְּרַחֲמָיו לְעֵינֵי כָּל-
חָי:

Congregation and Choir

יִמְלֹךְ יְיָ לְעוֹלָם אֱלֹהַיִךְ צִיּוֹן לְדוֹר וָדוֹר
הַלְלוּיָהּ:

(Congregation is seated)

### Reader

From generation to generation we declare Thy greatness and throughout all ages proclaim Thy holiness; Thy praise shall never cease from our lips. Praised be Thou, O Lord, the God of holiness.

### Congregation and Reader

We render thanks unto Thee that Thou hast called us from among all nations, and hast consecrated us to Thy service. Thou hast sanctified us through Thy commandments, that through Israel Thy great and holy name may become known in all the earth. Thou hast ordained for us feasts of joy, and seasons of gladness: this Feast of

(*Passover*—the season of our deliverance from Egypt.)

(*Weeks*—the time of the giving of the Law.)

(*Tabernacles*—the season of the harvest.)

(*Conclusion*—the season of our gladness.)

Bestow upon all who worship here the blessing of Thy holy festivals; and may we so celebrate them as to be worthy of Thy benediction. Praised be Thou, O Lord, who sanctifiest (the Sabbath,) Israel and the festivals.

### Choir: Amen.

Reader

לְדוֹר וָדוֹר נַגִּיד גָּדְלֶךָ. וּלְנֵצַח נְצָחִים קְדֻשָּׁתְךָ
נַקְדִּישׁ. וְשִׁבְחֲךָ אֱלֹהֵינוּ מִפִּינוּ לֹא יָמוּשׁ לְעוֹלָם
וָעֶד. בָּרוּךְ אַתָּה יְיָ הָאֵל הַקָּדוֹשׁ:

Congregation and Reader

אַתָּה בְחַרְתָּנוּ מִכָּל־הָעַמִּים. אָהַבְתָּ אוֹתָנוּ.
וְרָצִיתָ בָּנוּ. וְקִדַּשְׁתָּנוּ בְּמִצְוֹתֶיךָ. וְקֵרַבְתָּנוּ מַלְכֵּנוּ
לַעֲבוֹדָתֶךָ. וְשִׁמְךָ הַגָּדוֹל וְהַקָּדוֹשׁ עָלֵינוּ קָרָאתָ:
וַתִּתֶּן־לָנוּ יְיָ אֱלֹהֵינוּ בְּאַהֲבָה (שַׁבָּתוֹת לִמְנוּחָה וּ)
מוֹעֲדִים לְשִׂמְחָה חַגִּים וּזְמַנִּים לְשָׂשׂוֹן. אֶת ־יוֹם
(הַשַּׁבָּת הַזֶּה וְאֶת־יוֹם)

| הַשְּׁמִינִי חַג הָעֲצֶרֶת | חַג הַסֻּכּוֹת הַזֶּה. | חַג הַשָּׁבֻעוֹת הַזֶּה. | חַג הַמַּצּוֹת הַזֶּה. |
|---|---|---|---|
| הַזֶּה. זְמַן שִׂמְחָתֵנוּ | זְמַן שִׂמְחָתֵנוּ | זְמַן מַתַּן תּוֹרָתֵנוּ | זְמַן חֵרוּתֵנוּ |

(בְּאַהֲבָה) מִקְרָא קֹדֶשׁ זֵכֶר לִיצִיאַת מִצְרָיִם:
וְהַשִּׂיאֵנוּ יְיָ אֱלֹהֵינוּ אֶת־בִּרְכַּת מוֹעֲדֵי קָדְשֶׁךָ.
כַּאֲשֶׁר רָצִיתָ וְאָמַרְתָּ לְבָרְכֵנוּ. בָּרוּךְ אַתָּה יְיָ
מְקַדֵּשׁ (הַשַּׁבָּת) יִשְׂרָאֵל וְהַזְּמַנִּים:

### FOR THE FIRST DAY OF PESACH

*Responsive Reading*

Reader

I love Thee, O Lord, my Strength, my Rock, my Deliverer.

Congregation

My God, my Rock, in Him I take refuge.

He delivered me from mine enemy most strong and from them that hated me.

They confronted me in the day of my calamity but the Lord was a stay unto me.

For Thou dost save the afflicted people; but the haughty eyes Thou dost humble.

With the merciful Thou dost show Thyself merciful; with the upright man Thou dost show Thyself upright.

For Thou dost light my lamp; the Lord, my God, doth lighten my darkness.

Who is God, save the Lord, and who is a Rock, except our God?

The Lord liveth, and blessed be my Rock; and exalted be the God of my salvation.

Therefore I will give thanks unto Thee, O Lord, among the nations, and will sing praises unto Thy name.

### Reader

Gratefully we lift up our hearts to Thee, O God, and thank Thee for Thy never-ending goodness to the house of Israel. Our ancestors languished in Egyptian slavery; they ate the bread of affliction; the lash of the taskmaster drove them to their daily toil; but Thou wast mindful of the descendants of Abraham, Isaac and Jacob, Thy faithful servants. In the fulness of time Thou didst raise up a deliverer who, in Thy name, brought the message of redemption to the enslaved. Thou didst lead Israel from bondage to freedom, from darkness to light, from despair to hope. As on eagle's pinions, Thou didst bear him and bring him near unto Thee to be a kingdom of priests and a holy people. In thankful memory of Thy wondrous deliverance and of the consecration of our fathers unto Thy service, we celebrate this joyous feast of Passover.

Ofttimes since that early day has Israel been oppressed by kings unfeeling as Pharaoh, and trampled upon by men and nations as cruel as the Egyptians. But remembering that first deliverance, Thy people never again lost hope. Their trust in Thee, so firm and strong, buoyed them up. Ever and again Thy protecting love manifested itself, and they were saved from impending destruction. We pray unto Thee on this day of our feast that, as Thou hast protected the children of Israel throughout the past, so mayest Thou deliver them wherever they are still bowed beneath the oppressor's yoke. May all persecution cease, and every trace of bondage disappear from among men, so that at last a universal feast of freedom shall be celebrated in Thy name, God of Freedom, Father of mankind. Amen.

(Turn to page 240)

## FOR THE SEVENTH DAY OF PESACH

### Responsive Reading

Reader

I will make mention of the deeds of the Lord; I will remember Thy wonders of old.

Congregation

*I will meditate upon all Thy work, and muse on Thy doings.*

O God, Thy way is in holiness; who is like unto Thee?

*Thou, O God, doest wonders; Thou hast made known Thy strength among the peoples.*

Thou hast with Thine arm redeemed Thy people, the sons of Jacob and Joseph.

*Thou didst lead Thy people like a flock, by the hand of Moses and Aaron.*

Thy way was in the sea, and Thy path in the great waters.

*He turned the sea into dry land; they went through the river on foot.*

He ruleth by His might forever; His eyes keep watch upon the nations; let not the rebellious exalt themselves.

*Bless our God, ye peoples, and make the voice of His praise to be heard;*

Who hath set our soul in life, and suffered not our foot to be moved.

*For Thou, O God, hast tried us; Thou hast refined us, as silver is refined.*

We went through fire and through water; but Thou
    didst bring us out into abundance.

Praised be the Lord; day by day He beareth our
    burden, He is our salvation.

### Reader

A song of triumph and of joy rose unto Thee, O
God, from the lips of Israel's redeemed. They extolled
Thy name in ecstasy for the freedom which Thou
didst bestow upon them. Thou didst lead them in
love so that they might establish a new sanctuary, a
kingdom of the spirit, in which Thou alone shouldst
reign, and all men acknowledge Thee as the Ruler of
the universe. In lofty strains they praised Thy greatness and glory before which human greatness sinks into
nothingness and earthly glory vanishes. They had seen
how pride causes its own downfall, and how in the end
right conquers, not by might and not by power, but by
Thy spirit which rules nature and mankind. The idols
were powerless, for the spirit was not in them; the worshipers of false gods were put to shame and all their
plans came to naught when the time was ripe for the
redemption of Thy people.

We thank Thee, O God, for Thy providence which
keeps the spirit of truth, justice and peace alive in the
hearts of men. On this closing day of our feast, we
pray Thee to let Thy blessing rest upon our congregation; imbue us with holy zeal to work in the cause for
which it was established. Be Thou with the whole
house of Israel, so that we may live in freedom everywhere and unite with all men in singing a new song
of salvation and deliverance. Bestow Thy blessing, O

God, upon our country; may it always be the home of freedom, the refuge of the oppressed and downtrodden. Grant the blessing of liberty, justice and peace unto all Thy children now and evermore. Amen.

(Turn to page 240)

### FOR SHAVUOS

*Responsive Reading*

Reader

Happy are they that are upright in the way,

Congregation

*Who walk in the law of the Lord.*

Happy are they that keep His testimonies,

*That seek Him with the whole heart;*

With my whole heart have I sought Thee;

*O let me not err from Thy commandments.*

Unless Thy law had been my delight,

*I should then have perished in mine affliction.*

Thy word is a lamp unto my feet, and a light unto my path.

*I will delight in Thy statutes, I will not forget Thy word.*

*Choir*

Great peace have they that love Thy law and there shall be no stumbling for them. Great shall be the peace of Thy children.

*Reader*

With joy, O our God, we come before Thee in this gladsome season of the year, when nature sings Thy praise, when field and forest, hill and valley proclaim Thy goodness. Yet holier joy fills our hearts as we remember the day of Sinai, when Israel entered into covenant with Thee to become a kingdom of priests and a holy nation.

With Thy law in their hearts, Thy people has gone forth as Thy witness and midst deadly foes and devouring flames has proclaimed Thy name in all the earth. Through the ages Israel has been faithful to Thee. He found strength in trouble, light in darkness, hope in adversity, for he remembered Thy promise: I, the Lord, change not, and ye, O sons of Jacob, shall not be consumed. In the same faith we hold fast to Thy covenant, and bring our children unto Thine altar that they may renew the vow of their fathers. Grant, O God, that this covenant may be forever sealed upon their hearts as a covenant of life and peace. May Thy spirit which rested upon our fathers and Thy word which Thou didst put into their mouths not depart from our children and our children's children forever. Grant that the truths revealed to Israel may become the possession of all men, and that the time be not distant when all the children of earth shall recognize Thee as their God and Father. Amen.

(Turn to page 240)

## FOR SUCCOS

### Responsive Reading

Reader

O Thou that hearest prayer, unto Thee doth all flesh come.

Congregation

All the earth shall worship Thee, and shall sing praises unto Thee.

Thou turnest a wilderness into a pool of water.
  *And a dry land into springs of water.*
And there Thou makest the hungry to dwell,
  *And they establish a city of habitation;*
And sow fields and plant vineyards, which yield abundant fruits;
  *Thou blessest them also, so that they are multiplied greatly.*
Praised be the Lord; day by day He beareth our burden;
  He is our Salvation.
  *Yea, the Lord will give that which is good; and our land shall yield her produce.*
Thou crownest the year with Thy goodness
  *The earth hath yielded her increase.*
The meadows are clothed with flocks;
  *The valleys also are covered with corn.*
Let the peoples give thanks unto Thee, O God;
  *O let the nations be glad and sing for joy.*

### Reader

On this Feast of Tabernacles, O God, we recall with grateful hearts the loving care with which Thou didst watch over our fathers in the wilderness. When wearied by sultry sun and violent storm, they found shelter and refreshment in the booth of Thy protecting love. In drought Thou didst sustain them, in famine Thou didst preserve them. With a father's tender care Thou didst guide and shield them, and didst make them bearers of Thy truth, champions of Thy law.

We approach Thine altar, on this day of sacred memories, with the joyous symbols of our feast: the fruitful palm, the fragrant citron, the densely-leaved myrtle, and the low-hanging willow. They remind us of the time when Israel, the branch of Thy planting, began to bear fruit, when he first learned to know Thee and to proclaim Thy word in the world. They speak to us also of the unity of all Israel, of the common duties and tasks of a people consecrated unto Thee. Give us, we pray Thee, the strength and the courage to be true to our sacred trust. When storms of oppression beat down upon us and fires of persecution threaten to devour us, spread over us the tabernacle of Thy peace, and fortify our spirits with faith in Thee, the Guardian of Israel who sleepeth not nor slumbereth. Keep alive within us the memories of the past and the visions of the future. May we never cease to hope and to labor for that spiritual harvest, when all Thy children shall be gathered under Thy banner of truth, and stand united as one common brotherhood.

(Turn to page 240)

### FOR SHEMINI ATZERES

#### Responsive Reading

Reader
Give ear, O My people, to My teaching.

Congregation
Incline your ears to the words of My mouth.
That which we have heard and known,
And our fathers have told us, we will not hide from their children,

Telling to the generations to come the praises of the
Lord,

And His strength and His wondrous works that He
hath done.

For He established a testimony in Jacob, and appointed
a law in Israel

Which He commanded our fathers, that they should
make them known to their children;

That the generation to come might know them, even
the children that should be born;

Who should arise and tell them to their children,

That they might put their confidence in God,

And not forget the works of God, but keep His commandments.

### Reader

Throughout this festal season, O God, we have extolled Thee for the bounteous gifts of the earth. On
this sacred Feast of Conclusion, we return to render
our homage to Thee for the blessing with which Thou
crownest our days. Truly, O Lord, Thou art good to
all, and Thy lovingkindness is over all Thy works.

We thank Thee also for the spiritual joys of life, for
the eternal blessings that come from faithful obedience
to Thy law. We rejoice that Thou hast made Israel
the guardian of Thy truth, the keeper of the Torah,
the law of life, justice and peace for all men. We
delight in its possession as Israel's greatest boon, the
common heritage of our people. With ever renewed
devotion we read and reread it from year to year; and
we pray Thee, O Lord, that as we listen to its teachings,

we may grow in wisdom and understanding, in reverence of Thee and in love of man, and thus prove worthy of the crown of priesthood which Thou hast placed upon our head.

With unfaltering trust in Thee, O our God, and with heartfelt gratitude for Thy countless blessings, we conclude today the festive cycle of this month. May the spirit of reverence and devotion it has aroused cause us to rejoice in Thy law, to find in it the good tidings of justice and brotherhood unto all men. The Lord grant strength unto His people; may the Lord bless all His people with peace. Amen.

### Reader

Look with favor, O Lord, upon us, and may our service ever be acceptable unto Thee. Praised be Thou, O God, whom alone we serve in reverence.

### Congregation and Reader

We gratefully acknowledge, O Lord, our God, that Thou art our Creator and Preserver, the Rock of our life and the Shield of our help. We render thanks unto Thee for our lives which are in Thy hand, for our souls which are ever in Thy keeping, for Thy wondrous providence and for Thy continuous goodness, which Thou bestowest upon us day by day. Truly, Thy mercies never fail and Thy lovingkindness never ceases. Therefore do we forever put our trust in Thee.

### Reader

Our God and God of our fathers, may Thy blessing rest upon us, according to the gracious promise of Thy word:

### Reader and Choir

May the Lord bless thee and keep thee.

Amen.

May the Lord let His countenance shine upon thee and be gracious unto thee.

Amen.

May the Lord lift up His countenance upon thee and give thee peace.

Amen.

Reader

רְצֵה יְיָ אֱלֹהֵינוּ בְּעַמְּךָ יִשְׂרָאֵל וּתְפִלָּתָם
בְּאַהֲבָה תְקַבֵּל וּתְהִי לְרָצוֹן תָּמִיד עֲבֹדַת יִשְׂרָאֵל
עַמֶּךָ: בָּרוּךְ אַתָּה יְיָ שֶׁאוֹתְךָ לְבַדְּךָ בְּיִרְאָה נַעֲבוֹד:

Reader and Congregation

מוֹדִים אֲנַחְנוּ לָךְ שָׁאַתָּה הוּא יְיָ אֱלֹהֵינוּ וֵאלֹהֵי
אֲבוֹתֵינוּ לְעוֹלָם וָעֶד. צוּר חַיֵּינוּ מָגֵן יִשְׁעֵנוּ אַתָּה
הוּא לְדוֹר וָדוֹר נוֹדֶה לְּךָ וּנְסַפֵּר תְּהִלָּתֶךָ עַל־
חַיֵּינוּ הַמְּסוּרִים בְּיָדֶךָ וְעַל־נִשְׁמוֹתֵינוּ הַפְּקוּדוֹת
לָךְ וְעַל־נִסֶּיךָ שֶׁבְּכָל־יוֹם עִמָּנוּ וְעַל־נִפְלְאוֹתֶיךָ
וְטוֹבוֹתֶיךָ שֶׁבְּכָל־עֵת עֶרֶב וָבֹקֶר וְצָהֳרָיִם. הַטּוֹב
כִּי־לֹא כָלוּ רַחֲמֶיךָ וְהַמְרַחֵם כִּי לֹא־תַמּוּ חֲסָדֶיךָ
מֵעוֹלָם קִוִּינוּ לָךְ:

Reader

אֱלֹהֵינוּ וֵאלֹהֵי אֲבוֹתֵינוּ. בָּרְכֵנוּ בַבְּרָכָה
הַמְשֻׁלֶּשֶׁת הַכְּתוּבָה בַּתּוֹרָה:

Reader and Choir

יְבָרֶכְךָ יְיָ וְיִשְׁמְרֶךָ:

יָאֵר יְיָ פָּנָיו אֵלֶיךָ וִיחֻנֶּךָ:

יִשָּׂא יְיָ פָּנָיו אֵלֶיךָ וְיָשֵׂם לְךָ שָׁלוֹם:

Amen.

### Reader

Grant us peace, Thy most precious gift, O Thou eternal source of peace, and enable Israel to be its messenger unto the peoples of the earth. Bless our country that it may ever be a stronghold of peace, and its advocate in the council of nations. May contentment reign within its borders, health and happiness within its homes. Strengthen the bonds of friendship and fellowship among all the inhabitants of our land. Plant virtue in every soul, and may the love of Thy name hallow every home and every heart. Praised be Thou, O Lord, Giver of peace.

### Choir

Amen

### Silent Devotion

O God, keep my tongue from evil and my lips from speaking guile. Be my support when grief silences my voice, and my comfort when woe bends my spirit. Plant humility in my soul, and strengthen my heart with perfect faith in Thee. Help me to be strong in trial and temptation and to be patient and forgiving when others wrong me. Guide me by the light of Thy counsel, that I may ever find strength in Thee, my Rock and my Redeemer. Amen.

### Choir

May the words of my mouth and the meditations of my heart be acceptable in Thy sight, O Lord, my Rock and my Redeemer.

Reader

שִׂים שָׁלוֹם טוֹבָה וּבְרָכָה חֵן וָחֶסֶד וְרַחֲמִים
עָלֵינוּ וְעַל־כָּל־יִשְׂרָאֵי שְׁמֶךָ. בָּרְכֵנוּ אָבִינוּ כֻּלָּנוּ
כְּאֶחָד בְּאוֹר פָּנֶיךָ. כִּי בְאוֹר פָּנֶיךָ נָתַתָּ לָּנוּ יְיָ
אֱלֹהֵינוּ תּוֹרַת חַיִּים וְאַהֲבַת חֶסֶד וּצְדָקָה וּבְרָכָה
וְרַחֲמִים וְחַיִּים וְשָׁלוֹם. וְטוֹב בְּעֵינֶיךָ לְבָרֵךְ אֶת־
עַמְּךָ יִשְׂרָאֵל וְאֶת־כָּל־הָעַמִּים בְּרֹב עֹז וְשָׁלוֹם:
בָּרוּךְ אַתָּה יְיָ עֹשֵׂה הַשָּׁלוֹם:

Silent Prayer

אֱלֹהַי נְצוֹר לְשׁוֹנִי מֵרָע וּשְׂפָתַי מִדַּבֵּר מִרְמָה:
וְלִמְקַלְלַי נַפְשִׁי תִדּוֹם וְנַפְשִׁי כֶּעָפָר לַכֹּל תִּהְיֶה:
פְּתַח לִבִּי בְּתוֹרָתֶךָ וּבְמִצְוֹתֶיךָ תִּרְדּוֹף נַפְשִׁי: וְכָל
הַחוֹשְׁבִים עָלַי רָעָה מְהֵרָה הָפֵר עֲצָתָם וְקַלְקֵל
מַחֲשַׁבְתָּם. לְמַעַן יֵחָלְצוּן יְדִידֶיךָ הוֹשִׁיעָה יְמִינְךָ
וַעֲנֵנִי: יִהְיוּ לְרָצוֹן אִמְרֵי פִי וְהֶגְיוֹן לִבִּי לְפָנֶיךָ יְיָ
צוּרִי וְגֹאֲלִי:

## Responsive Reading

### הלל

#### (Psalms cxiii, cxviii)

Reader

Hallelujah. Praise, O ye servants of the Lord, praise
the name of the Lord.

Congregation

*Blessed be the name of the Lord from this time forth
and forever.*

From the rising of the sun unto the going down thereof,
the Lord's name is to be praised.

*The Lord is high above all nations; His glory is above
the heavens.*

Who is like unto the Lord our God, that is enthroned
on high, that looketh down low upon heaven
and upon the earth?

*Who raiseth up the poor out of the dust, and lifteth
up the needy out of the dunghill;*

That He may set him with princes, even with the
princes of His people.

*Who maketh the barren woman to dwell in her house
as a joyful mother of children. Hallelujah.*

### Reader and Choir

O give thanks unto the Lord, for He is good, for His
mercy endureth forever.

So let Israel now say, for His mercy endureth forever.

So let the house of Aaron now say, for His mercy
endureth forever.

So let them now that fear the Lord say, for His mercy
endureth forever.

## Responsive Reading

(Psalms cxiii, cxviii)

הַלְלוּיָהּ. הַלְלוּ עַבְדֵי יְיָ. הַלְלוּ אֶת־שֵׁם יְיָ:

יְהִי שֵׁם יְיָ מְבֹרָךְ מֵעַתָּה וְעַד־עוֹלָם:

מִמִּזְרַח־שֶׁמֶשׁ עַד־מְבוֹאוֹ מְהֻלָּל שֵׁם יְיָ:

רָם עַל־כָּל־גּוֹיִם יְיָ. עַל־הַשָּׁמַיִם כְּבוֹדוֹ:

מִי כַּייָ אֱלֹהֵינוּ הַמַּגְבִּיהִי לָשָׁבֶת:

הַמַּשְׁפִּילִי לִרְאוֹת בַּשָּׁמַיִם וּבָאָרֶץ:

מְקִימִי מֵעָפָר דָּל. מֵאַשְׁפֹּת יָרִים אֶבְיוֹן:

לְהוֹשִׁיבִי עִם־נְדִיבִים. עִם נְדִיבֵי עַמּוֹ:

מוֹשִׁיבִי עֲקֶרֶת הַבַּיִת. אֵם־הַבָּנִים שְׂמֵחָה הַלְלוּיָהּ:

הַלְלוּ אֶת־יְיָ כָּל־גּוֹיִם. שַׁבְּחוּהוּ כָּל־הָאֻמִּים:

כִּי נָבַר עָלֵינוּ חַסְדּוֹ. וֶאֱמֶת־יְיָ לְעוֹלָם הַלְלוּיָהּ:

## Reader and Choir

| כִּי לְעוֹלָם חַסְדּוֹ: | הוֹדוּ לַייָ כִּי־טוֹב |
|---|---|
| כִּי לְעוֹלָם חַסְדּוֹ: | יֹאמַר־נָא יִשְׂרָאֵל |
| כִּי לְעוֹלָם חַסְדּוֹ: | יֹאמְרוּ־נָא בֵית אַהֲרֹן |
| כִּי לְעוֹלָם חַסְדּוֹ: | יֹאמְרוּ־נָא יִרְאֵי יְיָ |

## FOR PESACH

### Responsive Reading

Reader
When Israel came forth out of Egypt,

Congregation
The house of Jacob from a people of strange language;
Judah became His sanctuary, Israel His dominion.

The sea saw it, and fled; the Jordan turned backward.
The mountains skipped like rams, the hills like young sheep.

What aileth thee, O thou sea, that thou fleest?
Thou Jordan, that thou turnest backward?

Ye mountains, that ye skip like rams; ye hills, like young sheep?

Tremble, thou earth, at the presence of the Lord,
At the presence of the God of Jacob;

Who turned the rock into a pool of water,
The flint into a fountain of waters.

(Turn to page 250)

### FOR SHAVUOS

## Responsive Reading

**Reader**

I love that the Lord should hear my voice and my
supplications.

**Congregation**

*Because He has inclined His ear unto me, I will call
upon Him all my days.*

Gracious is the Lord, and righteous; yea, our God is
compassionate.

*Return, O my soul, unto thy rest; for the Lord hath
dealt bountifully with thee.*

For Thou hast delivered my soul from death, mine eyes
from tears, and my feet from stumbling.

*I shall walk before the Lord in the land of the living.*

How can I repay unto the Lord all His bountiful dealings toward me?

*My vows will I pay unto the Lord, yea, in the presence
of all His people.*

I will lift up the cup of salvation, and call upon the
name of the Lord.

*I will offer to Thee the sacrifice of thanksgiving, and
will call upon the name of the Lord.*

(Turn to page 250)

## FOR SUCCOS

*Responsive Reading*

**Reader**

Not unto us, O Lord, not unto us, but unto Thy name give glory,

**Congregation**

*For Thy mercy, and for Thy truth's sake.*

Wherefore should the nations say: where is now their God?

*But our God is in the heavens; whatsoever pleased Him He hath done.*

Their idols are silver and gold, the work of men's hands.

*They have mouths, but they speak not; eyes have they, but they see not;*

They have ears, but they hear not; feet have they, but they walk not;

*They that make them shall be like unto them;*

Yea, every one that trusteth in them.

*O Israel, trust Thou in the Lord! He is our help and our shield!*

O house of Aaron, trust ye in the Lord! He is our help and our shield!

*Ye that fear the Lord, trust in the Lord! He is our help and our shield.*

(Turn to page 250)

## FOR SHEMINI ATZERES

*Responsive Reading*

Reader

The Lord hath been mindful of us, He will bless us.

Congregation

He will bless the house of Israel; He will bless the
house of Aaron.

He will bless them that fear the Lord, both small and
great.

The Lord increase you more and more, you and your
children.

Blessed be ye of the Lord, who made heaven and earth.

The heavens are the heavens of the Lord; but the
earth hath He given to the children of men.

The dead praise not the Lord, neither any that go down
into silence;

But we will bless the Lord from this time forth and
forever.

O praise the Lord, all ye nations; laud Him all ye
peoples.

For His mercy is great toward us; and the truth of
the Lord endureth forever. Hallelujah.

### Responsive Reading

**Reader**

In distress I called upon the Lord; He answered me with great deliverance.

**Congregation**

*The Lord is for me; I will not fear; what can man do unto me?*

The Lord is for me as my helper; and I shall gaze upon them that hate me.

*It is better to take refuge in the Lord than to trust in man.*

It is better to take refuge in the Lord than to trust in princes.

*All nations compass me about; verily, in the name of the Lord I will cut them off.*

They compass me about, yea, they compass me about; verily, in the name of the Lord I will cut them off.

*Thou didst thrust sore at me that I might fall; but the Lord helped me.*

The Lord is my strength and song; and He is become my salvation.

*The voice of rejoicing and salvation is in the tents of the righteous.*

The right hand of the Lord doeth valiantly; the right hand of the Lord is exalted.

*I shall not die, but live, and declare the works of the Lord.*

The Lord hath chastened me sore; but He hath not given me over unto death.

Responsive Reading

מִן־הַמֵּצַר קָרָאתִי יָּהּ עָנָנִי בַמֶּרְחָב יָהּ׃

יְיָ לִי לֹא אִירָא מַה־יַּעֲשֶׂה לִי אָדָם׃

יְיָ לִי בְּעֹזְרָי וַאֲנִי אֶרְאֶה בְשֹׂנְאָי׃

טוֹב לַחֲסוֹת בַּיְיָ מִבְּטֹחַ בָּאָדָם׃

טוֹב לַחֲסוֹת בַּיְיָ מִבְּטֹחַ בִּנְדִיבִים׃

כָּל־גּוֹיִם סְבָבוּנִי בְּשֵׁם יְיָ כִּי אֲמִילַם׃

סַבּוּנִי כִדְבֹרִים דֹּעֲכוּ כְּאֵשׁ קוֹצִים. בְּשֵׁם יְיָ כִּי אֲמִילַם׃

דָּחֹה דְחִיתַנִי לִנְפֹּל וַיְיָ עֲזָרָנִי׃

עָזִּי וְזִמְרָת יָהּ וַיְהִי־לִי לִישׁוּעָה׃

קוֹל רִנָּה וִישׁוּעָה בְּאָהֳלֵי צַדִּיקִים יְמִין יְיָ עֹשָׂה חָיִל׃

יְמִין יְיָ רוֹמֵמָה יְמִין יְיָ עֹשָׂה חָיִל׃

לֹא־אָמוּת כִּי־אֶחְיֶה וַאֲסַפֵּר מַעֲשֵׂי יָהּ׃

יַסֹּר יִסְּרַנִּי יָּהּ וְלַמָּוֶת לֹא נְתָנָנִי׃

פִּתְחוּ־לִי שַׁעֲרֵי־צֶדֶק אָבֹא בָם אוֹדֶה יָהּ׃

זֶה־הַשַּׁעַר לַיְיָ צַדִּיקִים יָבֹאוּ בוֹ׃

אוֹדְךָ כִּי עֲנִיתָנִי וַתְּהִי־לִי לִישׁוּעָה׃

Open to me the gates of righteousness; I will enter
into them; I will give thanks unto the Lord.

This is the gate of the Lord; the righteous shall enter
into it.

I will give thanks unto Thee, for Thou hast answered
me and art become my salvation.

The stone which the builders rejected is become the
chief corner-stone.

This is the Lord's doing; it is marvelous in our eyes.

This is the day which the Lord hath made; we will
rejoice and be glad in it.

### Reader and Choir

We beseech Thee, O Lord, save now!

We beseech Thee, O Lord, make us now to prosper!

**Reader**

Blessed be he that cometh in the name of the Lord;
we bless you out of the house of the Lord.

**Congregation**

Thou art my God, and I will give thanks unto Thee;
Thou art my God, I will exalt Thee.

O give thanks unto the Lord, for He is good, for His
mercy endureth forever.

אֶבֶן מָאֲסוּ הַבּוֹנִים הָיְתָה לְרֹאשׁ פִּנָּה:

מֵאֵת יְיָ הָיְתָה זֹּאת הִיא נִפְלָאת בְּעֵינֵינוּ:

זֶהַיּוֹם עָשָׂה יְיָ נָגִילָה וְנִשְׂמְחָה בוֹ:

Reader and Choir

אָנָּא יְיָ הוֹשִׁיעָה־נָּא:   אָנָּא יְיָ הוֹשִׁיעָה־נָּא:

אָנָּא יְיָ הַצְלִיחָה נָּא:   אָנָּא יְיָ הַצְלִיחָה נָּא:

בָּרוּךְ הַבָּא בְּשֵׁם יְיָ. בֵּרַכְנוּכֶם מִבֵּית יְיָ:

אֵלִי אַתָּה וְאוֹדֶךָּ. אֱלֹהַי אֲרוֹמְמֶךָּ:

הוֹדוּ לַיְיָ כִּי־טוֹב. כִּי לְעוֹלָם חַסְדּוֹ:

## READING OF SCRIPTURE

### Reader

(Isaiah II: 1–4)

And it shall come to pass in the end of days, that the mountain of the Lord's house shall be established as the top of the mountains, and shall be exalted above the hills; and all nations shall flow unto it. And many peoples shall go and say, Come ye, and let us go up to the mountain of the Lord, to the house of the God of Jacob; and He will teach us of His ways, and we will walk in His paths. For out of Zion shall go forth the law, and the word of the Lord from Jerusalem.

### Choir

There is none like unto Thee among the mighty, O Lord, and there are no works like unto Thine. Thy kingdom is an ever-lasting kingdom and Thy dominion endureth throughout all genera-tions. Thou art King eternal; Thou hast reigned and shalt reign for evermore. The Lord will give strength unto His people; the Lord will

אֵין כָּמוֹךָ בָאֱלֹהִים

אֲדֹנָי וְאֵין כְּמַעֲשֶׂיךָ:

מַלְכוּתְךָ מַלְכוּת כָּל־

עוֹלָמִים וּמֶמְשַׁלְתְּךָ בְּכָל־

דּוֹר וָדוֹר: יְיָ מֶלֶךְ יְיָ מָלָךְ

יְיָ יִמְלֹךְ לְעוֹלָם־וָעֶד: יְיָ

עֹז לְעַמּוֹ יִתֵּן. יְיָ יְבָרֵךְ

bless His people with peace.

אֶת־עַמּוֹ בַשָּׁלוֹם:

(Congregation rises)

### Reader, then Choir

The Lord, the Lord God is merciful and gracious, long-suffering and abundant in goodness and ever true: keeping mercy for thousands, forgiving iniquity, transgression and sin.

יְהֹוָה יְהֹוָה אֵל רַחוּם וְחַנּוּן. אֶרֶךְ אַפַּיִם וְרַב־חֶסֶד וֶאֱמֶת. נוֹצֵר חֶסֶד לָאֲלָפִים. נֹשֵׂא עָוֹן וָפֶשַׁע וְחַטָּאָה:

## TAKING THE SCROLL FROM THE ARK
### Reader

Let us declare the greatness of our God and render honor unto the Torah.

הָבוּ גֹדֶל לֵאלֹהֵינוּ וּתְנוּ כָבוֹד לַתּוֹרָה.

### Congregation and Choir

Praised be He who in His holiness has given the Torah unto Israel.

בָּרוּךְ שֶׁנָּתַן תּוֹרָה לְעַמּוֹ יִשְׂרָאֵל בִּקְדֻשָּׁתוֹ:

### Reader

O house of Jacob, let us walk in the light of the Lord.

בֵּית יַעֲקֹב לְכוּ וְנֵלְכָה בְּאוֹר יְהֹוָה:

*Congregation and Reader, then Choir*

Hear, O Israel: The Lord, our God, the Lord is One.

שְׁמַע יִשְׂרָאֵל יְהוָֹה אֱלֹהֵינוּ יְהוָֹה אֶחָד:

(Congregation is seated)

*Choir*

Thine, O Lord, is the greatness, and the power, the glory, and the victory, and the majesty; for all that is in the heaven and in the earth is Thine; Thine is the kingdom, O Lord, and Thou art exalted as head above all.

לְךָ יְיָ הַגְּדֻלָּה וְהַגְּבוּרָה.

וְהַתִּפְאֶרֶת וְהַנֵּצַח וְהַהוֹד

כִּי כֹל בַּשָּׁמַיִם וּבָאָרֶץ.

לְךָ יְיָ הַמַּמְלָכָה וְהַמִּתְנַשֵּׂא

לְכֹל לְרֹאשׁ:

(Before reading from the Torah)

*Reader*

Praise ye the Lord to whom all praise is due.

Praised be the Lord to whom all praise is due forever and ever.

Praised be Thou, O Lord our God, Ruler of the world, who hast

בָּרְכוּ אֶת־יְיָ הַמְבֹרָךְ:

בָּרוּךְ יְיָ הַמְבֹרָךְ

לְעוֹלָם וָעֶד:

בָּרוּךְ אַתָּה יְיָ אֱלֹהֵינוּ

מֶלֶךְ הָעוֹלָם. אֲשֶׁר בָּחַר־

called us from among all peoples and hast given us Thy law. Praised be Thou, O Lord, Giver of the Law.

בָּנוּ מִכָּל־הָעַמִּים וְנָתַן לָנוּ אֶת־תּוֹרָתוֹ. בָּרוּךְ אַתָּה יְיָ נוֹתֵן הַתּוֹרָה:

---

## READING FROM THE TORAH

---

(After reading from the Torah)

Praised be Thou, O Lord our God, Ruler of the world, who hast given us the law of truth and hast implanted within us everlasting life. Praised be Thou, O Lord, Giver of the Law.

בָּרוּךְ אַתָּה יְיָ אֱלֹהֵינוּ מֶלֶךְ הָעוֹלָם. אֲשֶׁר נָתַן לָנוּ תּוֹרַת אֱמֶת וְחַיֵּי עוֹלָם נָטַע בְּתוֹכֵנוּ. בָּרוּךְ אַתָּה יְיָ נוֹתֵן הַתּוֹרָה:

(Before reading the Haftarah)

Praised be the Lord our God, for the law of truth and righteousness revealed in Israel, for the words of the prophets filled with His spirit and for the teachings of the sages whom He raised up aforetime and in these days.

## READING OF THE HAFTARAH

(Turn to page 265)

## READING OF SCRIPTURE FOR
## SHEMINI ATZERES

### Reader
(Isaiah II: 1–4)

And it shall come to pass in the end of days, that the mountain of the Lord's house shall be established as the top of the mountains, and shall be exalted above the hills; and all nations shall flow unto it. And many peoples shall go and say, Come ye, and let us go up to the mountain of the Lord, to the house of the God of Jacob; and He will teach us of His ways, and we will walk in His paths. For out of Zion shall go forth the law, and the word of the Lord from Jerusalem.

### Choir

| | |
|---|---|
| It has been shown thee that thou mightest know that the Lord, He is God, there is none beside Him. | אַתָּה הָרְאֵתָ לָדַעַת כִּי יְיָ הוּא הָאֱלֹהִים. אֵין עוֹד מִלְבַדּוֹ: |
| That He alone doeth wonders, for His mercy endureth forever. | לְעוֹשֶׂה נִפְלָאוֹת גְּדֹלוֹת לְבַדּוֹ. כִּי לְעוֹלָם חַסְדּוֹ: |
| The glory of the Lord is eternal, the Lord rejoices in His works. | יְהִי כְבוֹד יְיָ לְעוֹלָם. יִשְׂמַח יְיָ בְּמַעֲשָׂיו: |
| Blessed be the name of the Lord from this time forth and forever. | יְהִי שֵׁם יְיָ מְבֹרָךְ. מֵעַתָּה וְעַד עוֹלָם: |
| Be with us as Thou wast | יְהִי יְיָ אֱלֹהֵינוּ עִמָּנוּ כַּאֲשֶׁר הָיָה עִם |

with our fathers; forsake us not.

אֲבֹתֵינוּ. אַל יַעַזְבֵנוּ וְאַל יִטְּשֵׁנוּ: וְיִהְיוּ נָא אֲמָרֵינוּ

May our words be acceptable before Thee, O Lord of all.

לְרָצוֹן. לִפְנֵי אֲדוֹן כֹּל:

(The scrolls are taken from the Ark by the president or other officer of the congregation and handed to the rabbi. The rabbi handing the Torah to the three generations recites these verses:)

For out of Zion goeth forth the law and the word of God from Jerusalem.

כִּי מִצִּיּוֹן תֵּצֵא תוֹרָה. וּדְבַר יְיָ מִירוּשָׁלָיִם:

Praised be He who in His holiness has given the Law to His people Israel.

בָּרוּךְ שֶׁנָּתַן תּוֹרָה לְעַמּוֹ יִשְׂרָאֵל בִּקְדֻשָּׁתוֹ:

But ye that did cleave unto the Lord your God are alive, everyone of you, this day.

וְאַתֶּם הַדְּבֵקִים בַּיָי אֱלֹהֵיכֶם חַיִּים כֻּלְּכֶם הַיּוֹם:

(Then all face congregation and say: שמע ישראל יהוה אלהינו יהוה Hear, O Israel, the Lord our God, the Lord is one.)    אחד:

(Then they proceed with the Hakofos, one or more circuits of the Temple, in procession, the choir singing:)

## Choir

| | |
|---|---|
| We beseech Thee, O Lord, save us now. | אָנָּא יְיָ הוֹשִׁיעָה נָּא. אָנָּא |
| We beseech Thee, O Lord, make us now to prosper. | יְיָ הַצְלִיחָה נָּא: אָנָּא יְיָ |
| | עֲנֵנוּ בְיוֹם קָרְאֵנוּ: |
| O Lord, answer us on the day that we call. | אֱלֹהֵי הָרוּחוֹת הוֹשִׁיעָה |
| God of all spirits, save us now. | נָּא: בּוֹחֵן לְבָבוֹת |
| Searcher of hearts, make us now to prosper. | הַצְלִיחָה נָּא: גּוֹאֵל |
| | חָזָק עֲנֵנוּ בְיוֹם קָרְאֵנוּ: |
| Mighty Redeemer, answer us on the day that we call. | דּוֹבֵר צְדָקוֹת הוֹשִׁיעָה נָּא: |
| Proclaimer of righteousness, save now. | הָדוּר בִּלְבוּשׁוֹ הַצְלִיחָה |
| Appareled in glory, make us now to prosper. | נָּא: וָתִיק וְעוֹשֶׂה חֶסֶד |
| | עֲנֵנוּ בְיוֹם קָרְאֵנוּ: |
| Omnipotent and gracious, answer us on the day that we call. | יוֹדֵעַ מַחֲשָׁבוֹת הוֹשִׁיעָה |
| Thou who knowest our thoughts, save now. | נָּא: כַּבִּיר וְנָאוֹר |
| Powerful and resplendent, make us now to prosper. | הַצְלִיחָה נָּא: לוֹבֵשׁ |
| Clothed in righteousness, answer us on the day that we call. | צְדָקוֹת עֲנֵנוּ בְיוֹם |
| | קָרְאֵנוּ: |
| Holy and revered, save now. | קָדוֹשׁ וְנוֹרָא הוֹשִׁיעָה נָּא: |
| | רַחוּם וְחַנּוּן הַצְלִיחָה |

Merciful and Gracious, make us now to prosper.

נָא: שׁוֹמֵר הַבְּרִית עֲנֵנוּ בְּיוֹם קָרְאֵנוּ:

Keeper of the covenant, answer us on the day that we call.

תּוֹמֵךְ תְּמִימִים הוֹשִׁיעָה

Upholder of the upright, save now.

נָא: תַּקִּיף לָעַד

Eternal Sovereign, make us now to prosper.

הַצְלִיחָה נָא: תָּמִים

Thou who art perfect in Thy ways, answer us on the day that we call.

בְּמַעֲשָׂיו עֲנֵנוּ בְּיוֹם קָרְאֵנוּ:

(When all have returned to the platform which they reascend, two of the scrolls are taken to the pulpit and opened, one at Vezos Hab'rocho and the other at Bereshis. The rabbi then reads the following prayer:)

This law shall not depart out of thy mouth; but thou shalt meditate thereon day and night. All the commandments which I command you this day shall ye observe to do, that ye may live and that ye may know that not by bread alone doth man live but by all that proceedeth out of the mouth of the Lord.

We thank Thee, our God and God of our fathers, that Thou hast given unto us this book of the law. As we complete its reading and begin it anew each year, may we grow in wisdom and understanding, in truth and in goodness. Amen.

(The choir then sings Lecho, the rabbi recites the B'rocho and reads from the Scroll. After the reading of the two passages from the Scroll and their translations and the Haftarah (Joshua I) and while the fathers and sons remain on the pulpit, the organ begins its processional. The consecrants enter, carrying flowers. They ascend the pulpit and with the rabbi repeat: Sh'ma Yisroel, Adonoi Elohenu Adonoi Echod. The rabbi then blesses the consecrants.)

Our Father, we pray Thee, bless these little children. Shelter them under the wings of Thy protecting love. May their souls grow in knowledge and find delight in the worship of Thee. May they be dedicated this day to lives of loyalty and goodness that they bring joy to those who love them and honor to the household of Israel. Shield and guide them in all their ways.

יְבָרֶכְךָ יְיָ וְיִשְׁמְרֶךָ:

May the Lord bless thee and keep thee.

Amen.

יָאֵר יְיָ פָּנָיו אֵלֶיךָ וִיחֻנֶּךָ:

May the Lord let His countenance shine upon thee and be gracious unto thee.

Amen.

יִשָּׂא יְיָ פָּנָיו אֵלֶיךָ וְיָשֵׂם לְךָ שָׁלוֹם:

May the Lord lift up His countenance upon thee and give thee peace.

Amen.

(The children leave the platform and return to their families. The fathers and sons stand before the rabbi at the open ark to receive his blessing:)

Eternal God, our dwelling-place, Thine everlasting arms uphold us. Thy counsels stand forever and Thy thoughts to all generations.

Into our hands hast Thou placed Thy law to be handed from father to son and taught by one generation to another. Through all the ages, whatever befell them, our people remained steadfast in loyalty to Thy Torah. It was carried into exile in the arms of fathers that their sons might not lose their birthright.

We pray, O God, that we may be worthy of this inheritance. May we take its teachings into our hearts and transmit it to those who follow us. May those who stand befor Thee this day be symbols of all the fathers and sons in Israel, of their loyalty to knowledge and to truth, to justice and to peace. Thus shall we labor for the day when the Lord shall be one and His name shall be one.

יְיָ עֹז לְעַמּוֹ יִתֵּן. יְיָ יְבָרֵךְ אֶת־עַמּוֹ בַשָּׁלוֹם:

O Lord, give strength unto Thy people; O Lord, bless Thy people with peace.

(The Scrolls are given back to the rabbi one by one and placed within the Ark. While the Scrolls are being returned, the choir sings:)

## Choir

| | |
|---|---|
| Rejoice and be glad in | שִׂישׂוּ וְשִׂמְחוּ בְּשִׂמְחַת |
| this Feast of the Law. | תּוֹרָה, וּתְנוּ כָבוֹד לַתּוֹרָה. |
| Render honor unto the | נָגִיל וְנָשִׂישׂ בְּזֹאת הַתּוֹרָה, |
| Torah. It is our light | כִּי הִיא לָנוּ עֹז וְאוֹרָה: |
| and our strength, a tree | תּוֹרָה הִיא עֵץ חַיִּים, |
| of life unto all who take | לְכֻלָּם חַיִּים, כִּי עַמְּךָ |

hold of it. Happy are מְקוֹר חַיִּים: אַשְׁרֵיכֶם

ye, O Israel, blessed by יִשְׂרָאֵל, אֲשֶׁר בָּחַר בָּכֶם

God to inherit the Law. אֵל, וְהִנְחִילְכֶם הַתּוֹרָה:

(The fathers and sons return to their pews and the service continues.)

(For the First day of Passover and the Feast of Conclusion)

## Reader

Thou, O Lord, art the source of life, the fountain of light and of truth. Let Thy doctrine descend as the rain, Thy word distil as the dew. Open Thou our hearts that they may receive the good seeds of Thine instruction, and let Thy blessing ripen them into fruits of righteousness. Let Thy gracious promise be fulfilled: I will pour water upon the thirsty land and streams upon the dry ground; I will pour My spirit upon thy seed and My blessing upon thine offspring.

Let rain and dew descend upon the fields of our land,

## Reader and Choir

For the blessing of all and the hurt of none.

For the joy of all and the woe of none.

For the life of all and the death of none.

לִבְרָכָה וְלֹא לִקְלָלָה:

לְשׂוֹבַע וְלֹא לְרָזוֹן:

לְחַיִּים וְלֹא לְמָוֶת:

(For last day of Passover, Shavuos and first day of Succos)

## Reader

O our God and Father, our Protector and Savior, we invoke Thy blessings on the House of Israel. Whatever be our portion in the countries of the earth, may we remain true to our heritage. Bestow Thy favor on this blessed land. Prosper our nation in all its industries and its commerce, on land and on sea so that there may be no want nor scarcity anywhere. Grant that they whom the people have placed in authority may be filled with Thy spirit, the spirit of wisdom and understanding, the spirit of knowledge and the fear of Thee. May Thy blessing rest upon our free institutions, that this land remain forever the home of liberty. May peace abide within its borders and righteousness among its inhabitants. Be Thou with us now and ever. Help Thou us in all our ways. Amen.

(If Memorial Service is used, insert here.)

### RETURNING THE SCROLL TO THE ARK
(Congregation rises)

*Reader*

O magnify the Lord with me and let us exalt His name together.

גַּדְּלוּ לַיָי אִתִּי . וּנְרוֹמְמָה שְׁמוֹ יַחְדָּו:

*Choir*

His glory is in the earth and in the heavens. He is the strength of all His servants, the praise of them that truly love Him, the hope of Israel, the people He brought nigh to Himself. Halle-lujah.

הוֹדוֹ עַל־אֶרֶץ וְשָׁמָיִם
וַיָּרֶם קֶרֶן לְעַמּוֹ תְּהִלָּה
לְכָל־חֲסִידָיו לִבְנֵי
יִשְׂרָאֵל עַם קְרֹבוֹ
הַלְלוּיָהּ:

## Reader

The law of the Lord is perfect, restoring the soul; the testimony of the Lord is sure, making wise the simple. The precepts of the Lord are right, rejoicing the heart; the judgments of the Lord are true; they are righteous altogether. Behold, a good doctrine has been given unto you; forsake it not.

תּוֹרַת יְיָ תְּמִימָה.
מְשִׁיבַת נָפֶשׁ. עֵדוּת יְיָ
נֶאֱמָנָה. מַחְכִּימַת פֶּתִי:
פִּקוּדֵי יְיָ יְשָׁרִים. מְשַׂמְּחֵי
לֵב. מִשְׁפְּטֵי יְיָ אֱמֶת
צָדְקוּ יַחְדָּו: כִּי לֶקַח
טוֹב נָתַתִּי לָכֶם תּוֹרָתִי
אַל־תַּעֲזֹבוּ:

(Congregation is seated)

## Choir

It is a tree of life to them that lay hold of it, and the supporters thereof are happy. Its ways are ways of pleasantness, and all its paths are peace.

עֵץ־חַיִּים הִיא לַמַּחֲזִיקִים
בָּהּ וְתוֹמְכֶיהָ מְאֻשָּׁר:
דְּרָכֶיהָ דַרְכֵי נֹעַם וְכָל־
נְתִיבוֹתֶיהָ שָׁלוֹם:

**SERMON**

## MEMORIAL SERVICE FOR THE SEVENTH DAY OF PASSOVER

### Choir

**(Psalm xxiii)**

The Lord is my shepherd, I shall not want. He maketh me to lie down in green pastures; He leadeth me beside the still waters. He restoreth my soul; He guideth me in straight paths for His name's sake. Yea, though I walk through the valley of the shadow of death I will fear no evil, for Thou art with me; Thy rod and Thy staff, they comfort me. Thou preparest a table before me in the presence of mine enemies; Thou hast anointed my head with oil; my cup runneth over. Surely goodness and mercy shall follow me all the days of my life, and I shall dwell in the house of the Lord forever.

מִזְמוֹר לְדָוִד יְהֹוָה
רֹעִי לֹא אֶחְסָר: בִּנְאוֹת
דֶּשֶׁא יַרְבִּיצֵנִי עַל־מֵי
מְנֻחוֹת יְנַהֲלֵנִי: נַפְשִׁי
יְשׁוֹבֵב יַנְחֵנִי בְמַעְגְּלֵי־
צֶדֶק לְמַעַן שְׁמוֹ: גַּם כִּי־
אֵלֵךְ בְּגֵיא צַלְמָוֶת לֹא־
אִירָא רָע כִּי־אַתָּה עִמָּדִי
שִׁבְטְךָ וּמִשְׁעַנְתֶּךָ הֵמָּה
יְנַחֲמֻנִי: תַּעֲרֹךְ לְפָנַי
שֻׁלְחָן נֶגֶד צֹרְרָי דִּשַּׁנְתָּ
בַשֶּׁמֶן רֹאשִׁי כּוֹסִי רְוָיָה:
אַךְ טוֹב וָחֶסֶד יִרְדְּפוּנִי
כָּל־יְמֵי חַיָּי וְשַׁבְתִּי בְּבֵית
יְהֹוָה לְאֹרֶךְ יָמִים:

### Reader

Everliving God, Thou abidest amidst the ceaseless tides of change which sweep away the generations of man! In the springtime of the year when field and forest reawaken from the seeming death of winter, when earth and sky resound with the song of life reborn, a renewed faith and confidence surge through our hearts. The clouds that darkened our spirits are dispelled by the miracle of reviving nature. The gloom of the valley of the shadow is pierced by the light of Thy presence. Beyond the winter of death smiles Thine eternal springtime. It cannot be that in a world of unending life, we, Thy children, are given over to destruction; that fashioned in Thine image we are doomed to annihilation. The spirit, implanted within us, cannot be only a passing breath. Thou art our dwelling place in life and in death.

### Responsive Reading

**Reader**

O Lord, Thou art my God, earnestly will I seek Thee.

**Congregation**

*My soul thirsteth for Thee, my flesh longeth for Thee.*

Whom have I in heaven but Thee?

*And beside Thee I desire none upon earth.*

My flesh and my heart fail;

*But God is the rock of my heart and my portion forever.*

Thou wilt guide me with Thy counsel,

*And afterward receive me with glory.*

But as for me, the nearness of God is my good;
  I have made the Lord God my refuge.
How precious is Thy lovingkindness, O God,
  And the children of men take refuge in the shadow
    of Thy wings.
For with Thee is the fountain of life;
  In Thy light do we see light.
O continue Thy lovingkindness unto them that know
    Thee
  And Thy righteousness to the upright in heart.

## Choir

(Psalm xvi, 8–11)

I have set the Lord always before me; surely He is at my right hand, I shall not be moved. Therefore my heart is glad and my glory rejoiceth; my flesh also dwelleth in safety. For Thou wilt not abandon my soul to the grave; neither wilt Thou suffer Thy faithful to see destruction. Thou makest me to know the path of life. In Thy presence is fulness of joy, at Thy right hand, bliss for evermore.

שִׁוִּיתִי יְיָ לְנֶגְדִּי תָמִיד.

כִּי מִימִינִי בַּל־אֶמּוֹט: לָכֵן

שָׂמַח לִבִּי וַיָּגֶל כְּבוֹדִי. אַף־

בְּשָׂרִי יִשְׁכֹּן לָבֶטַח: כִּי

לֹא־תַעֲזֹב נַפְשִׁי לִשְׁאוֹל.

לֹא־תִתֵּן חֲסִידְךָ לִרְאוֹת

שָׁחַת: תּוֹדִיעֵנִי אֹרַח חַיִּים.

שֹׂבַע שְׂמָחוֹת אֶת־פָּנֶיךָ.

נְעִימוֹת בִּימִינְךָ נֶצַח:

### Reader

Heavenly Father! The solemn call of this hour revives within our memories the beloved who have passed through the portal of death. We recall the happy days when they walked among us on earth, when, blessed with their love, we lived our lives. They are near us though the snows of many winters may have covered their graves. Now, as in the hour when they laid off the raiment of mortality, our hearts yearn for them. Precious links binding heart to heart still are broken. Transfigured by memory, our dear ones stand again before us in this sacred hour. We remember them with gratitude and name them with a benediction.

We recall the men and women who but yesterday were part of this congregation and shared in the tasks of our community. We pay our tribute of respect and affection to all those whose self-sacrificing devotion has contributed to the growth of our sacred institutions and to the well-being of our people.

We think, too, of the whole household of Israel. We behold the vacant places once filled by brave and consecrated spirits, who by noble teaching and personal example stood forth as faithful guides unto Israel, and a pride to all mankind. Reverently we reflect upon the unnumbered hosts who lived and died for the sanctification of Thy name. We know the names of but few of the vast army of martyrs and heroes, who were swifter than eagles and stronger than lions in doing Thy will. We treasure their unnamed memory, the beauty of their life, the glory of their death.

In gratitude for all the blessings they brought to us, to Israel and to humanity, we dedicate ourselves anew

to the sacred tasks they bequeathed. Mayest Thou
remember them for blessing among the righteous of
the world.

## Silent Prayer

יִזְכּוֹר אֱלֹהִים נִשְׁמַת אָבִי מוֹרִי (אִמִּי מוֹרָתִי)
שֶׁהָלַךְ לְעוֹלָמוֹ (שֶׁהָלְכָה לְעוֹלָמָהּ). אָנָּא תְּהִי נַפְשׁוֹ
(נַפְשָׁהּ) צְרוּרָה בִּצְרוֹר הַחַיִּים וּתְהִי מְנוּחָתוֹ
(מְנוּחָתָהּ) כָּבוֹד. שְׂבַע שְׂמָחוֹת אֶת־פָּנֶיךָ נְעִימוֹת
בִּימִינְךָ נֶצַח. אָמֵן:

Remember, O God, unto life eternal the soul of my
beloved who has gone to his (her) repose and shelter
him (her) beneath the wing of Thy love and grace
for evermore. Strengthen me in my loss, O God of
mercy, that I may honor the memory of my departed
by kindly deeds unto the living. Help me to continue
the noble tasks which gave meaning to his (her) life,
and to contribute in his (her) spirit to the well-being
of our fellowmen and to the sanctification of Thy name.

## Choir

O God, full of compas-
sion, Thou who dwellest
on high! Beneath the
sheltering wings of Thy
presence, among the holy
and pure who shine as
the brightness of the fir-

אֵל מָלֵא רַחֲמִים שׁוֹכֵן
בַּמְּרוֹמִים. הַמְצֵא מְנוּחָה
נְכוֹנָה תַּחַת כַּנְפֵי הַשְּׁכִינָה.
עִם קְדוֹשִׁים וּטְהוֹרִים

mament, grant perfect rest unto the souls of our dear ones who have gone unto eternity. Lord of mercy, bring them under the cover of Thy wings, and let their souls be bound up in the bond of eternal life. Be Thou their portion, and may they rest in peace. Amen.

כְּזֹהַר הָרָקִיעַ מַזְהִירִים. לְנִשְׁמוֹת יַקִּירֵינוּ שֶׁהָלְכוּ לְעוֹלָמָם: בַּעַל הָרַחֲמִים יַסְתִּירֵם בְּסֵתֶר כְּנָפָיו לְעוֹלָמִים וְיִצְרוֹר בִּצְרוֹר הַחַיִּים אֶת נִשְׁמָתָם. יְיָ הוּא נַחֲלָתָם. וְיָנוּחוּ בְּשָׁלוֹם עַל מִשְׁכָּבָם. וְנֹאמַר אָמֵן:

**RETURN OF SCROLL**

(Turn to page 266)

## ADORATION

---

(Congregation rises)

### Congregation and Reader

Let us adore the ever-living God, and render praise unto Him who spread out the heavens and established the earth, whose glory is revealed in the heavens above and whose greatness is manifest throughout the world. He is our God; there is none else.

We bow the head in reverence, and worship the King of kings, the Holy One, praised be He.

### Choir and Congregation

וַאֲנַחְנוּ כֹּרְעִים וּמִשְׁתַּחֲוִים וּמוֹדִים לִפְנֵי מֶלֶךְ
מַלְכֵי הַמְּלָכִים הַקָּדוֹשׁ בָּרוּךְ הוּא:

(Congregation is seated)

### Reader

May the time not be distant, O God, when Thy name shall be worshiped in all the earth, when unbelief shall disappear and error be no more. We fervently pray that the day may come when all men shall invoke Thy name, when corruption and evil shall give way to purity and goodness, when superstition shall no longer enslave the mind, nor idolatry blind the eye, when all who dwell on earth shall know that to Thee alone every knee must bend and every tongue give homage. O may all, created in Thine image, recognize that they are brethren, so that, one in spirit and one in fellowship, they may be forever united before Thee. Then shall Thy kingdom be established on earth and the word of Thine ancient seer be fulfilled: The Lord will reign forever and ever.

## Congregation (or Choir)

On that day the Lord shall be One and His name shall be One.

## Reader

God is the source of life, the fountain of all good. He has given us dear ones and we rejoice in their love, grow strong through their care, and are ennobled by their influence. He has also fixed an end for life and earthly companionship. Ofttimes we cannot fathom His purpose, yet we trust in Him. Though the longing within us seems more than we can bear, we know that our grief is according to our blessing. The sorrow of separation is the inevitable price of days and years of precious love; tears are the tender tribute of yearning affection for those who have passed away but cannot be forgotten.

Death is not the end; the earthly body vanishes, the immortal spirit lives on with God. In our hearts, also, our loved ones never die. Their love and memory abide as a lasting inspiration, moving us to noble deeds and blessing us evermore.

In humble gratitude for their life and love, and with steadfast faith, let us sanctify God's name.

(Mourners rise)

### Reader

Extolled and hallowed be the name of God throughout the world which He has created according to His will. And may He speedily establish His kingdom of righteousness on earth. Amen.

### Congregation

Praised be His glorious name unto all eternity.

### Reader

Praised and glorified be the name of the Holy One, though He be above all the praises which we can utter. Our guide is He in life and our redeemer through all eternity.

### Congregation

Our help cometh from Him, the creator of heaven and earth.

### Reader

The departed whom we now remember have entered into the peace of life eternal. They still live on earth in the acts of goodness they performed and in the hearts of those who cherish their memory. May the beauty of their life abide among us as a loving benediction.

### Congregation: Amen.

### Reader

May the Father of peace send peace to all who mourn, and comfort all the bereaved among us.

### Congregation: Amen.

(Mourners are seated)

(Mourners rise)

Reader

יִתְגַּדַּל וְיִתְקַדַּשׁ שְׁמֵהּ רַבָּא. בְּעָלְמָא דִי־בְרָא
כִרְעוּתֵהּ. וְיַמְלִיךְ מַלְכוּתֵהּ. בְּחַיֵּיכוֹן וּבְיוֹמֵיכוֹן
וּבְחַיֵּי דְכָל־בֵּית יִשְׂרָאֵל. בַּעֲגָלָא וּבִזְמַן קָרִיב.
וְאִמְרוּ אָמֵן:

Congregation

יְהֵא שְׁמֵהּ רַבָּא מְבָרַךְ לְעָלַם וּלְעָלְמֵי עָלְמַיָּא:

Reader

יִתְבָּרַךְ וְיִשְׁתַּבַּח וְיִתְפָּאַר וְיִתְרוֹמַם וְיִתְנַשֵּׂא
וְיִתְהַדָּר וְיִתְעַלֶּה וְיִתְהַלָּל שְׁמֵהּ דְּקוּדְשָׁא. בְּרִיךְ
הוּא. לְעֵלָּא מִן כָּל־בִּרְכָתָא וְשִׁירָתָא. תֻּשְׁבְּחָתָא
וְנֶחָמָתָא. דַּאֲמִירָן בְּעָלְמָא. וְאִמְרוּ אָמֵן:

עַל יִשְׂרָאֵל וְעַל צַדִּיקַיָּא. וְעַל־כָּל־מַן דְּאִתְפְּטַר
מִן עָלְמָא הָדֵין כִּרְעוּתֵהּ דֶּאֱלָהָא. יְהֵא לְהוֹן
שְׁלָמָא רַבָּא וְחִנָּא וְחִסְדָּא מִן־קֳדָם מָרֵא שְׁמַיָּא
וְאַרְעָא. וְאִמְרוּ אָמֵן:

יְהֵא שְׁלָמָא רַבָּא מִן־שְׁמַיָּא וְחַיִּים. עָלֵינוּ וְעַל־
כָּל־יִשְׂרָאֵל. וְאִמְרוּ אָמֵן:

עֹשֶׂה שָׁלוֹם בִּמְרוֹמָיו. הוּא יַעֲשֶׂה שָׁלוֹם עָלֵינוּ
וְעַל־כָּל־יִשְׂרָאֵל. וְאִמְרוּ אָמֵן:

(Mourners are seated)

## THE MOURNER'S KADDISH

### Reader

Yis-gad-dal v'yis-kad-dash sh'meh rab-bo, b'ol-mo di'v-ro kir'-u-seh v'yam-lich mal-chu-seh, b'cha-ye-chon u-v'yo-me-chon u-v'cha-yeh d'chol bes yis-ro-el, ba-a-go-lo u-viz-man ko-riv, v'im-ru O-men.

### Congregation

Y'heh sh'meh rab-bo m'vo-rach, l'o-lam ul'ol'meh ol-ma-yo:

### Reader

Yis-bo-rach v'yish-tab-bach, v'yis-po-ar, v'yis-ro-mam, v'yis-nas-seh, v'yis-had-dor, v'yis-al-leh, v'yis-hal-lol, sh'-meh d'kud'-sho, b'rich hu. L'e-lo min kol bir-cho-so v'shi-ro-so, tush-b'cho-so v'ne-cho-mo-so, da-a-mi-ron b'ol-mo, v'im-ru O-men:

Al yis-ro-el v'al tsa-de-ka-yo, v'al kol man d'isp'tar min ol-mo ho-dain kir-ooseh de-e-lo-ho y'hai l'hon shlo-mo rab-bo v'chino v'chis-do min ko-dom mo-rai sh'ma-yo v'ar-o, v'im-ru O-men:

Y'heh sh'lo-mo rab-bo min sh'ma-yo v'cha-yim, o-le-nu v'al kol yis-ro-el, v'imru O-men:

O-seh sho-lom bim'-ro-mov, hu ya-a-seh sho-lom, o-le-nu v'al kol yis-ro-el, v'imru O-men.

# Services for Week-Days

---

## Evening Service
## Service at House of Mourning
## Morning Service

# Evening Service for Week-Days

### Choir

Bless ye the Lord, all ye servants of the Lord, that stand in the house of the Lord in the night seasons. Lift up your hands unto the Lord and worship Him in holiness. The Lord who made heaven and earth will bless thee out of Zion. By day the Lord will command his lovingkindness and in the night His song shall be with me. I will call unto the Lord with my voice, and He answereth me out of His holy mountain. But as for me, in Thy mercy do I trust; my heart shall rejoice in Thy salvation. I will sing unto the Lord, because He hath dealt bountifully with me.

הִנֵּה בָּרְכוּ אֶת־יְיָ
כָּל־עַבְדֵי יְיָ הָעוֹמְדִים
בְּבֵית יְיָ בַּלֵּילוֹת: שְׂאוּ
יְדֵיכֶם קֹדֶשׁ וּבָרְכוּ אֶת־
יְיָ: יְבָרֶכְךָ יְיָ מִצִּיּוֹן.
עֹשֵׂה שָׁמַיִם וָאָרֶץ:
יוֹמָם יְצַוֶּה יְיָ חַסְדּוֹ:
וּבַלַּיְלָה שִׁירֹה עִמִּי.
קוֹלִי אֶל־יְיָ אֶקְרָא.
וַיַּעֲנֵנִי מֵהַר קָדְשׁוֹ סֶלָה:
וַאֲנִי בְּחַסְדְּךָ בָטַחְתִּי. יָגֵל
לִבִּי בִּישׁוּעָתֶךָ. אָשִׁירָה
לַיְיָ כִּי גָמַל עָלָי:

## Responsive Readings

### I

**Reader**

The heavens declare the glory of God, and the firmament showeth His handiwork.

**Congregation**

Day unto day uttereth speech, and night unto night revealeth knowledge.

There is no speech, there are no words, neither is their voice heard.

Their line is gone out through all the earth, and their words to the ends of the world.

The law of the Lord is perfect, restoring the soul;

The testimony of the Lord is sure, making wise the simple.

The precepts of the Lord are right, rejoicing the heart;

The commandment of the Lord is pure, enlightening the eyes.

The fear of the Lord is clean, enduring forever;

The ordinances of the Lord are true; they are righteous altogether.

More to be desired are they than gold, yea, than much fine gold; sweeter also than honey and the honeycomb.

Moreover by them is thy servant warned; in keeping of them there is great reward.

Who can discern errors? Clear Thou me from hidden faults.

Keep back Thy servant also from presumptuous sins,
that they may not have dominion over me;

Then shall I be faultless, and I shall be clear from great
transgression.

Let the words of my mouth and the meditation of
my heart be acceptable before Thee, O Lord, my
Rock, and my Redeemer.

(Turn to page 288)

---

## II

**Reader**

O give thanks unto the Lord, for He is good; for His
mercy endureth forever.

**Congregation**

Who can express the mighty acts of the Lord, or make
all His praise to be heard?

Happy are they that keep justice, that do righteousness
at all times.

Remember me, O Lord, when Thou favorest Thy
people; think of me at Thy salvation;

That I may behold the prosperity of Thy chosen, that
I may rejoice in the gladness of Thy nation.

All nations shall come and worship before Thee, they
shall glorify Thy name.

Surely His salvation is nigh them that fear Him, that
glory may dwell in our land.

Mercy and truth are met together; righteousness and
peace have kissed each other.

Truth springeth out of the earth, and righteousness hath looked down from heaven.

Show us Thy mercy, O Lord, and grant us Thy salvation.

(Turn to page 288)

---

## III

Reader

How lovely are Thy tabernacles, O Lord of hosts!

Congregation

My soul yearneth, yea, even pineth for the courts of the Lord;

My heart and my flesh sing for joy unto the living God.

Happy are they that dwell in Thy house, they are ever praising Thee.

Happy is the man whose strength is in Thee; in whose heart are the highways.

They go from strength to strength, every one of them appeareth before God.

I had rather stand at the threshold of the house of God, than to dwell in the tents of wickedness.

For the Lord God is a sun and a shield; the Lord giveth grace and glory;

No good thing will He withhold from them that walk uprightly.

O Lord of hosts, happy is the man that trusteth in Thee.

(Turn to page 288)

## IV.

**Reader**

I will bless the Lord at all times; His praise shall continually be in my mouth.

**Congregation**

*My soul shall glory in the Lord; the humble shall hear thereof and be glad.*

O magnify the Lord with me, and let us exalt His name together.

*I sought the Lord, and He answered me, and delivered me from all my fears.*

They looked unto Him, and were radiant; and their faces shall never be abashed.

*This poor man cried, and the Lord heard, and saved him from all his troubles.*

The angel of the Lord encampeth round about them that fear Him, and delivereth them.

*O consider and see that the Lord is good; happy is the man that taketh refuge in Him.*

O fear the Lord, ye His holy ones; for there is no want to them that fear Him.

*The eyes of the Lord are toward the righteous, and His ears are open unto their cry.*

The Lord is nigh unto them that are of a broken heart, and saveth such as are of a contrite spirit.

*The Lord redeemeth the soul of His servants; and none of them that take refuge in Him shall be desolate.*

(Turn to page 288)

# V

**Reader**

Marvelous things of the Lord, our God, have we heard, and our fathers have told us.

**Congregation**

Repeat to their children His ancient praise, that the generations may set their hope in God.

They that trust in the Lord are as mount Zion, which cannot be removed, but abideth forever.

As the mountains are round about Jerusalem, so the Lord is round about His people.

The counsel of the Lord is with them that fear Him; in the time of trouble, He hideth them in His pavilion.

In the daytime He leadeth them with a cloud, and in the night with a light of fire.

Though they fall, they shall not be utterly cast down, for the Lord upholdeth them with His arm.

They shall not be afraid of evil tidings, for their times are in His hands.

Because their heart is not haughty, nor their eyes lofty, and they are quiet as a weaned child;

Therefore He lifteth them up and girdeth them with might, though they know it not.

Commit thy way unto the Lord, wait patiently for Him, and thou shalt never be forsaken.

He will draw thee out of the dark waters and show thee the path of life.

Who is among you that feareth the Lord, yet walketh
in darkness, and hath no light?

*Let him surely trust in the Lord and stay upon his
God.*

Lift up your eyes to the heavens and look upon the
earth beneath;

*For the heavens shall vanish away like smoke, and
the earth shall wax old like a garment;*

And they that dwell therein shall die in like manner;

*But My salvation shall be forever, and My favor shall
not be abolished.*

(Turn to page 288)

---

## VI

**Reader**

Happy is the nation whose God is the Lord; the people
whom He hath chosen for His inheritance.

**Congregation**

*Open ye the gates that the righteous nation that
keepeth faithfulness may enter in.*

For when the righteous are increased the people rejoice;
but when the wicked bear rule, the people sigh.

*Woe to thee, O land, when equity cannot enter; when
judgment is turned backward.*

Blessed art thou, O land, when thy law is not slackened.

*I will make thy officers peace, and righteousness thy
magistrates.*

When each despiseth the gain of oppression, and shak-
eth his hands from holding bribes;

And respecteth not the person of the poor, nor honoreth the person of the mighty;

But in righteousness serveth the people, and establisheth true judgment in the gates;

Then shall violence be no more heard in thy land, nor wasting and destruction within thy borders.

Then shall justice roll down as waters, and righteousness as a mighty stream.

And thou shalt call thy walls Salvation, and thy gates Praise.

For righteousness exalteth a nation, and injustice is a reproach to the people;

And in righteousness hath the Lord called thee, and given thee for a light to the nations.

O God, we have heard with our ears, and our fathers have told us, what works Thou didst in their days, and in the times before them.

Our lines have fallen unto us in pleasant places, yea, we have a goodly heritage.

(Congregation rises)

### Reader

Praise ye the Lord, to whom all praise is due.

### Choir and Congregation

Praised be the Lord to whom all praise is due forever and ever.

(Congregation is seated)

### Reader

Praised be Thou, O Lord our God, ruler of the world, by whose law the shadows of evening fall and the gates of morn are opened. In wisdom hast Thou established the changes of times and seasons and ordered the ways of the stars in their heavenly courses. Creator of heaven and earth, O living God, rule Thou over us forever. Praised be Thou, O Lord, for the day and its work and for the night and its rest.

### Congregation and Reader

Infinite as is Thy power even so is Thy love. Thou didst manifest it through Israel Thy people. By laws and commandments, by statutes and ordinances hast Thou led us in the way of righteousness and brought us to the light of truth. Therefore at our lying down and our rising up, we will meditate on Thy teachings and find in Thy laws true life and length of days. O that Thy love may never depart from our hearts. Praised be Thou, O Lord, who hast revealed Thy love through Israel.

(Congregation rises)

Reader

בָּרְכוּ אֶת־יְיָ הַמְבֹרָךְ׃

Choir and Congregation

בָּרוּךְ יְיָ הַמְבֹרָךְ לְעוֹלָם וָעֶד:

(Congregation is seated)

Reader

בָּרוּךְ אַתָּה יְיָ אֱלֹהֵינוּ מֶלֶךְ הָעוֹלָם. אֲשֶׁר
בִּדְבָרוֹ מַעֲרִיב עֲרָבִים. בְּחָכְמָה פּוֹתֵחַ שְׁעָרִים.
וּבִתְבוּנָה מְשַׁנֶּה עִתִּים וּמַחֲלִיף אֶת־הַזְּמַנִּים. וּמְסַדֵּר
אֶת־הַכּוֹכָבִים בְּמִשְׁמְרוֹתֵיהֶם בָּרָקִיעַ כִּרְצוֹנוֹ.
בּוֹרֵא יוֹם וָלָיְלָה. יְיָ צְבָאוֹת שְׁמוֹ. אֵל חַי וְקַיָּם
תָּמִיד יִמְלֹךְ עָלֵינוּ לְעוֹלָם וָעֶד. בָּרוּךְ אַתָּה יְיָ
הַמַּעֲרִיב עֲרָבִים:

אַהֲבַת עוֹלָם בֵּית יִשְׂרָאֵל עַמְּךָ אָהַבְתָּ. תּוֹרָה
וּמִצְוֹת חֻקִּים וּמִשְׁפָּטִים אוֹתָנוּ לִמַּדְתָּ. עַל־כֵּן יְיָ
אֱלֹהֵינוּ בְּשָׁכְבֵּנוּ וּבְקוּמֵנוּ נָשִׂיחַ בְּחֻקֶּיךָ. וְנִשְׂמַח
בְּדִבְרֵי תוֹרָתֶךָ וּבְמִצְוֹתֶיךָ לְעוֹלָם וָעֶד. כִּי הֵם
חַיֵּינוּ וְאֹרֶךְ יָמֵינוּ. וּבָהֶם נֶהְגֶּה יוֹמָם וָלָיְלָה.
וְאַהֲבָתְךָ אַל־תָּסִיר מִמֶּנּוּ לְעוֹלָמִים. בָּרוּךְ אַתָּה
יְיָ אוֹהֵב עַמּוֹ יִשְׂרָאֵל:

(Congregation rises)

### Reader

Hear, O Israel: The Lord our God, the Lord is One. Praised be His name whose glorious kingdom is forever and ever.

(Congregation is seated)

### Congregation and Reader

Thou shalt love the Lord, thy God, with all thy heart, with all thy soul, and with all thy might. And these words, which I command thee this day, shall be upon thy heart. Thou shalt teach them diligently unto thy children, and shalt speak of them when thou sittest in thy house, when thou walkest by the way, when thou liest down, and when thou risest up. Thou shalt bind them for a sign upon thy hand, and they shall be for frontlets between thine eyes. Thou shalt write them upon the doorposts of thy house and upon thy gates: That ye may remember and do all My commandments and be holy unto your God.

### Responsive Reading

Reader
Eternal truth it is that Thou alone art God, and there is none else.

Congregation
And through Thy power alone has Israel been redeemed from the hand of oppressors.

Great deeds hast Thou wrought in our behalf and wonders without number.

Thou hast kept us in life; our footsteps have not faltered.

(Congregation rises)

Reader, then Choir and Congregation

שְׁמַע יִשְׂרָאֵל יְהֹוָה אֱלֹהֵינוּ יְהֹוָה אֶחָד:

בָּרוּךְ שֵׁם כְּבוֹד מַלְכוּתוֹ לְעוֹלָם וָעֶד:

(Congregation is seated)

Reader

וְאָהַבְתָּ אֵת יְיָ אֱלֹהֶיךָ בְּכָל־לְבָבְךָ וּבְכָל־נַפְשְׁךָ

וּבְכָל־מְאֹדֶךָ: וְהָיוּ הַדְּבָרִים הָאֵלֶּה אֲשֶׁר אָנֹכִי

מְצַוְּךָ הַיּוֹם עַל־לְבָבֶךָ: וְשִׁנַּנְתָּם לְבָנֶיךָ וְדִבַּרְתָּ בָּם.

בְּשִׁבְתְּךָ בְּבֵיתֶךָ וּבְלֶכְתְּךָ בַדֶּרֶךְ וּבְשָׁכְבְּךָ וּבְקוּמֶךָ:

וּקְשַׁרְתָּם לְאוֹת עַל־יָדֶךָ. וְהָיוּ לְטֹטָפֹת בֵּין עֵינֶיךָ:

וּכְתַבְתָּם עַל־מְזֻזוֹת בֵּיתֶךָ וּבִשְׁעָרֶיךָ:

לְמַעַן תִּזְכְּרוּ וַעֲשִׂיתֶם אֶת־כָּל־מִצְוֹתָי וִהְיִיתֶם

קְדוֹשִׁים לֵאלֹהֵיכֶם: אֲנִי יְיָ אֱלֹהֵיכֶם:

Responsive Reading

אֱמֶת וֶאֱמוּנָה כָּל־זֹאת וְקַיָּם עָלֵינוּ. כִּי הוּא יְיָ

אֱלֹהֵינוּ וְאֵין זוּלָתוֹ. וַאֲנַחְנוּ יִשְׂרָאֵל עַמּוֹ:

הַפּוֹדֵנוּ מִיַּד מְלָכִים. מַלְכֵּנוּ הַגּוֹאֲלֵנוּ מִכַּף כָּל־

הֶעָרִיצִים:

הָעֹשֶׂה גְדֹלוֹת עַד־אֵין חֵקֶר. וְנִפְלָאוֹת עַד־אֵין

מִסְפָּר:

Thy love has watched over us in the night of oppression;
*Thy mercy has sustained us in the hour of trial.*

And now that we live in a land of freedom may we continue to be faithful to Thee and Thy word.
*May Thy law rule the life of all Thy children and Thy truth unite their hearts in fellowship.*

O God, our refuge and our hope, we glorify Thy name now as did our fathers in ancient days:

### Choir

Who is like unto Thee, O Lord? Who is like unto Thee, glorious in holiness, revered in worship, wondrous in works?

### Reader

Thy children acknowledged Thy sovereign power, and exclaimed:

### Choir

The Lord shall reign forever and ever.

### Reader

As Thou hast redeemed Israel and saved him from arms stronger than his own, so mayest Thou redeem all who are oppressed and persecuted. Praised be Thou, O Lord, Redeemer of Israel.

הַשָּׂם נַפְשֵׁנוּ בַּחַיִּים. וְלֹא נָתַן לַמּוֹט רַגְלֵנוּ:

הָעֹשֶׂה לָּנוּ נִסִּים בְּמִצְרָיִם. אוֹתוֹת וּמוֹפְתִים בְּאַדְמַת בְּנֵי חָם:

הַמַּכֶּה בְּעֶבְרָתוֹ כָּל־בְּכוֹרֵי מִצְרָיִם וַיּוֹצֵא אֶת־עַמּוֹ יִשְׂרָאֵל מִתּוֹכָם לְחֵירוּת עוֹלָם.

וְרָאוּ בָנָיו גְבוּרָתוֹ. שִׁבְּחוּ וְהוֹדוּ לִשְׁמוֹ:

וּמַלְכוּתוֹ בְּרָצוֹן קִבְּלוּ עֲלֵיהֶם מֹשֶׁה וּבְנֵי יִשְׂרָאֵל:

לְךָ עָנוּ שִׁירָה בְּשִׂמְחָה רַבָּה וְאָמְרוּ כֻלָּם:

Choir

מִי־כָמֹכָה בָּאֵלִים יְיָ. מִי כָּמֹכָה נֶאְדָּר בַּקֹּדֶשׁ נוֹרָא תְהִלֹּת עֹשֵׂה־פֶלֶא:

Reader

מַלְכוּתְךָ רָאוּ בָנֶיךָ. זֶה אֵלִי עָנוּ וְאָמְרוּ:

Choir

יְיָ יִמְלֹךְ לְעֹלָם וָעֶד:

Reader

וְנֶאֱמַר כִּי־פָדָה יְהוָה אֶת־יַעֲקֹב וּגְאָלוֹ מִיַּד חָזָק מִמֶּנּוּ. בָּרוּךְ אַתָּה יְיָ גָּאַל יִשְׂרָאֵל:

*Reader*

Praised be Thou, O Lord, God of our fathers, God of Abraham, Isaac and Jacob, great, mighty, and exalted. Thou bestowest lovingkindness upon all Thy children. Thou rememberest the devotion of the fathers, and, in love, bringest redemption to their descendants for the sake of Thy name. Thou art our King and Helper, Savior and Protector. Praised be Thou, O Lord, Shield of Abraham.

Eternal is Thy power, O Lord, Thou art mighty to save. In lovingkindness Thou sustainest the living; in the multitude of Thy mercies, Thou preservest all. Thou upholdest the falling, healest the sick; bringest freedom to the captives and keepest faith with Thy children in death as in life. Who is like unto Thee, Almighty God, Author of life and death, Source of salvation? Praised be Thou, O Lord, who hast implanted within us immortal life.

*Reader*

בָּרוּךְ אַתָּה יְיָ אֱלֹהֵינוּ וַאלֹהֵי אֲבוֹתֵינוּ. אֱלֹהֵי
אַבְרָהָם אֱלֹהֵי יִצְחָק וַאלֹהֵי יַעֲקֹב. הָאֵל הַגָּדוֹל
הַגִּבּוֹר וְהַנּוֹרָא. אֵל עֶלְיוֹן. גּוֹמֵל חֲסָדִים טוֹבִים.
וְקֹנֵה הַכֹּל וְזוֹכֵר חַסְדֵי אָבוֹת. וּמֵבִיא גְאֻלָּה לִבְנֵי
בְנֵיהֶם. לְמַעַן שְׁמוֹ בְּאַהֲבָה: מֶלֶךְ עוֹזֵר וּמוֹשִׁיעַ
וּמָגֵן. בָּרוּךְ אַתָּה יְיָ מָגֵן אַבְרָהָם:

אַתָּה גִבּוֹר לְעוֹלָם אֲדֹנָי. רַב לְהוֹשִׁיעַ. מְכַלְכֵּל
חַיִּים בְּחֶסֶד. מְחַיֵּה הַכֹּל בְּרַחֲמִים רַבִּים. סוֹמֵךְ
נוֹפְלִים וְרוֹפֵא חוֹלִים וּמַתִּיר אֲסוּרִים. וּמְקַיֵּם
אֱמוּנָתוֹ לִישֵׁנֵי עָפָר. מִי כָמוֹךְ בַּעַל גְּבוּרוֹת. וּמִי
דּוֹמֶה־לָּךְ. מֶלֶךְ מֵמִית וּמְחַיֶּה. וּמַצְמִיחַ יְשׁוּעָה:
בָּרוּךְ אַתָּה יְיָ נֹטֵעַ בְּתוֹכֵנוּ חַיֵּי עוֹלָם:

*Reader*

Heavenly Father, who graciously bestowest knowledge on man and endowest him with reason, send us the light of Thy truth, that we may gain an ever clearer insight into the wisdom of Thy ways. Banish from our hearts every desire and thought of evil, that we may truly revere Thy holy name. Forgive our sins, pardon our failings, and remove from us suffering and sorrow. May the erring and the wayward be led to know Thy loving-kindness, and to serve Thee in newness of heart; and may those who love virtue and do the right, ever be glad of Thy favor. Bless our land with plenty and our nation with peace; may righteousness dwell in our midst and virtue reign among us.

O Thou, who knowest our needs before we utter them, and ordainest all things for the best, in Thee do we forever put our trust.

*Congregation:* Amen.

Reader

אַתָּה חוֹנֵן לְאָדָם דַּעַת וּמְלַמֵּד לֶאֱנוֹשׁ בִּינָה.
חָנֵּנוּ מֵאִתְּךָ דֵּעָה בִּינָה וְהַשְׂכֵּל: הֲשִׁיבֵנוּ אָבִינוּ
לְתוֹרָתֶךָ. וְקָרְבֵנוּ מַלְכֵּנוּ לַעֲבוֹדָתֶךָ: וְהַחֲזִירֵנוּ
בִּתְשׁוּבָה שְׁלֵמָה לְפָנֶיךָ: סְלַח־לָנוּ אָבִינוּ כִּי־חָטָאנוּ.
מְחַל־לָנוּ מַלְכֵּנוּ כִּי־פָשָׁעְנוּ. כִּי־מוֹחֵל וְסוֹלֵחַ אָתָּה:
רְפָאֵנוּ יְיָ וְנֵרָפֵא הוֹשִׁיעֵנוּ וְנִוָּשֵׁעָה כִּי־תְהִלָּתֵנוּ אָתָּה.
וְהַעֲלֵה רְפוּאָה שְׁלֵמָה לְכָל־מַכּוֹתֵינוּ כִּי־אֵל מֶלֶךְ
רוֹפֵא נֶאֱמָן וְרַחֲמָן אָתָּה: שְׁמַע קוֹלֵנוּ יְיָ אֱלֹהֵינוּ.
חוּס וְרַחֵם עָלֵינוּ. וְקַבֵּל בְּרַחֲמִים וּבְרָצוֹן אֶת־
תְּפִלָּתֵנוּ. כִּי־אֵל שׁוֹמֵעַ תְּפִלּוֹת וְתַחֲנוּנִים אָתָּה.
וּמִלְּפָנֶיךָ מַלְכֵּנוּ רֵיקָם אַל־תְּשִׁיבֵנוּ. כִּי אַתָּה שׁוֹמֵעַ
תְּפִלַּת עַמְּךָ יִשְׂרָאֵל בְּרַחֲמִים. בָּרוּךְ אַתָּה יְיָ שׁוֹמֵעַ
תְּפִלָּה:

Congregation: Amen.

### PRAYER FOR PURIM

*Reader*

Thou, O Lord, pleadest the cause of the just, and defeatest the devices of the cruel. The counsel of the heathen, Thou bringest to nought; the devices of the crafty, Thou makest of no effect.

We bless Thee, O Lord our God, that Thou hast sustained us in life and preserved the house of Israel unto this day. Thou didst work miracles for our fathers in the days of old, and hast enabled us to survive the enemies of Thy truth. When Haman rose up against us, Thou didst cause the devotion of Mordecai and the lovingkindness of Esther to triumph over unjust wrath and hate. The righteous were delivered out of the hand of the wicked, and those who sought to destroy were themselves destroyed. Thou hast ever been Israel's salvation, our hope in every generation. None that trusts in Thee shall be put to shame.

We pray Thee, O Father, that in the presence of cruelty and wrong our hearts remain steadfast and true. When evil men plot against us and seek to uproot us, let not despair drain our strength nor fear chill our faith. Teach us to meet enmity with courage and hope, and to battle against adversity with resolute will and unyielding self-possession. Keep alive within us the vision of our higher purposes and nobler destiny, and renew our zeal for the divine tasks of life. Open our hearts to the cry of the persecuted and the despoiled. Hasten the day when hate and strife shall cease to divide the family of men, and justice and love reign supreme in the world.

## Silent Prayer

Grant, O heavenly Father, that we lie down to rest with a quiet mind, and rise again in health and strength, to take up the duties of the new day. Receive into Thy keeping our lives and the lives of our loved ones. May Thy protection be a shield around our homes during our sleeping hours. Preserve us from all evil, from the sword of the foe, from pestilence, famine and destruction. May we be freed from care and worry. May we readily forgive those who wrong us, and seek forgiveness of those whom we have wronged. So shall Thy blessing attend us, and Thy peace, O God, abide within us. Amen.

## Choir

May the words of my mouth and the meditation of my heart be acceptable before Thee, O Lord, my Rock and my Redeemer.

(Adoration and Kaddish, Page 274)
(Reading of Selections from Book of Esther)
For Hanukkah, turn to page 85

# Evening Service At the House of Mourning

*Reader*

We are assembled with our friends in the shadow that has fallen on their home. We raise our voices together in prayer to the Father above, asking for comfort and strength. We need light when gloom darkens our home; whence can it come but from the Creator of light? We need fortitude and resignation under the chastening of the Lord; whence can these come save from Him who lays the burden upon us? Who among us has not passed through trials and bereavements! Some bear fresh wounds in their hearts and therefore feel the more keenly the kinship of sorrow. Others whose days of mourning are more remote, still recall the comfort that sympathy brought to their sorrowing hearts. And those of us who have not yet tasted of the bitter cup cannot know how soon we may be called on to drink of it. All that we prize is but lent to us and we must surrender it when God demands. We are travelers on the same road which leads to the same end.

*Responsive Reading*

Reader

I lift mine eyes unto the mountains: Whence cometh
my help?

Congregation

*My help cometh from the Lord who made heaven and
earth.*

He will not suffer thy foot to be moved; He that keepeth
thee doth not slumber.

*Behold, He that keepeth Israel doth neither slumber nor sleep.*

The Lord is thy keeper; the Lord is thy shade upon thy right hand.

*The sun shall not smite thee by day nor the moon by night,*

The Lord shall keep thee from all evil; He shall keep thy soul.

*The Lord shall guard thy going out and thy coming in from this time forth and forever.*

(Congregation rises)

### Reader

בָּרְכוּ אֶת־יְיָ הַמְבֹרָךְ:

Praise ye the Lord, to whom all praise is due.

בָּרוּךְ יְיָ הַמְבֹרָךְ לְעוֹלָם וָעֶד:

Praised be the Lord to whom all praise is due forever and ever.

(Congregation is seated)

### Reader

Praised be Thou, O Eternal our God, Ruler of the world. Thy word calleth forth the evening twilight. Thy wisdom openeth the gates of heaven so that morning shall alternate with eventide. In human life, too, Thou hast ordained that the daylight of joy shall follow the night of sorrow. Thy wisdom hath established the succession of life and death, of grief and hope. All things change but Thou alone changest not. Thou abidest to all eternity.

(Congregation rises)

## Congregation and Reader

Hear, O Israel: The Lord our God, the Lord is One.
Praised be His name whose glorious kingdom is forever and ever.

(Congregation is seated)

## Congregation and Reader

Thou shalt love the Lord, thy God, with all thy heart,
with all thy soul, and with all thy might. And these
words, which I command thee this day, shall be upon
thy heart. Thou shalt teach them diligently unto thy
children, and shalt speak of them when thou sittest in
thy house, when thou walkest by the way, when thou
liest down, and when thou risest up. Thou shalt bind
them for a sign upon thy hand, and they shall be for
frontlets between thine eyes. Thou shalt write them
upon the doorposts of thy house and upon thy gates:
That ye may remember and do all My commandments
and be holy unto your God.

(Congregation rises)

Congregation and Reader

שְׁמַע יִשְׂרָאֵל יְהֹוָה אֱלֹהֵינוּ יְהֹוָה אֶחָד:

בָּרוּךְ שֵׁם כְּבוֹד מַלְכוּתוֹ לְעוֹלָם וָעֶד:

(Congregation is seated)

Reader

וְאָהַבְתָּ אֵת יְיָ אֱלֹהֶיךָ בְּכָל־לְבָבְךָ וּבְכָל־נַפְשְׁךָ
וּבְכָל־מְאֹדֶךָ: וְהָיוּ הַדְּבָרִים הָאֵלֶּה אֲשֶׁר אָנֹכִי
מְצַוְּךָ הַיּוֹם עַל־לְבָבֶךָ: וְשִׁנַּנְתָּם לְבָנֶיךָ וְדִבַּרְתָּ
בָּם. בְּשִׁבְתְּךָ בְּבֵיתֶךָ וּבְלֶכְתְּךָ בַדֶּרֶךְ וּבְשָׁכְבְּךָ
וּבְקוּמֶךָ: וּקְשַׁרְתָּם לְאוֹת עַל־יָדֶךָ. וְהָיוּ לְטֹטָפֹת
בֵּין עֵינֶיךָ: וּכְתַבְתָּם עַל־מְזֻזוֹת בֵּיתֶךָ וּבִשְׁעָרֶיךָ:
לְמַעַן תִּזְכְּרוּ וַעֲשִׂיתֶם אֶת־כָּל־מִצְוֹתָי וִהְיִיתֶם
קְדֹשִׁים לֵאלֹהֵיכֶם: אֲנִי יְיָ אֱלֹהֵיכֶם:

## Responsive Reading

Reader

In my distress I cried unto the Lord and He heard me.

Congregation

*He healeth the broken in heart and bindeth up their wounds.*

As one whom his mother comforteth, so will I comfort you, saith the Lord.

*I am the Lord thy God who sheltereth thee with the shadow of My hand.*

The Eternal God is thy dwelling place and underneath are the everlasting arms.

*The Lord is a stronghold in the day of trouble.*

## Reader

Eternal is Thy power, O Lord, Thou art mighty to save. In lovingkindness Thou sustainest the living; in the multitude of Thy mercies, Thou preservest all. Thou upholdest the falling and healest the sick, freest the captives, and keepest faith with Thy children in death as in life. Who is like unto Thee, Almighty God, Author of life and death, Source of salvation? Praised be Thou, O Lord, who hast implanted within us eternal life.

## Silent Prayer

### (Psalm xxiii)

The Lord is my shepherd, I shall not want. He maketh me to lie down in green pastures; He leadeth me beside the still waters. He restoreth my soul; He guideth me in straight paths for His name's sake. Yea, though I walk through the valley of the shadow of death I will fear no evil, for Thou art with me; Thy rod and Thy staff, they comfort me. Thou preparest a table before me in the presence of mine enemies; Thou hast anointed my head with oil; my cup runneth over. Surely goodness and mercy shall follow me all the days of my life, and I shall dwell in the house of the Lord forever.

### ADORATION

---

(Congregation rises)

## Congregation and Reader

Let us adore the ever-living God, and render praise unto Him who spread out the heavens and established the earth, whose glory is revealed in the heavens above and whose greatness is manifest throughout the world. He is our God; there is none else.

We bow the head in reverence, and worship the King of kings, the Holy One, praised be He.

וַאֲנַחְנוּ כֹּרְעִים וּמִשְׁתַּחֲוִים וּמוֹדִים לִפְנֵי מֶלֶךְ
מַלְכֵי הַמְּלָכִים הַקָּדוֹשׁ בָּרוּךְ הוּא:

(Congregation is seated)

## Reader

May the time not be distant, O God, when Thy name shall be worshiped in all the earth, when unbelief shall disappear and error be no more. We fervently pray that the day may come when all men shall invoke Thy name, when corruption and evil shall give way to purity and goodness, when superstition shall no longer enslave the mind, nor idolatry blind the eye, when all who dwell on earth shall know that to Thee alone every knee must bend and every tongue give homage. O may all, created in Thine image, recognize that they are brethren, so that, one in spirit and one in fellowship, they may be forever united before Thee. Then shall Thy kingdom be established on earth and the word of Thine ancient seer be fulfilled: The Lord will reign forever and ever.

### Congregation

On that day the Lord shall be One and His name shall be One.

### Reader

At Thy command, O God, we have laid to rest a dearly beloved one. We murmur not at Thine inscrutable decree; we pray for strength to bear what Thou hast laid on us. Let Thy light shine on us in the night of our sorrow that we may find the path of life and follow it towards the goal which Thou hast appointed to each of Thy children. We thank Thee for the life which in Thy goodness Thou hadst given and in Thy wisdom hast taken away. Make us to know Thy ways that in our love we may triumph over grief and despair. Calm Thou our troubled spirits that athwart our tears may arch the rainbow of Thine eternal promise. Praised be Thou, O Lord, who comfortest the mourners. Amen.

(Mourners rise)

### Reader

Extolled and hallowed be the name of God throughout the world which He has created according to His will. And may He speedily establish His kingdom of righteousness on earth. Amen.

### Congregation

Praised be His glorious name unto all eternity.

### Reader

Praised and glorified be the name of the Holy One, though He be above all the praises which we can utter. Our guide is He in life and our redeemer through all eternity.

### Congregation

Our help cometh from Him, the creator of heaven and earth.

### Reader

The departed whom we now remember have entered into the peace of life eternal. They still live on earth in the acts of goodness they performed and in the hearts of those who cherish their memory. May the beauty of their life abide among us as a loving benediction.

### Congregation: Amen.

### Reader

May the Father of peace send peace to all who mourn, and comfort all the bereaved among us.

### Congregation: Amen.

(Mourners are seated)

(Mourners rise)

Reader

יִתְגַּדַּל וְיִתְקַדַּשׁ שְׁמֵהּ רַבָּא. בְּעָלְמָא דִי־בְרָא
כִרְעוּתֵהּ. וְיַמְלִיךְ מַלְכוּתֵהּ. בְּחַיֵּיכוֹן וּבְיוֹמֵיכוֹן
וּבְחַיֵּי דְכָל־בֵּית יִשְׂרָאֵל. בַּעֲגָלָא וּבִזְמַן קָרִיב.
וְאִמְרוּ אָמֵן:

Congregation

יְהֵא שְׁמֵהּ רַבָּא מְבָרַךְ לְעָלַם וּלְעָלְמֵי עָלְמַיָּא:

Reader

יִתְבָּרַךְ וְיִשְׁתַּבַּח וְיִתְפָּאַר וְיִתְרוֹמַם וְיִתְנַשֵּׂא
וְיִתְהַדַּר וְיִתְעַלֶּה וְיִתְהַלָּל שְׁמֵהּ דְּקוּדְשָׁא. בְּרִיךְ
הוּא. לְעֵלָּא מִן כָּל־בִּרְכָתָא וְשִׁירָתָא. תֻּשְׁבְּחָתָא
וְנֶחָמָתָא. דַּאֲמִירָן בְּעָלְמָא. וְאִמְרוּ אָמֵן:

עַל יִשְׂרָאֵל וְעַל צַדִּיקַיָּא. וְעַל־כָּל־מַן דְּאִתְפְּטַר
מִן עָלְמָא הָדֵין כִּרְעוּתֵהּ דֶּאֱלָהָא. יְהֵא לְהוֹן
שְׁלָמָא רַבָּא וְחִנָּא וְחִסְדָּא מִן־קֳדָם מָרֵא שְׁמַיָּא
וְאַרְעָא. וְאִמְרוּ אָמֵן:

יְהֵא שְׁלָמָא רַבָּא מִן־שְׁמַיָּא וְחַיִּים. עָלֵינוּ וְעַל־
כָּל־יִשְׂרָאֵל. וְאִמְרוּ אָמֵן:

עֹשֶׂה שָׁלוֹם בִּמְרוֹמָיו. הוּא יַעֲשֶׂה שָׁלוֹם עָלֵינוּ
וְעַל־כָּל־יִשְׂרָאֵל. וְאִמְרוּ אָמֵן:

(Mourners are seated)

## THE MOURNER'S KADDISH

### Reader

Yis-gad-dal v'yis-kad-dash sh'meh rab-bo, b'ol-mo
di'v-ro kir'-u-seh v'yam-lich mal-chu-seh, b'cha-ye-chon
u-v'yo-me-chon u-v'cha-yeh d'chol bes yis-ro-el, ba-a-go-lo
u-viz-man ko-riv, v'im-ru O-men.

### Congregation

Y'heh sh'meh rab-bo m'vo-rach, l'o-lam ul'ol'meh ol-
ma-yo:

### Reader

Yis-bo-rach v'yish-tab-bach, v'yis-po-ar, v'yis-ro-mam,
v'yis-nas-seh, v'yis-had-dor, v'yis-al-leh, v'yis-hal-lol, sh'-
meh d'kud'-sho, b'rich hu. L'e-lo min kol bir-cho-so
v'shi-ro-so, tush-b'cho-so v'ne-cho-mo-so, da-a-mi-ron
b'ol-mo, v'im-ru O-men:

Al yis-ro-el v'al tsa-de-ka-yo, v'al kol man d'isp'tar min
ol-mo ho-dain kir-ooseh de-e-lo-ho y'hai l'hon shlo-mo
rab-bo v'chino v'chis-do min ko-dom mo-rai sh'ma-yo
v'ar-o, v'im-ru O-men:

Y'heh sh'lo-mo rab-bo min sh'ma-yo v'cha-yim, o-le-nu
v'al kol yis-ro-el, v'imru O-men:

O-seh sho-lom bim'-ro-mov, hu ya-a-seh sho-lom,
o-le-nu v'al kol yis-ro-el, v'imru O-men.

# Morning Services for Week-Days

How goodly are thy tents, O Jacob, thy dwellings, O Israel! Through Thy great mercy, O God, I come to Thy house and bow down in Thy holy temple in the fear of Thee. O Lord, I love the place of Thy house and the abode in which Thy glory dwelleth. And so I bow down, and adore Thee, O God, my Maker. May my prayer be offered in an acceptable time; mayest Thou, in the greatness of Thy mercy, answer me according to Thy faithfulness.

מַה־טֹּבוּ אֹהָלֶיךָ יַעֲקֹב מִשְׁכְּנֹתֶיךָ יִשְׂרָאֵל: וַאֲנִי בְּרֹב חַסְדְּךָ אָבֹא בֵיתֶךָ אֶשְׁתַּחֲוֶה אֶל־הֵיכַל קָדְשְׁךָ בְּיִרְאָתֶךָ: יְיָ אָהַבְתִּי מְעוֹן בֵּיתֶךָ וּמְקוֹם מִשְׁכַּן כְּבוֹדֶךָ: וַאֲנִי אֶשְׁתַּחֲוֶה וְאֶכְרָעָה אֶבְרְכָה לִפְנֵי־יְיָ עֹשִׂי: וַאֲנִי תְפִלָּתִי לְךָ יְיָ עֵת רָצוֹן אֱלֹהִים בְּרָב חַסְדֶּךָ עֲנֵנִי בֶּאֱמֶת יִשְׁעֶךָ:

311

### Reader

Happy are they who dwell in Thy house, they are continually praising Thee. Incline Thine ear and answer us, be gracious unto us, O God, and cause us to rejoice, for unto Thee we lift up our souls. Teach us Thy way that we may walk firmly in Thy truth. Show us Thy kindness, grant us Thy salvation. Be with us this day and at all times, O Thou, our God and our Father, our Rock and our Redeemer.

The soul which Thou, O God, hast given unto me came pure from Thee. Thou hast created it, Thou hast formed it, Thou hast breathed it into me; Thou hast preserved it in this body; and, at the appointed time, Thou wilt take it from this earth that it may enter upon life everlasting. While the breath of life is within me I will worship Thee, Sovereign of the world and Lord of all souls. Praised be Thou, O God, in whose hands are the souls of all the living and the spirits of all flesh.

### Choir

### Amen

### Responsive Reading

**Reader**

I will extol Thee, my God, O King, and I will bless Thy name forever and ever.

**Congregation**

*Every day I will bless Thee, and I will praise Thy name forever and ever.*

Great is the Lord and highly to be praised; and His greatness is beyond our finding out.

One generation shall praise Thy works to another, and shall declare Thy mighty acts.

I will speak of the splendor of Thy majesty and of Thy wondrous works.

And men shall tell of Thy mighty acts, and I will declare Thy greatness.

They shall herald Thy great goodness, and shall sing of Thy righteousness.

The Lord is gracious and full of compassion, slow to anger and of great mercy.

The Lord is good to all, and His tender mercies are over all His works.

Thy kingdom is a kingdom for all ages, and Thy dominion endureth throughout all generations.

The Lord upholdeth those who fall, and raiseth up those who are bowed down.

The eyes of all wait upon Thee, and Thou givest them their food in due season.

Thou openest Thy hand and satisfiest the desire of every living being.

The Lord is righteous in all His ways, and gracious in all His works.

The Lord is near unto all who call upon Him, to all who call upon Him in truth.

My mouth shall utter the praise of the Lord; and let all flesh bless His holy name forever and ever.

(Congregation rises)

### Reader

Praise ye the Lord to whom all praise is due.

### Choir and Congregation

Praised be the Lord to whom all praise is due forever and ever.

(Congregation is seated)

### Reader

Praised be Thou, O Lord our God, Ruler of the world, who in Thy mercy makest light to shine over the earth and all its inhabitants, and renewest daily the work of creation. How manifold are Thy works, O Lord! In wisdom hast Thou made them all. The heavens declare Thy glory. The earth reveals Thy creative power. Thou formest light and darkness, ordainest good out of evil, bringest harmony into nature and peace to the heart of man.

Great has been Thy love for us and Thy compassion boundless. Our fathers put their trust in Thee and Thou didst teach them the law of life. Be gracious also unto us that we may understand and fulfill the teachings of Thy word. Enlighten our eyes in Thy law that we may cling unto Thy commandments. Unite our hearts

(Congregation rises)

### Reader

בָּרְכוּ אֶת יְיָ הַמְבֹרָךְ:

### Choir and Congregation

בָּרוּךְ יְיָ הַמְבֹרָךְ לְעוֹלָם וָעֶד:

(Congregation is seated)

### Reader

בָּרוּךְ אַתָּה יְיָ אֱלֹהֵינוּ מֶלֶךְ הָעוֹלָם. יוֹצֵר אוֹר
וּבוֹרֵא חֹשֶׁךְ. עֹשֶׂה שָׁלוֹם וּבוֹרֵא אֶת־הַכֹּל:
הַמֵּאִיר לָאָרֶץ וְלַדָּרִים עָלֶיהָ בְּרַחֲמִים. וּבְטוּבוֹ
מְחַדֵּשׁ בְּכָל־יוֹם תָּמִיד מַעֲשֵׂה בְרֵאשִׁית: מָה רַבּוּ
מַעֲשֶׂיךָ יְיָ. כֻּלָּם בְּחָכְמָה עָשִׂיתָ. מָלְאָה הָאָרֶץ
קִנְיָנֶךָ: תִּתְבָּרַךְ יְיָ אֱלֹהֵינוּ עַל־שֶׁבַח מַעֲשֵׂה יָדֶיךָ.
וְעַל־מְאוֹרֵי־אוֹר שֶׁעָשִׂיתָ יְפָאֲרוּךָ סֶּלָה: בָּרוּךְ אַתָּה
יְיָ יוֹצֵר הַמְּאוֹרוֹת:

אַהֲבָה רַבָּה אֲהַבְתָּנוּ יְיָ אֱלֹהֵינוּ. חֶמְלָה
גְדוֹלָה וִיתֵרָה חָמַלְתָּ עָלֵינוּ: אָבִינוּ מַלְכֵּנוּ. בַּעֲבוּר
אֲבוֹתֵינוּ שֶׁבָּטְחוּ בְךָ וַתְּלַמְּדֵם חֻקֵּי חַיִּים. כֵּן תְּחָנֵּנוּ
וּתְלַמְּדֵנוּ: הָאֵר עֵינֵינוּ בְּתוֹרָתֶךָ. וְדַבֵּק לִבֵּנוּ

to love and revere Thee. We trust in Thee and rejoice in Thy saving power, for from Thee cometh our help. Thou hast called us and drawn us nigh unto Thee to serve Thee in faithfulness. Joyfully do we lift up our voices and proclaim Thy unity. Praised be Thou, O God, who in Thy love hast called Thy people Israel to serve Thee.

(Congregation rises)

### Reader

Hear, O Israel: The Lord our God, the Lord is One. Praised be His name whose glorious kingdom is forever and ever.

(Congregation is seated)

### Congregation and Reader

Thou shalt love the Lord, thy God, with all thy heart, with all thy soul, and with all thy might. And these words, which I command thee this day, shall be upon thy heart. Thou shalt teach them diligently unto thy children, and shalt speak of them when thou sittest in thy house, when thou walkest by the way, when thou liest down, and when thou risest up. Thou shalt bind them for a sign upon thy hand, and they shall be for frontlets between thine eyes. Thou shalt write them upon the doorposts of thy house and upon thy gates: That ye may remember and do all My commandments and be holy unto your God.

בְּמִצְוֹתֶיךָ. וְיַחֵד לְבָבֵנוּ לְאַהֲבָה וּלְיִרְאָה שְׁמֶךָ.
כִּי בְשֵׁם קָדְשְׁךָ בָּטָחְנוּ. נָגִילָה וְנִשְׂמְחָה בִּישׁוּעָתֶךָ.
כִּי אֵל פּוֹעֵל יְשׁוּעוֹת אָתָּה. וּבָנוּ בָחַרְתָּ וְקֵרַבְתָּנוּ
לְשִׁמְךָ הַגָּדוֹל סֶלָה בֶּאֱמֶת. לְהוֹדוֹת לְךָ וּלְיַחֶדְךָ
בְּאַהֲבָה. בָּרוּךְ אַתָּה יְיָ הַבּוֹחֵר בְּעַמּוֹ יִשְׂרָאֵל
בְּאַהֲבָה:

(Congregation rises)

Reader, then Choir and Congregation

שְׁמַע יִשְׂרָאֵל יְהֹוָה אֱלֹהֵינוּ יְהֹוָה אֶחָד:
בָּרוּךְ שֵׁם כְּבוֹד מַלְכוּתוֹ לְעוֹלָם וָעֶד:

(Congregation is seated)

Reader

וְאָהַבְתָּ אֵת יְיָ אֱלֹהֶיךָ בְּכָל־לְבָבְךָ וּבְכָל־נַפְשְׁךָ
וּבְכָל־מְאֹדֶךָ: וְהָיוּ הַדְּבָרִים הָאֵלֶּה אֲשֶׁר אָנֹכִי
מְצַוְּךָ הַיּוֹם עַל־לְבָבֶךָ: וְשִׁנַּנְתָּם לְבָנֶיךָ וְדִבַּרְתָּ
בָּם. בְּשִׁבְתְּךָ בְּבֵיתֶךָ וּבְלֶכְתְּךָ בַדֶּרֶךְ וּבְשָׁכְבְּךָ
וּבְקוּמֶךָ: וּקְשַׁרְתָּם לְאוֹת עַל־יָדֶךָ. וְהָיוּ לְטֹטָפֹת
בֵּין עֵינֶיךָ: וּכְתַבְתָּם עַל־מְזֻזוֹת בֵּיתֶךָ וּבִשְׁעָרֶיךָ:
לְמַעַן תִּזְכְּרוּ וַעֲשִׂיתֶם אֶת־כָּל־מִצְוֹתָי וִהְיִיתֶם
קְדוֹשִׁים לֵאלֹהֵיכֶם: אֲנִי יְיָ אֱלֹהֵיכֶם:

## Responsive Reading

**Reader**

True and enduring is Thy word which Thou hast spoken
through Thy prophets.

**Congregation**

Thou art the living God, Thy words bring life and
light to the soul.

Thou art the strength of our life, the rock of our salvation; Thy kingdom and Thy truth abide for-
ever.

Thou hast been the help of our fathers in time of
trouble and art our refuge in all generations.

Thou art the first and the last, and besides Thee there
is no redeemer nor helper.

As Thou hast saved Israel from Egyptian bondage,
so mayest Thou send Thy help to all who are
oppressed.

May Thy law rule in the hearts of all Thy children,
and Thy truth unite them in bonds of fellowship.

May the righteous of all nations rejoice in Thy grace
and triumph by Thy power.

O God, who art our refuge and our hope, we glorify
Thy name now as did our fathers in ancient
days:

## Choir

Who is like unto Thee, O Lord? Who is like unto
Thee, glorious in holiness, awe-inspiring, working wonders?

מִי־כָמְכָה בָּאֵלִים יְיָ. מִי כָּמְכָה נֶאְדָּר בַּקֹּדֶשׁ
נוֹרָא תְהִלֹּת עֹשֵׂה־פֶלֶא:

### Reader

A new song the redeemed sang unto Thy name.
They proclaimed Thy sovereignty and said:

### Choir

The Lord shall reign forever and ever.

יְיָ יִמְלֹךְ לְעֹלָם וָעֶד:

### Reader

O Rock of Israel, redeem those who are oppressed
and deliver those who are persecuted. Praised be Thou,
our Redeemer, the Holy One of Israel.

צוּר יִשְׂרָאֵל. קוּמָה בְּעֶזְרַת יִשְׂרָאֵל. גוֹאֲלֵנוּ יְיָ
צְבָאוֹת שְׁמוֹ. קְדוֹשׁ יִשְׂרָאֵל. בָּרוּךְ אַתָּה יְיָ גָּאַל
יִשְׂרָאֵל:

### Choir: Amen.

### Reader

בָּרוּךְ אַתָּה יְיָ אֱלֹהֵינוּ וֵאלֹהֵי אֲבוֹתֵינוּ. אֱלֹהֵי
אַבְרָהָם אֱלֹהֵי יִצְחָק וֵאלֹהֵי יַעֲקֹב. הָאֵל הַגָּדוֹל
הַגִּבּוֹר וְהַנּוֹרָא. אֵל עֶלְיוֹן. גּוֹמֵל חֲסָדִים טוֹבִים.
וְקֹנֵה הַכֹּל וְזוֹכֵר חַסְדֵי אָבוֹת. וּמֵבִיא גְאֻלָּה לִבְנֵי
בְנֵיהֶם לְמַעַן שְׁמוֹ בְּאַהֲבָה: מֶלֶךְ עוֹזֵר וּמוֹשִׁיעַ
וּמָגֵן. בָּרוּךְ אַתָּה יְיָ מָגֵן אַבְרָהָם:

אַתָּה גִבּוֹר לְעוֹלָם אֲדֹנָי. רַב לְהוֹשִׁיעַ. מְכַלְכֵּל
חַיִּים בְּחֶסֶד. מְחַיֵּה הַכֹּל בְּרַחֲמִים רַבִּים. סוֹמֵךְ
נוֹפְלִים וְרוֹפֵא חוֹלִים וּמַתִּיר אֲסוּרִים וּמְקַיֵּם
אֱמוּנָתוֹ לִישֵׁנֵי עָפָר. מִי כָמוֹךָ בַּעַל גְּבוּרוֹת. וּמִי
דוֹמֶה לָּךְ. מֶלֶךְ מֵמִית וּמְחַיֶּה. וּמַצְמִיחַ יְשׁוּעָה:
בָּרוּךְ אַתָּה יְיָ נֹטֵעַ בְּתוֹכֵנוּ חַיֵּי עוֹלָם:

### Reader

Praised be Thou, O Lord, God of our fathers, God
of Abraham, Isaac and Jacob, great, mighty, and exalted.
Thou bestowest lovingkindness upon all Thy children.
Thou rememberest the devotion of the fathers. In Thy
love Thou bringest redemption to their descendants
for the sake of Thy name. Thou art our King and
Helper, our Savior and Protector. Praised be Thou, O
Lord, Shield of Abraham.

Eternal is Thy power, O Lord, Thou art mighty to
save. In lovingkindness Thou sustainest the living; in

the multitude of Thy mercies Thou preservest all. Thou upholdest the falling and healest the sick; freest the captives and keepest faith with Thy children in death as in life. Who is like unto Thee, Almighty God, Author of life and death, Source of salvation? Praised be Thou, O Lord, who hast implanted within us eternal life.

## SANCTIFICATION

(Congregation rises)

### Reader

We sanctify Thy name on earth, as the heavens declare Thy glory; and in the words of the prophet we say:

Holy, holy, holy is the Lord of hosts; the whole earth is full of His glory.

### Choir and Congregation

קָדוֹשׁ קָדוֹשׁ קָדוֹשׁ יְיָ צְבָאוֹת. מְלֹא כָל־הָאָרֶץ כְּבוֹדוֹ:

### Reader

Praised be the glory of God in all the world.

### Choir and Congregation

בָּרוּךְ כְּבוֹד יְיָ מִמְּקוֹמוֹ:

### Reader

The Lord will reign forever, thy God, O Zion, from generation to generation. Hallelujah!

### Choir and Congregation

יִמְלֹךְ יְיָ לְעוֹלָם אֱלֹהַיִךְ צִיּוֹן לְדוֹר וָדוֹר הַלְלוּיָהּ:

(Congregation is seated)

## Responsive Reading

**Reader**

Thou who dost graciously endow man with reason and teachest him understanding, imbue us with true knowledge and discernment.

**Congregation**

*Praised be Thou, O Lord, gracious giver of knowledge.*

Cause us to return, O our Father, unto Thy law; and through perfect repentance restore us to Thy presence.

*Praised be Thou, O Lord, who desirest repentance.*

Forgive our sins, O Father, pardon our transgressions, for Thou art a merciful God.

*Praised be Thou, O Lord, with whom is abundant forgiveness.*

Look upon all the afflicted and the oppressed. Let wickedness and hatred cease, and reign Thou over us in justice and in love.

*Praised be Thou, O Lord, who lovest righteousness and justice.*

Heal us, O Lord, and we shall be healed; save us and we shall be saved; for Thou art our God. Thou art a faithful and merciful healer.

*Praised be Thou, O Lord, who healest the sick.*

Hear, O Father, the voice of our supplication, and accept in favor our prayers and the prayers of all Thy children who seek Thy help. Sustain us in trial and in danger, and direct our hearts to serve Thee in truth.

*Praised be Thou, O Lord, who hearest prayer.*

## Responsive Reading

אַתָּה חוֹנֵן לְאָדָם דַּעַת וּמְלַמֵּד לָאֱנוֹשׁ בִּינָה. חָנֵּנוּ מֵאִתְּךָ דֵּעָה בִּינָה וְהַשְׂכֵּל: בָּרוּךְ אַתָּה יְיָ חוֹנֵן הַדָּעַת:

הֲשִׁיבֵנוּ אָבִינוּ לְתוֹרָתֶךָ. וְקָרְבֵנוּ מַלְכֵּנוּ לַעֲבוֹדָתֶךָ: וְהַחֲזִירֵנוּ בִּתְשׁוּבָה שְׁלֵמָה לְפָנֶיךָ: בָּרוּךְ אַתָּה יְיָ הָרוֹצֶה בִּתְשׁוּבָה:

סְלַח־לָנוּ אָבִינוּ כִּי־חָטָאנוּ. מְחַל־לָנוּ מַלְכֵּנוּ כִּי־פָשָׁעְנוּ. כִּי־מוֹחֵל וְסוֹלֵחַ אָתָּה: בָּרוּךְ אַתָּה יְיָ חַנּוּן הַמַּרְבֶּה לִסְלוֹחַ:

רְפָאֵנוּ יְיָ וְנֵרָפֵא הוֹשִׁיעֵנוּ וְנִוָּשֵׁעָה כִּי־תְהִלָּתֵנוּ אָתָּה. וְהַעֲלֵה רְפוּאָה שְׁלֵמָה לְכָל־מַכּוֹתֵינוּ כִּי־אֵל מֶלֶךְ רוֹפֵא נֶאֱמָן וְרַחֲמָן אָתָּה: בָּרוּךְ אַתָּה יְיָ רוֹפֵא חוֹלֵי עַמּוֹ יִשְׂרָאֵל:

שְׁמַע קוֹלֵנוּ יְיָ אֱלֹהֵינוּ. חוּס וְרַחֵם עָלֵינוּ. וְקַבֵּל בְּרַחֲמִים וּבְרָצוֹן אֶת־תְּפִלָּתֵנוּ. כִּי־אֵל שׁוֹמֵעַ תְּפִלּוֹת וְתַחֲנוּנִים אָתָּה. וּמִלְּפָנֶיךָ מַלְכֵּנוּ רֵיקָם אַל־תְּשִׁיבֵנוּ. כִּי אַתָּה שׁוֹמֵעַ תְּפִלַּת עַמְּךָ יִשְׂרָאֵל בְּרַחֲמִים. בָּרוּךְ אַתָּה יְיָ שׁוֹמֵעַ תְּפִלָּה:

*Reader*

Look with favor, O Lord, upon us, and may our service be acceptable unto Thee. Praised be Thou, O God, whom alone we serve in reverence.

*Congregation and Reader*

We gratefully acknowledge, O Lord, our God, that Thou art our Creator and Preserver, the Rock of our life and the Shield of our help. We render thanks unto Thee for our lives which are in Thy hand, for our souls which are ever in Thy keeping; for Thy wondrous providence and for Thy continuous goodness, which Thou bestowest upon us day by day. Truly, Thy mercies never fail and Thy lovingkindness never ceases. Therefore do we forever put our trust in Thee.

(Special Prayers for Hanukkah and Purim, p. 135)

*Reader*

Grant us peace, Thy most precious gift, O Thou eternal source of peace, and enable Israel to be its messenger unto the peoples of the earth. Bless our country that it may ever be a stronghold of peace, and its advocate in the council of nations. May contentment reign within its borders, health and happiness within its homes. Strengthen the bonds of friendship and fellowship among all the inhabitants of our land. Plant virtue in every soul, and may the love of Thy name hallow every home and every heart. Praised be Thou, O Lord, Giver of peace.

**Choir: Amen.**

Reader

רְצֵה יְיָ אֱלֹהֵינוּ בְּעַמְּךָ יִשְׂרָאֵל וּתְפִלָּתָם
בְּאַהֲבָה תְקַבֵּל וּתְהִי לְרָצוֹן תָּמִיד עֲבֹדַת יִשְׂרָאֵל
עַמֶּךָ: בָּרוּךְ אַתָּה יְיָ שֶׁאוֹתְךָ לְבַדְּךָ בְּיִרְאָה נַעֲבוֹד:

Congregation and Reader

מוֹדִים אֲנַחְנוּ לָךְ שָׁאַתָּה הוּא יְיָ אֱלֹהֵינוּ וֵאלֹהֵי
אֲבוֹתֵינוּ לְעוֹלָם וָעֶד . צוּר חַיֵּינוּ מָגֵן יִשְׁעֵנוּ אַתָּה
הוּא לְדוֹר וָדוֹר נוֹדֶה לְךָ וּנְסַפֵּר תְּהִלָּתֶךָ עַל־
חַיֵּינוּ הַמְּסוּרִים בְּיָדֶךָ וְעַל־נִשְׁמוֹתֵינוּ הַפְּקוּדוֹת
לָךְ וְעַל־נִסֶּיךָ שֶׁבְּכָל־יוֹם עִמָּנוּ וְעַל־נִפְלְאוֹתֶיךָ
וְטוֹבוֹתֶיךָ שֶׁבְּכָל־עֵת עֶרֶב וָבֹקֶר וְצָהֳרָיִם . הַטּוֹב
כִּי־לֹא כָלוּ רַחֲמֶיךָ וְהַמְרַחֵם כִּי־לֹא תַמּוּ חֲסָדֶיךָ
מֵעוֹלָם קִוִּינוּ לָךְ:

Reader

שִׂים שָׁלוֹם טוֹבָה וּבְרָכָה חֵן וָחֶסֶד וְרַחֲמִים
עָלֵינוּ וְעַל־כָּל־יִרְאֵי שְׁמֶךָ . בָּרְכֵנוּ אָבִינוּ כֻּלָּנוּ
כְּאֶחָד בְּאוֹר פָּנֶיךָ . כִּי בְאוֹר פָּנֶיךָ נָתַתָּ־לָּנוּ יְיָ
אֱלֹהֵינוּ תּוֹרַת חַיִּים וְאַהֲבַת חֶסֶד וּצְדָקָה וּבְרָכָה
וְרַחֲמִים וְחַיִּים וְשָׁלוֹם . וְטוֹב בְּעֵינֶיךָ לְבָרֵךְ אֶת־
עַמְּךָ יִשְׂרָאֵל וְאֶת־כָּל־הָעַמִּים בְּרֹב עֹז וְשָׁלוֹם:
בָּרוּךְ אַתָּה יְיָ עֹשֵׂה הַשָּׁלוֹם:

## Silent Prayer

(or such other prayer as the heart may prompt)

O God, keep my tongue from evil and my lips from speaking guile. Be my support when grief silences my voice, and my comfort when woe bends my spirit. Implant humility in my soul, and strengthen my heart with perfect faith in Thee. Help me to be strong in temptation and trial and to be patient and forgiving when others wrong me. Guide me by the light of Thy counsel, that I may ever find strength in Thee, my Rock and my Redeemer. Amen.

## Choir

May the words of my mouth and the meditation of my heart be acceptable unto Thee, O Lord, my Rock and my Redeemer.

יִהְיוּ לְרָצוֹן אִמְרֵי־פִי וְהֶגְיוֹן לִבִּי לְפָנֶיךָ ۰ יְיָ צוּרִי
וְגוֹאֲלִי:

**READING FROM SCRIPTURE**

(For ADORATION and KADDISH, see p. 365)

## II

### Choir

(Psalm cxxii)

I rejoiced when they said unto me: Let us go unto the house of the Lord. Our feet are standing within thy gates, O Jerusalem. Pray for the peace of Jerusalem; may

שָׂמַחְתִּי בְּאֹמְרִים לִי
בֵּית יְהֹוָה נֵלֵךְ: עֹמְדוֹת
הָיוּ רַגְלֵינוּ בִּשְׁעָרֵיִךְ
יְרוּשָׁלָיִם: שַׁאֲלוּ שְׁלוֹם

they prosper that love thee. Peace be within thy walls, and prosperity within thy palaces. For my brethren and companions' sakes, I will now say: Peace be within thee. For the sake of the house of the Lord our God I will seek thy good.

יְרוּשָׁלָ֑ם יִשְׁלָ֥יוּ אֹהֲבָֽיִךְ׃
יְהִי־שָׁל֥וֹם בְּחֵילֵ֑ךְ שַׁלְוָ֖ה
בְּאַרְמְנוֹתָֽיִךְ׃ לְמַ֖עַן אַחַ֣י
וְרֵעָ֑י אֲדַבְּרָה־נָּ֥א שָׁל֖וֹם
בָּ֑ךְ׃ לְמַ֖עַן בֵּית־יְהוָ֣ה
אֱלֹהֵ֑ינוּ אֲבַקְשָׁ֖ה ט֥וֹב לָֽךְ׃

### Reader

The synagogue is the sanctuary of Israel. It was born out of Israel's longing for the living God. It has been to Israel throughout his endless wanderings a visible token of the presence of God in the midst of the people. It has shed a beauty that is the beauty of holiness and has ever stood on the high places as the champion of justice and brotherhood and peace. It is Israel's sublime gift to the world. Its truths are true for all men, its love is a love for all men, its God is the God of all men, even as was prophesied of old, My house shall be called a house of prayer for all peoples. Come then, ye who inherit and ye who share the fellowship of Israel, ye who hunger for righteousness, ye who seek the Lord of Hosts, come and together let us lift up our hearts in worship.

(Congregation rises)

### Reader

Praise ye the Lord to whom all praise is due.

### Choir and Congregation

Praised be the Lord to whom all praise is due forever and ever.

(Congregation is seated)

### Reader

Praised be Thou, O Lord our God, who formest light and darkness, ordainest good out of evil, bringest harmony into nature and peace to the heart of man.

Great has been Thy love for us and Thy compassion boundless. Our fathers put their trust in Thee and Thou didst teach them the law of life. Be gracious also unto us that we may understand and fulfil the teachings of Thy word. Enlighten our eyes in Thy law that we may cling unto Thy commandments. Unite our hearts to love and revere Thee. We trust in Thee and rejoice in Thy saving power, for from Thee cometh our help. Thou hast chosen us and drawn us nigh unto Thee to serve Thee in faithfulness. Joyfully do we lift up our voices and proclaim Thy unity. Praised be Thou, O God, who in Thy love hast called Thy people Israel to serve Thee.

Let us now proclaim the supreme truth of our faith. It is heard round the world. In every crisis of his life, even in the presence of death, has the Jew affirmed his faith in the one and only God. By this he has endured the fury and suffering of the centuries and risen to a sublime ministry of service. So do we take up the ancient watchword of our fathers which binds generation to generation in an everlasting covenant:

(Congregation rises)

Reader

בָּרְכוּ אֶת יְיָ הַמְבֹרָךְ:

Choir and Congregation

בָּרוּךְ יְיָ הַמְבֹרָךְ לְעוֹלָם וָעֶד:

(Congregation is seated)

Reader

בָּרוּךְ אַתָּה יְיָ אֱלֹהֵינוּ מֶלֶךְ הָעוֹלָם. יוֹצֵר אוֹר
וּבוֹרֵא חְשֶׁךְ. עֹשֶׂה שָׁלוֹם וּבוֹרֵא אֶת־הַכֹּל:
אַהֲבָה רַבָּה אֲהַבְתָּנוּ יְיָ אֱלֹהֵינוּ. חֶמְלָה גְדוֹלָה
וִיתֵרָה חָמַלְתָּ עָלֵינוּ: אָבִינוּ מַלְכֵּנוּ. בַּעֲבוּר
אֲבוֹתֵינוּ שֶׁבָּטְחוּ בְךָ וַתְּלַמְּדֵם חֻקֵּי חַיִּים. כֵּן תְּחָנֵּנוּ
וּתְלַמְּדֵנוּ: הָאֵר עֵינֵינוּ בְּתוֹרָתֶךָ. וְדַבֵּק לִבֵּנוּ
בְּמִצְוֹתֶיךָ. וְיַחֵד לְבָבֵנוּ לְאַהֲבָה וּלְיִרְאָה שְׁמֶךָ:
כִּי בְשֵׁם קָדְשְׁךָ בָּטָחְנוּ. נָגִילָה וְנִשְׂמְחָה בִּישׁוּעָתֶךָ.
כִּי אֵל פּוֹעֵל יְשׁוּעוֹת אָתָּה. וּבָנוּ בָחַרְתָּ וְקֵרַבְתָּנוּ
לְשִׁמְךָ הַגָּדוֹל סֶלָה בֶּאֱמֶת. לְהוֹדוֹת לְךָ וּלְיַחֶדְךָ
בְּאַהֲבָה. בָּרוּךְ אַתָּה יְיָ הַבּוֹחֵר בְּעַמּוֹ יִשְׂרָאֵל
בְּאַהֲבָה:

(Congregation rises)

*Reader*

שְׁמַע יִשְׂרָאֵל יְהוָֹה אֱלֹהֵינוּ יְהוָֹה אֶחָד:

בָּרוּךְ שֵׁם כְּבוֹד מַלְכוּתוֹ לְעוֹלָם וָעֶד:

(Congregation is seated)

*Congregation and Reader*

וְאָהַבְתָּ אֵת יְיָ אֱלֹהֶיךָ בְּכָל־לְבָבְךָ וּבְכָל־נַפְשְׁךָ

וּבְכָל־מְאֹדֶךָ: וְהָיוּ הַדְּבָרִים הָאֵלֶּה אֲשֶׁר אָנֹכִי

מְצַוְּךָ הַיּוֹם עַל־לְבָבֶךָ: וְשִׁנַּנְתָּם לְבָנֶיךָ וְדִבַּרְתָּ

בָּם. בְּשִׁבְתְּךָ בְּבֵיתֶךָ וּבְלֶכְתְּךָ בַדֶּרֶךְ וּבְשָׁכְבְּךָ

וּבְקוּמֶךָ: וּקְשַׁרְתָּם לְאוֹת עַל־יָדֶךָ. וְהָיוּ לְטֹטָפֹת

בֵּין עֵינֶיךָ. וּכְתַבְתָּם עַל־מְזֻזוֹת בֵּיתֶךָ וּבִשְׁעָרֶיךָ:

לְמַעַן תִּזְכְּרוּ וַעֲשִׂיתֶם אֶת־כָּל־מִצְוֹתָי וִהְיִיתֶם

קְדֹשִׁים לֵאלֹהֵיכֶם: אֲנִי יְיָ אֱלֹהֵיכֶם:

*Reader*

Hear, O Israel: The Lord our God, the Lord is One.
Praised be His name whose glorious kingdom is forever and ever.

*Congregation and Reader*

Thou shalt love the Lord, thy God, with all thy
heart, with all thy soul, and with all thy might. And

these words, which I command thee this day, shall be upon thy heart. Thou shalt teach them diligently unto thy children, and shalt speak of them when thou sittest in thy house, when thou walkest by the way, when thou liest down, and when thou risest up. Thou shalt bind them for a sign upon thy hand, and they shall be for frontlets between thine eyes. Thou shalt write them upon the doorposts of thy house and upon thy gates: That ye may remember and do all My commandments and be holy unto your God.

## Responsive Reading

**Reader**

And now, O Israel, what doth the Lord thy God require of thee;

**Congregation**

*But to serve the Lord thy God, to love and serve Him with all thy heart and with all thy soul.*

Ye are My witnesses, saith the Lord, and My servant whom I have chosen, that ye may know and believe that I, even I, am the Lord, and beside Me there is no savior.

*Now, therefore, if ye will indeed keep My covenant, ye shall be unto Me a kingdom of priests and a holy people.*

Behold My servant, whom I uphold; Mine elect, in whom My soul delighteth.

*I have put My spirit upon him; he shall make the right to go forth to the nations.*

I, the Lord, have called thee in righteousness, and have taken hold of thy hand,

*And* kept thee and set thee for a covenant of the people for a light to the nations.

Also the sons of the stranger that join themselves to the Lord and hold fast to His covenant, even them will I bring to My holy mountain and make them joyful in My house of prayer.

For My house shall be called a house of prayer for all peoples.

### Reader

Who is like unto Thee, O Lord? Who is like unto Thee, glorious in holiness, awe-inspiring, working wonders?

### Choir and Congregation

מִי־כָמֹכָה בָּאֵלִים יְיָ. מִי כָּמֹכָה נָאְדָּר בַּקֹּדֶשׁ
נוֹרָא תְהִלֹּת עֹשֵׂה־פֶלֶא:

### Reader

A new song the redeemed sang unto Thy name. They proclaimed Thy sovereignty and said:

### Choir and Congregation

The Lord shall reign forever and ever.

יְיָ יִמְלֹךְ לְעֹלָם וָעֶד:

*Reader*

צוּר יִשְׂרָאֵל. קוּמָה בְּעֶזְרַת יִשְׂרָאֵל. וּגְאַלְנוּ יְיָ
צְבָאוֹת שְׁמוֹ. קְדוֹשׁ יִשְׂרָאֵל. בָּרוּךְ אַתָּה יְיָ גָּאַל
יִשְׂרָאֵל:

O Rock of Israel, redeem those who are oppressed and deliver those who are persecuted. Praised be Thou, our Redeemer, the Holy One of Israel.

*Choir:* Amen.

*Reader*

Praised be Thou, O Lord, God of our fathers, God of Abraham, Isaac and Jacob, great, mighty, and exalted. Thou bestowest lovingkindness upon all Thy children. Thou rememberest the devotion of the fathers. In Thy love Thou bringest redemption to their descendants for the sake of Thy name. Thou art our King and Helper, our Savior and Protector. Praised be Thou, O Lord, Shield of Abraham.

Eternal is Thy power, O Lord, Thou art mighty to save. In lovingkindness Thou sustainest the living; in the multitude of Thy mercies Thou preservest all. Thou upholdest the falling and healest the sick; freest the captives and keepest faith with Thy children in death as in life. Who is like unto Thee, Almighty God, Author of life and death, Source of salvation? Praised be Thou, O Lord, who hast implanted within us eternal life.

## SANCTIFICATION

(Congregation rises)

*Reader*

We sanctify Thy name on earth, as the heavens declare Thy glory; and in the words of the prophet we say:

Holy, holy, holy is the Lord of hosts; the whole earth is full of His glory.

*Choir and Congregation*

קָדוֹשׁ קָדוֹשׁ קָדוֹשׁ יְיָ צְבָאוֹת. מְלֹא כָל־הָאָרֶץ כְּבוֹדוֹ:

*Reader*

Praised be the glory of God in all the world.

*Choir and Congregation*

בָּרוּךְ כְּבוֹד יְיָ מִמְּקוֹמוֹ:

*Reader*

The Lord will reign forever, thy God, O Zion, from generation to generation.   Hallelujah!

*Choir and Congregation*

יִמְלֹךְ יְיָ לְעוֹלָם אֱלֹהַיִךְ צִיּוֹן לְדֹר וָדֹר הַלְלוּיָהּ:

(Congregation is seated)

### Reader

O Thou who givest meaning to the strivings of men, attune our hearts for communion with Thee. How often, when everything else fails us, do we yearn for Thee. In the stillness of the night, in the press of the crowd, in the agony of inner conflict, we bow our heads, and lo, Thou art in our hearts and we are at peace. We know not, O Lord, whether the gifts for which we ask are for our good, whether our trials and tribulations may not be blessings in disguise, whether even the fragment of our shattered hopes and love may not minister to the upbuilding of other lives and the fulfillment of Thine unfathomable plan. So we do not pray unto Thee to make our lives easy, to give us happiness without alloy. Rather do we pray Thee to aid us to be uncomplaining and unafraid. Teach us to face life with faith and courage that we may see the blessings hidden away even in its discords and struggles. Help us to wrest victory from the discipline of pain. May we realize that life calls us not merely to enjoy the fatness of the earth but to exult in heights attained after the toil of climbing. Thus will our darkness be illumined by Thy light and our weakness made strong by Thy strength, lifting us above fear and defeat, and sustaining our steps with an immortal hope. Praised be Thou, O Lord, the stay and trust of the righteous.

### Congregation and Reader

We gratefully acknowledge, O Lord, our God, that Thou art our Creator and Preserver, the Rock of our life and the Shield of our help. We render thanks unto Thee for our lives which are in Thy hand, for our souls which are ever in Thy keeping; for Thy wondrous providence and for Thy continuous goodness, which Thou bestowest upon us day by day. Truly, Thy mercies never fail and Thy lovingkindness never ceases. Therefore do we forever put our trust in Thee.

## Silent Prayer

### (or such other prayer as the heart may prompt)

O Lord, I shut out the din and fret and littleness of things that I may feel myself alone with Thee in the silence. As a child yields itself to loving arms, I yield myself to Thee, asking for nothing, complaining about nothing. What if my labor is hard, what if my lot is humble, what if my dreams turn into futile tears, if only there is the peace of Thy nearness in my heart. There comes to me in the stillness, despite the terror and tumult of life, a trust in a goodness that nourishes the roots of the grassblade, that glows in the flaming star, and attains fulfillment in the soul of man. How healing and strengthening is this communion with Thee, O God! If only I could always abide in it! But I must go forth again to the struggle for daily bread, to the restlessness of desire and the fear of pain, to the disillusionment of dreams that never come true. Let me not go forth alone, O God. Abide Thou deep in the solitude of my heart, that I may trust in Thee and be unafraid in the face of the inscrutable years, and see that everything happens for the best. Amen.

*Choir*

May the words of my mouth and the meditation of
my heart be acceptable unto Thee, O Lord, my Rock
and my Redeemer.

יִהְיוּ לְרָצוֹן אִמְרֵי־פִי וְהֶגְיוֹן לִבִּי לְפָנֶיךָ. יְיָ
צוּרִי וְגוֹאֲלִי:

### READING FROM SCRIPTURE

(For ADORATION and KADDISH, see p. 365)

## III

*Choir*

(Psalm v)

Give ear to my words, O Lord, consider my meditation. Hearken unto the voice of my cry, my King, and my God; for unto Thee do I pray. O Lord, in the morning shalt Thou hear my voice; in the morning will I order my prayer unto Thee, and will look forward. For Thou art not a God that hath pleasure in wickedness; evil shall not sojourn with Thee. But as for me, in the abundance of Thy loving-kindness will I come into Thy house; I will bow down toward Thy holy temple in the fear of Thee.

אֲמָרַי הַאֲזִינָה יְהֹוָה

בִּינָה הֲגִיגִי: הַקְשִׁיבָה

לְקוֹל שַׁוְעִי מַלְכִּי וֵאלֹהָי

כִּי־אֵלֶיךָ אֶתְפַּלָּל: בֹּקֶר

תִּשְׁמַע קוֹלִי בֹּקֶר אֶעֱרָךְ־

לְךָ וַאֲצַפֶּה: כִּי לֹא אֵל

חָפֵץ רֶשַׁע אָתָּה לֹא יְגֻרְךָ

רָע: וַאֲנִי בְּרֹב חַסְדְּךָ

אָבוֹא בֵיתֶךָ אֶשְׁתַּחֲוֶה

אֶל־הֵיכַל קָדְשְׁךָ

בְּיִרְאָתֶךָ:

*Reader*

O God, and God of our fathers, we come into Thy house with gladness, we enter Thy courts with praise. Here we are reminded of the high and holy purpose which Thou hast set for us. Open our eyes that we may behold wondrous things out of Thy law; give us understanding that we may keep Thy commandments. Then shall we truly serve Thee and declare Thy name amongst the peoples.

## Responsive Reading

Reader

O give thanks unto the Lord, call upon His name; make known His doings among the peoples.

Congregation

Sing unto Him, sing praises unto Him; speak ye of all His marvelous works.

Glory ye in His holy name; let the heart of them rejoice that seek the Lord.

Seek ye the Lord and His strength; seek His presence continually.

He is the Lord our God;

His judgments are in all the earth.

Remember His covenant forever, the word which He commanded to a thousand generations;

The covenant which He made with Abraham, and His oath unto Isaac.

And He established it unto Jacob for a statute, to Israel for an everlasting covenant.

When they went about from nation to nation, and from one kingdom to another,

He did suffer no man to destroy them, yea, for their sake He reproved kings:

Touch not Mine anointed ones and do My prophets no harm.

(Congregation rises)

### Reader

Praise ye the Lord to whom all praise is due.

### Choir and Congregation

Praised be the Lord to whom all praise is due forever and ever.

(Congregation is seated)

### Reader

O Lord of all the worlds, in Thy lovingkindness Thou causest the morning dawn to give light to all earth's creatures. By Thy will the marvels of creation are daily renewed. The heavens declare Thy glory and the earth reveals Thy handiwork. Creator of light and of darkness, Thou art praised day by day in the beauty and harmony of all Thy works.

### Congregation and Reader

Great has been Thy love for us and Thy compassion boundless. Our fathers put their trust in Thee and Thou didst teach them the law of life. Be gracious also unto us that we may understand and fulfil the teachings of Thy word. Enlighten our eyes in Thy law that we may cling unto Thy commandments. Unite our hearts to love and revere Thee. We trust in Thee and rejoice in Thy saving power, for from Thee cometh our help. Thou hast chosen us and drawn us nigh unto

(Congregation rises)

### Reader

בָּרְכוּ אֶת יְיָ הַמְבֹרָךְ׃

### Choir and Congregation

בָּרוּךְ יְיָ הַמְבֹרָךְ לְעוֹלָם וָעֶד׃

(Congregation is seated)

### Reader

בָּרוּךְ אַתָּה יְיָ אֱלֹהֵינוּ מֶלֶךְ הָעוֹלָם. יוֹצֵר אוֹר
וּבוֹרֵא חֹשֶׁךְ. עֹשֶׂה שָׁלוֹם וּבוֹרֵא אֶת־הַכֹּל׃
הַמֵּאִיר לָאָרֶץ וְלַדָּרִים עָלֶיהָ בְּרַחֲמִים. וּבְטוּבוֹ
מְחַדֵּשׁ בְּכָל־יוֹם תָּמִיד מַעֲשֵׂה־בְרֵאשִׁית׃ מָה רַבּוּ
מַעֲשֶׂיךָ יְיָ. כֻּלָּם בְּחָכְמָה עָשִׂיתָ. מָלְאָה הָאָרֶץ
קִנְיָנֶךָ׃ תִּתְבָּרַךְ יְיָ אֱלֹהֵינוּ עַל־שֶׁבַח מַעֲשֵׂה יָדֶיךָ.
וְעַל־מְאוֹרֵי־אוֹר שֶׁעָשִׂיתָ יְפָאֲרוּךָ סֶּלָה׃ בָּרוּךְ אַתָּה
יְיָ יוֹצֵר הַמְּאוֹרוֹת׃

אַהֲבָה רַבָּה אֲהַבְתָּנוּ יְיָ אֱלֹהֵינוּ. חֶמְלָה גְדוֹלָה
וִיתֵרָה חָמַלְתָּ עָלֵינוּ׃ אָבִינוּ מַלְכֵּנוּ. בַּעֲבוּר
אֲבוֹתֵינוּ שֶׁבָּטְחוּ בְךָ וַתְּלַמְּדֵם חֻקֵּי חַיִּים. כֵּן
תְּחָנֵּנוּ וּתְלַמְּדֵנוּ׃

Thee to serve Thee in faithfulness. Joyfully do we lift up our voices and proclaim Thy unity. Praised be Thou, O God, who in Thy love hast called Thy people Israel to serve Thee.

(Congregation rises)

Reader

Hear, O Israel: The Lord our God, the Lord is One. Praised be His name whose glorious kingdom is forever and ever.

(Congregation is seated)

Congregation and Reader

Thou shalt love the Lord, thy God, with all thy heart, with all thy soul, and with all thy might. And these words, which I command thee this day, shall be upon thy heart. Thou shalt teach them diligently unto thy children, and shalt speak of them when thou sittest in thy house, when thou walkest by the way, when thou liest down, and when thou risest up. Thou shalt bind them for a sign upon thy hand, and they shall be for frontlets between thine eyes. Thou shalt write them upon the doorposts of thy house and upon thy gates: That ye may remember and do all My commandments and be holy unto your God.

הָאֵר עֵינֵינוּ בְּתוֹרָתֶךָ. וְדַבֵּק לִבֵּנוּ בְּמִצְוֹתֶיךָ.
וְיַחֵד לְבָבֵנוּ לְאַהֲבָה וּלְיִרְאָה שְׁמֶךָ: כִּי בְשֵׁם
קָדְשְׁךָ בָּטָחְנוּ. נָגִילָה וְנִשְׂמְחָה בִּישׁוּעָתֶךָ. כִּי
אֵל פּוֹעֵל יְשׁוּעוֹת אָתָּה. וּבָנוּ בָחַרְתָּ וְקֵרַבְתָּנוּ
לְשִׁמְךָ הַגָּדוֹל סֶלָה בֶּאֱמֶת. לְהוֹדוֹת לְךָ וּלְיַחֶדְךָ
בְּאַהֲבָה. בָּרוּךְ אַתָּה יְיָ הַבּוֹחֵר בְּעַמּוֹ יִשְׂרָאֵל
בְּאַהֲבָה:

(Congregation rises)<br>
Reader then Choir and Congregation

שְׁמַע יִשְׂרָאֵל יְהֹוָה אֱלֹהֵינוּ יְהֹוָה אֶחָד:
בָּרוּךְ שֵׁם כְּבוֹד מַלְכוּתוֹ לְעוֹלָם וָעֶד:

(Congregation is seated)<br>
Reader and Congregation

וְאָהַבְתָּ אֵת יְיָ אֱלֹהֶיךָ בְּכָל־לְבָבְךָ וּבְכָל־נַפְשְׁךָ
וּבְכָל־מְאֹדֶךָ: וְהָיוּ הַדְּבָרִים הָאֵלֶּה אֲשֶׁר אָנֹכִי
מְצַוְּךָ הַיּוֹם עַל־לְבָבֶךָ: וְשִׁנַּנְתָּם לְבָנֶיךָ וְדִבַּרְתָּ
בָּם. בְּשִׁבְתְּךָ בְּבֵיתֶךָ וּבְלֶכְתְּךָ בַדֶּרֶךְ וּבְשָׁכְבְּךָ
וּבְקוּמֶךָ: וּקְשַׁרְתָּם לְאוֹת עַל־יָדֶךָ. וְהָיוּ לְטֹטָפֹת
בֵּין עֵינֶיךָ: וּכְתַבְתָּם עַל־מְזֻזוֹת בֵּיתֶךָ וּבִשְׁעָרֶיךָ:
לְמַעַן תִּזְכְּרוּ וַעֲשִׂיתֶם אֶת־כָּל־מִצְוֹתָי וִהְיִיתֶם
קְדֹשִׁים לֵאלֹהֵיכֶם: אֲנִי יְיָ אֱלֹהֵיכֶם:

### Responsive Reading

Reader

The heavens shall acknowledge Thy wonders, and the voice of the waters shall glorify Thee.

Congregation

*Yea, all the people shall give thanks unto Thee, and all the nations shall praise Thee.*

Our fathers chose Thee alone to serve, and no strange god beside Thee.

*We also will serve Thee alone, and, as a son his father, will we honor Thee.*

Lo! Thy works are very many and very great, and all of them shall praise Thy name, O Lord.

*Yea, the everlasting arms support the world from the beginning to the end of time and grow not weary.*

How shall I come before God, the most High? and how shall I bow before the God of old?

*I will build an altar of the broken fragments of my heart, and humble my spirit within me.*

In sacrifice and meat-offering Thou delightest not; sin-offering and burnt-offering Thou hast not asked.

*My broken spirit—that is Thy sacrifice; let it be acceptable upon Thine altar.*

From everlasting unto everlasting all things are in Thee, and Thou art in all.

*Without Thy power, there is no strength; and without Thy might, there is no help.*

*Choir*

Who is like unto Thee, O Lord?  Who is like unto Thee, glorious in holiness, awe-inspiring, working wonders?

מִי־כָמְכָה בָּאֵלִים יְיָ. מִי כָּמְכָה נֶאְדָּר בַּקֹּדֶשׁ.
נוֹרָא תְהִלֹת עֹשֵׂה־פֶלֶא:

*Reader*

A new song the redeemed sang unto Thy name. They proclaimed Thy sovereignty and said:

שִׁירָה חֲדָשָׁה שִׁבְּחוּ גְאוּלִים לְשִׁמְךָ עַל־שְׂפַת
הַיָּם יַחַד כֻּלָּם הוֹדוּ וְהִמְלִיכוּ וְאָמְרוּ:

*Choir*

The Lord shall reign forever and ever.

יְיָ יִמְלֹךְ לְעֹלָם וָעֶד:

*Reader*

O Rock of Israel, redeem those who are oppressed and deliver those who are persecuted.  Praised be Thou, our Redeemer, the Holy One of Israel.

צוּר יִשְׂרָאֵל. קוּמָה בְּעֶזְרַת יִשְׂרָאֵל. גֹּאֲלֵנוּ יְיָ
צְבָאוֹת שְׁמוֹ. קְדוֹשׁ יִשְׂרָאֵל. בָּרוּךְ אַתָּה יְיָ גָּאַל
יִשְׂרָאֵל:

**Choir: Amen.**

### Reader

Praised be Thou, O Lord, God of our fathers, God
of Abraham, Isaac and Jacob, great, mighty, and exalted.
Thou bestowest lovingkindness upon all Thy children.
Thou rememberest the devotion of the fathers. In
Thy love, Thou bringest redemption to their descend-
ents for the sake of Thy name. Thou art our King
and Helper, our Savior and Protector. Praised be Thou,
O Lord, Shield of Abraham.

Eternal is Thy power, O Lord, Thou art mighty to
save. In lovingkindness Thou sustainest the living; in
the multitude of Thy mercies, Thou preservest all.
Thou upholdest the falling and healest the sick; freest
the captives and keepest faith with Thy children in
death as in life. Who is like unto Thee, Almighty God,
Author of life and death, Source of salvation? Praised
be Thou, O Lord, who hast implanted within us eternal
life.

*Reader*

בָּרוּךְ אַתָּה יְיָ אֱלֹהֵינוּ וֵאלֹהֵי אֲבוֹתֵינוּ. אֱלֹהֵי
אַבְרָהָם אֱלֹהֵי יִצְחָק וֵאלֹהֵי יַעֲקֹב. הָאֵל הַגָּדוֹל
הַגִּבּוֹר וְהַנּוֹרָא. אֵל עֶלְיוֹן. גּוֹמֵל חֲסָדִים טוֹבִים.
וְקֹנֵה הַכֹּל וְזוֹכֵר חַסְדֵי אָבוֹת. וּמֵבִיא גוֹאֵל לִבְנֵי
בְנֵיהֶם. לְמַעַן שְׁמוֹ בְּאַהֲבָה: מֶלֶךְ עוֹזֵר וּמוֹשִׁיעַ
וּמָגֵן. בָּרוּךְ אַתָּה יְיָ מָגֵן אַבְרָהָם:

אַתָּה גִבּוֹר לְעוֹלָם אֲדֹנָי. רַב לְהוֹשִׁיעַ. מְכַלְכֵּל
חַיִּים בְּחֶסֶד. מְחַיֶּה הַכֹּל בְּרַחֲמִים רַבִּים. סוֹמֵךְ
נוֹפְלִים וְרוֹפֵא חוֹלִים וּמַתִּיר אֲסוּרִים. וּמְקַיֵּם
אֱמוּנָתוֹ לִישֵׁנֵי עָפָר. מִי כָמוֹךָ בַּעַל גְּבוּרוֹת. וּמִי
דוֹמֶה־לָּךְ. מֶלֶךְ מֵמִית וּמְחַיֶּה. וּמַצְמִיחַ יְשׁוּעָה:
בָּרוּךְ אַתָּה יְיָ נֹטֵעַ בְּתוֹכֵנוּ חַיֵּי עוֹלָם:

## SANCTIFICATION

(Congregation rises)

### Reader

We sanctify Thy name on earth, as the heavens declare Thy glory, and in the words of the prophet we say:

Holy, holy, holy is the Lord of hosts; the whole earth is full of His glory.

### Choir and Congregation

קָדוֹשׁ קָדוֹשׁ קָדוֹשׁ יְיָ צְבָאוֹת. מְלֹא כָל־הָאָרֶץ
כְּבוֹדוֹ:

### Reader

Praised be the glory of God in all the world.

### Choir and Congregation

בָּרוּךְ כְּבוֹד יְיָ מִמְּקוֹמוֹ:

### Reader

The Lord will reign forever, thy God, O Zion, from generation to generation. Hallelujah!

### Choir and Congregation

יִמְלֹךְ יְיָ לְעוֹלָם אֱלֹהַיִךְ צִיּוֹן לְדוֹר וָדוֹר
הַלְלוּיָהּ:

(Congregation is seated)

*Congregation and Reader*

Heavenly Father, who hast graciously endowed mankind with reason and understanding, send us the light of Thy truth, that we may gain insight into the wisdom of Thy ways. Banish from our hearts every desire and thought of evil, that we may truly revere Thy holy name. Forgive our sins, pardon our failings, and remove from us suffering and sorrow. May the erring and the wayward be led to know Thy lovingkindness, and to serve Thee in newness of heart; and may those who love virtue and do the right, ever be glad of Thy favor. Bless our land with plenty and our nation with peace; may righteousness dwell in our midst and virtue reign among us.

Thou knowest our needs before we utter them, and ordainest all things for the best. Praised be Thou, O Lord, who hearest prayer.

*Congregation and Reader*

הֲבִינֵנוּ יְיָ אֱלֹהֵינוּ לָדַעַת דְּרָכֶיךָ. וּמוֹל אֶת־
לְבָבֵנוּ לְיִרְאָתֶךָ. וְתִסְלַח לָנוּ לִהְיוֹת גְּאוּלִים.
וְרַחֲקֵנוּ מִמַּכְאוֹב. וְדַשְּׁנֵנוּ בִּנְאוֹת אַרְצֶךָ. וְהַתְּוֹעִים
עַל־דַּעְתְּךָ יִשָּׁפֵטוּ. יְהִי רָצוֹן לְפָנֶיךָ יְיָ אֱלֹהֵינוּ
וֵאלֹהֵי אֲבוֹתֵינוּ. שֶׁתִּתֵּן לְכָל־אֶחָד וְאֶחָד כְּדֵי
פַרְנָסָתוֹ וּלְכָל־גְּוִיָּה וּגְוִיָּה דֵּי מַחְסוֹרָהּ. וְהַטּוֹב
בְּעֵינֶיךָ עֲשֵׂה. בָּרוּךְ אַתָּה יְיָ שׁוֹמֵעַ תְּפִלָּה:

## Reader

O Lord God, Creator of all the world, Thou hast blessed man with noble powers. Teach us to seek the good that we may wisely use these powers. We thank Thee for the duty of bearing Thy word unto the children of men. Enlighten us that we may approach this sacred task with an understanding of the message that we bring. May we be filled with zeal for knowledge lest ignorance leave us powerless. Strengthen Thou our faith, that we may kindle the light of Thy presence in the hearts of others.

## Congregation and Reader

O Lord, God of all the world, show Thou the pathway of peace unto all the children of men. Imbue them with the desire for brotherliness and goodwill which alone can bring enduring peace. May the nations realize that the triumphs of war turn to ashes and that justice and righteousness are better than conquest and dominion; for it is not by might nor by power, but by Thy spirit that the blessings of peace can be made secure. Amen.

## Silent Prayer

(or such other prayer .as the heart may prompt)

O God, grant that I may understand my duty to Thee and to my people. May my life be a sanctification of Thy name. Let me not be discouraged by the sneers of the cynical, or dismayed by the attacks of the hostile. Grant me the courage to proclaim Thy name. Strengthen me, O Father, when I am weak; help me to hasten the day when all mankind shall be joined in fellowship, and acknowledge Thee as their God and Father.

## Choir

May the words of my mouth and the meditation of my heart be acceptable in Thy sight, O Lord, my Rock and my Redeemer.

### READING FROM SCRIPTURE
(For ADORATION and KADDISH, see p. 365)

## IV

### Choir

(Psalm xxxvi)

How precious is Thy lovingkindness, O God! The children of men take refuge in the shadow of Thy wings. They are satisfied with the abundance of Thy house; and Thou makest them drink of the river of Thy pleasures. For with Thee is the fountain of life; in Thy light, do we see light.

מַה־יָּקָר חַסְדְּךָ אֱלֹהִים

וּבְנֵי אָדָם בְּצֵל כְּנָפֶיךָ

יֶחֱסָיוּן: יִרְוְיֻן מִדֶּשֶׁן בֵּיתֶךָ

וְנַחַל עֲדָנֶיךָ תַשְׁקֵם: כִּי־

עִמְּךָ מְקוֹר חַיִּים בְּאוֹרְךָ

נִרְאֶה־אוֹר:

### Responsive Reading

**Reader**

How lovely are Thy tabernacles, O Lord of hosts! My soul yearneth, yea, even pineth for the courts of the Lord;

**Congregation**

My heart and my flesh sing for joy unto the living God.

Yea, the sparrow hath found a house, and the swallow a nest where she may lay her young;

So to me are Thine altars, O Lord of hosts, my King, and my God.

Happy are they that dwell in Thy house, they are ever
   praising Thee.

*Happy is the man whose strength is in Thee, in whose
   heart are Thy ways.*

They go from strength to strength, everyone of them
   appeareth before God in Zion.

*O Lord God of hosts, hear my prayer; give ear, O
   God of Jacob.*

For a day in Thy courts is better than a thousand elsewhere; I had rather stand at the threshold of
   the house of my God, than to dwell in the tents
   of wickedness.

*For the Lord God is a sun and a shield; the Lord
   giveth grace and glory;*

No good thing will He withhold from them that walk
   uprightly.

*O Lord of hosts, happy is the man that trusteth in
   Thee.*

### Reader

O God, Thou art hidden from the eyes of all the
living and art beyond the comprehension of all creatures.  The keenest eye fails to penetrate beyond the
smallest portion of Thy universe, and the mind of
genius cannot comprehend more than a broken fragment of Thy glory.  The tongues of poets and sages
falter as they seek to express Thine incomparable wisdom and splendor.  Yet though Thy greatness sur-

passes our understanding, we feel Thy nearness and
are overcome with wonder and with awe as we behold
the signs of Thy majesty. Thy laws guide the creatures
of earth even as they direct the planets on high. Within
ourselves, we feel the stirrings of a heaven-soaring spirit.
This emboldens us to seek Thy presence, O infinite
Creator, firm in the faith that we shall find Thee if,
with sincere hearts, we seek Thee. As the flowers of
the field drink of the dew of heaven and of the radiance
of the sun, so would we, lifting our spirits unto Thee,
drink of the pure fountains of holiness. In Thee our
souls rejoice, for Thou art our life and our song. Amen.

(Congregation rises)

### Reader

בָּרְכוּ אֶת־יְיָ הַמְבֹרָךְ:

Praise ye the Lord, to whom all praise is due.

### Choir and Congregation

בָּרוּךְ יְיָ הַמְבֹרָךְ לְעוֹלָם וָעֶד:

Praised be the Lord to whom all praise is due forever
and ever.

(Congregation is seated)

### Reader

Thine, O Lord, are the heavens, Thine also the earth;
the world and the fulness thereof. Thou hast founded
them. The universe with its myriads of wonders sings
of Thy wisdom, and daily proclaims the marvels of

creation. Thy might upholds the circling spheres and guides their courses in the heights of heaven. Though they wax old as a garment, Thou wilt endure forever; Thy years have no end. The mysteries of decay and death, as of life and growth, manifest Thy workings. Thy throne is established from of old; Thou art from everlasting. The whole universe, O ever-living God, is Thy sanctuary, resounding with praise of Thy glory.

## Congregation and Reader

In the heart of man, too, Thou reignest supreme. Above the floods of passion and hate, we hear Thy voice proclaim the law of right and duty. Open our eyes to Thy truth, endow our spirits with faith in Thy life-giving behests, and imbue our hearts with courage to translate them into deeds of lovingkindness. Consecrate us anew to the task to which our fathers joyfully dedicated themselves: to speed the dawn of the new day when all men will be united in brotherhood, and, with one accord, will acclaim Thee their Father and their God.

(Congregation rises)

Reader and Congregation

שְׁמַע יִשְׂרָאֵל יְהֹוָה אֱלֹהֵינוּ יְהֹוָה אֶחָד:

בָּרוּךְ שֵׁם כְּבוֹד מַלְכוּתוֹ לְעוֹלָם וָעֶד:

(Congregation is seated)

Reader

וְאָהַבְתָּ אֵת יְיָ אֱלֹהֶיךָ בְּכָל־לְבָבְךָ וּבְכָל־נַפְשְׁךָ
וּבְכָל־מְאֹדֶךָ: וְהָיוּ הַדְּבָרִים הָאֵלֶּה אֲשֶׁר אָנֹכִי
מְצַוְּךָ הַיּוֹם עַל־לְבָבֶךָ: וְשִׁנַּנְתָּם לְבָנֶיךָ וְדִבַּרְתָּ
בָּם. בְּשִׁבְתְּךָ בְּבֵיתֶךָ וּבְלֶכְתְּךָ בַדֶּרֶךְ וּבְשָׁכְבְּךָ
וּבְקוּמֶךָ: וּקְשַׁרְתָּם לְאוֹת עַל־יָדֶךָ. וְהָיוּ לְטֹטָפֹת
בֵּין עֵינֶיךָ: וּכְתַבְתָּם עַל־מְזוּזוֹת בֵּיתֶךָ וּבִשְׁעָרֶיךָ:
לְמַעַן תִּזְכְּרוּ וַעֲשִׂיתֶם אֶת־כָּל־מִצְוֹתָי וִהְיִיתֶם
קְדֹשִׁים לֵאלֹהֵיכֶם: אֲנִי יְיָ אֱלֹהֵיכֶם:

Reader

Hear, O Israel: The Lord our God, the Lord is One.
Praised be His name whose glorious kingdom is
forever and ever.

Congregation and Reader

Thou shalt love the Lord, thy God, with all thy
heart, with all thy soul, and with all thy might. And
these words, which I command thee this day, shall be
upon thy heart. Thou shalt teach them diligently unto
thy children, and shalt speak of them when thou sittest

in thy house, when thou walkest by the way, when thou liest down, and when thou risest up. Thou shalt bind them for a sign upon thy hand, and they shall be for frontlets between thine eyes. Thou shalt write them upon the doorposts of thy house and upon thy gates: That ye may remember and do all My commandments and be holy unto your God.

## Responsive Reading

Reader

Thou, O Lord, givest being to all things and sustainest all creation.

Congregation

*In Thee Israel has found the strength to meet every trial and peril.*

We trust not in the might of arms; neither do we rely upon our own power to save us.

*Thou hast been our deliverer, our guardian and our guide.*

Trusting in Thee we have carried aloft undismayed the torch of Thy truth unto the nations.

*Continue to be our inspiration in the tasks which confront us, in the noon-tide of joy or in the night of adversity.*

Send forth Thy light and Thy truth to lead us; let them bring us unto Thy holy mountain.

*When doubts and confusion assail us, aid us to remain constant in our devotion unto Thee.*

Deepen our loyalty to the sacred obligations which rest upon us as children of Israel.

*Let not our hearts turn away from Thy covenant, and let our lives testify to our faith in Thee.*

*Choir*

Who is like unto Thee, O Lord?  Who is like unto Thee, glorious in holiness, awe-inspiring, working wonders?

*Reader*

A new song the redeemed sang unto Thy name. They proclaimed Thy sovereignty and said:

*Choir*

The Lord shall reign forever and ever.

*Reader*

O Rock of Israel, redeem those who are oppressed and deliver those who are persecuted.  Praised be Thou, our Redeemer, the Holy One of Israel.

*Choir: Amen.*

*Reader*

Praised be Thou, O Lord, God of our fathers, God of Abraham, Isaac and Jacob, great, mighty, and exalted. Thou bestowest lovingkindness upon all Thy children. Thou rememberest the devotion of the fathers.  In Thy love Thou bringest redemption to their descendants for the sake of Thy name.  Thou art our King and Helper, our Savior and Protector.  Praised be Thou, O Lord, Shield of Abraham.

Choir and Congregation

מִי־כָמְכָה בָּאֵלִים יְיָ. מִי כָּמְכָה נֶאְדָּר בַּקֹּדֶשׁ.
נוֹרָא תְהִלֹּת עֹשֵׂה־פֶלֶא:

Reader

שִׁירָה חֲדָשָׁה שִׁבְּחוּ גְאוּלִים לְשִׁמְךָ עַל־שְׂפַת
הַיָּם יַחַד כֻּלָּם הוֹדוּ וְהִמְלִיכוּ וְאָמְרוּ:

Choir

יְיָ יִמְלֹךְ לְעֹלָם וָעֶד:

Reader

צוּר יִשְׂרָאֵל. קוּמָה בְּעֶזְרַת יִשְׂרָאֵל. וּגְאָלֵנוּ יְיָ
צְבָאוֹת שְׁמוֹ. קְדוֹשׁ יִשְׂרָאֵל. בָּרוּךְ אַתָּה יְיָ גָּאַל
יִשְׂרָאֵל:

Choir: Amen.

Reader

בָּרוּךְ אַתָּה יְיָ אֱלֹהֵינוּ וֵאלֹהֵי אֲבוֹתֵינוּ. אֱלֹהֵי
אַבְרָהָם אֱלֹהֵי יִצְחָק וֵאלֹהֵי יַעֲקֹב. הָאֵל הַגָּדוֹל
הַגִּבּוֹר וְהַנּוֹרָא. אֵל עֶלְיוֹן. גּוֹמֵל חֲסָדִים טוֹבִים.
וְקֹנֵה הַכֹּל וְזוֹכֵר חַסְדֵי אָבוֹת. וּמֵבִיא גְאֻלָּה לִבְנֵי
בְנֵיהֶם. לְמַעַן שְׁמוֹ בְּאַהֲבָה: מֶלֶךְ עוֹזֵר וּמוֹשִׁיעַ
וּמָגֵן. בָּרוּךְ אַתָּה יְיָ מָגֵן אַבְרָהָם:

Eternal is Thy power, O Lord, Thou art mighty to save. In lovingkindness Thou sustainest the living; in the multitude of Thy mercies, Thou preservest all. Thou upholdest the falling and healest the sick; freest the captives and keepest faith with Thy children in death as in life. Who is like unto Thee, Almighty God, Author of life and death, Source of salvation? Praised be Thou, O Lord, who hast implanted within us eternal life.

## Reader

Gracious and merciful God! Thou hast dowered us above all earth-born creatures with a spark of Thy spirit. We thank Thee, O God, for the gift of reason whereby we may search after knowledge and gain mastery over nature. Let us not misuse this gift to darken Thy light and defeat Thy sacred purposes. In the pride of intellect may we not become a law unto ourselves and reject Thy benign statutes. O God, our hearts are filled with discord as they grow estranged from Thee. Lower desires often threaten to defeat our nobler inclinations. As we grow in knowledge, may we grow also in reverence and humility. Let the fruit of the tree of knowledge yield more abundant life and happiness and not pain, misery, and death. May the consciousness of Thy presence be the music of our lives, bringing harmony into our existence and raising us to the heights of true humanity. Praised be Thou, O Lord, gracious Giver of knowledge.

## Silent Prayer

(or such other prayer as the heart may prompt)

Heavenly Father! Thou art near us whenever we forsake evil and turn unto Thee in sincerity. We pray for Thy support as we struggle to free ourselves from thoughts that lead astray and from desires that defile our better nature. Give us unity of heart and firmness of will to follow Thy laws of goodness and truth. When we stray from Thee into places of darkness and of the

shadow of death, aid us to find our way back to Thee.
Deliver us from idolatry of self, from vain pride and
from arrogance, and imbue us with a deeper regard for
others. Let the fire of sacrificial service ever glow upon
the altar of our hearts, and zeal for brotherhood and
for peace burn within our souls. Restore us to the joy
of Thy presence that we may behold Thy way in holiness and Thy will in truth, in justice and in love. Amen.

## Choir

May the words of my mouth and the meditation of my
  heart be acceptable unto Thee, O Lord, my Rock
  and my Redeemer.

יִהְיוּ לְרָצוֹן אִמְרֵי־פִי וְהֶגְיוֹן לִבִּי לְפָנֶיךָ יְיָ צוּרִי
וְגוֹאֲלִי:

## READING FROM SCRIPTURE

## III

### Reader

To you, who mourn the loss of loved ones, let there come the comfort of the hope that, though the dust returns to the earth as it was, the spirit returns to God who gave it. Death is not the end. Our dear ones have passed through the gateway of the grave into the peace of life that endureth always. We know that all of us must tread the same path, though we know not when the hour may strike. Let us so live that the coming of that hour shall find us unafraid. May our deeds do honor to the memory of our beloved whom Thou hast taken unto Thyself. In unshaken trust in Thy wisdom and lovingkindness, we give praise unto Thy name:

(Kaddish, pages 370–371)

## IV

### Reader

O Living Fountain, whence our healing flows, unto Thee the stricken look for comfort, and the sorrow-laden for consolation. In grief Thou art our refuge and

---

## ADORATION
### (Congregation rises)

### Reader and Congregation

Let us adore the ever-living God, and render praise unto Him who spread out the heavens and established the earth, whose glory is revealed in the heavens above and whose greatness is manifest throughout the world. He is our God; there is none else.

### Choir and Congregation

We bow the head in reverence, and worship the King of kings, the Holy One, praised be He.

### Choir and Congregation

וַאֲנַחְנוּ כֹּרְעִים וּמִשְׁתַּחֲוִים וּמוֹדִים לִפְנֵי מֶלֶךְ
מַלְכֵי הַמְּלָכִים הַקָּדוֹשׁ בָּרוּךְ הוּא:

### (Congregation is seated)

### Reader

May the time not be distant, O God, when Thy name shall be worshiped in all the earth, when unbelief shall disappear and error be no more. Fervently we pray that the day may come when all men shall invoke Thy name, when corruption and evil shall give way to purity and goodness, when superstition shall no longer enslave the mind, nor idolatry blind the eye; when all who dwell on earth shall know that to Thee alone every knee must bend and every tongue give homage. O may all, created in Thine image, recognize that they are brethren, so that, one in spirit and one in fellowship, they may be forever united before Thee. Then shall Thy kingdom be established on earth and the word of Thine ancient seer be fulfilled: The Lord will reign forever and ever.

## Congregation

On that day the Lord shall be One and His name shall be One.

## I

### Reader

O Eternal Father, the generations of men come and go before Thee. Brief is their existence. Many are the tasks still unfinished, the plans unfulfilled, the dreams unrealized when we are summoned to leave this earthly home. Yet we lift up our souls to Thee, that our little day may find its permanence as part of Thine eternity and our work its completeness in Thee.

At this hallowed hour we turn our thoughts to our beloved departed and recall the tender companionship of their earthly presence. Though their mortal career has ended, they have not vanished from our hearts. By love are they remembered and in memory they live.

Grant us, O God, strength and blessing through the memory of our departed. May the noble purposes which inspired them and the high ideals which they cherished endure in our thoughts and live in our actions. We rise in reverence of Thee who dost bind the generations each to each and conquerest death forever. Amen.

(Kaddish, pages 370–371)

## II

### Reader

At this time of sacred memory, we recall those who are bound to us by the ties of love and sweet remembrance. The thought of them moves us to gentle impulses and a wider fellowship with sorrow. They whisper to us of a world where years and horizons have no meaning and where the heart's desires come abidingly into their own. Help us to understand, O Lord, that grief and love go hand in hand, that the sorrow of loss is but a token of the love that is stronger than death. Even though we cry in the bereavement of our hearts when our beloved are taken from this earth, may it be as a child cries who knows his father is near and wh clings unafraid to a trusted hand. In this spirit, Thou who art the Master of our destiny, do we comr all that is precious to us into Thy keeping, as repeat the words hallowed by generations:

(Kaddish, pages 370–371)

in distress our deliverer.  Though we walk in the valley of the shadow of death, we shall fear no evil for Thou art with us.  Thy rod and Thy staff, they comfort us. Cause Thy peace to abide with all troubled spirits. Turn our sorrow into gladness, and our grief into joy. Amid the darkness that envelops us, may we behold Thy light; and, in submission to Thine inscrutable will, find strength for our daily tasks.

(Mourners rise)

Extolled and hallowed be the name of God throughout the world which He has created according to His will. And may He speedily establish His kingdom of righteousness on earth. Amen.

### Congregation

Praised be His glorious name unto all eternity.

### Reader

Praised and glorified be the name of the Holy One, though He be above all the praises which we can utter. Our guide is He in life and our redeemer through all eternity.

### Congregation

Our help cometh from Him, the creator of heaven and earth.

### Reader

The departed whom we now remember have entered into the peace of life eternal. They still live on earth in the acts of goodness they performed and in the hearts of those who cherish their memory. May the beauty of their life abide among us as a loving benediction.

### Congregation

Amen

### Reader

May the Father of peace send peace to all who mourn, and comfort all the bereaved among us.

### Congregation

Amen

(Mourners are seated)

(Mourners rise)

יִתְגַּדַּל וְיִתְקַדַּשׁ שְׁמֵהּ רַבָּא. בְּעָלְמָא דִי־בְרָא
כִרְעוּתֵהּ. וְיַמְלִיךְ מַלְכוּתֵהּ. בְּחַיֵּיכוֹן וּבְיוֹמֵיכוֹן
וּבְחַיֵּי דְכָל־בֵּית יִשְׂרָאֵל. בַּעֲגָלָא וּבִזְמַן קָרִיב.
וְאִמְרוּ אָמֵן:

Congregation

יְהֵא שְׁמֵהּ רַבָּא מְבָרַךְ לְעָלַם וּלְעָלְמֵי עָלְמַיָּא:

Reader

יִתְבָּרַךְ וְיִשְׁתַּבַּח וְיִתְפָּאַר וְיִתְרוֹמַם וְיִתְנַשֵּׂא
וְיִתְהַדָּר וְיִתְעַלֶּה וְיִתְהַלָּל שְׁמֵהּ דְּקוּדְשָׁא. בְּרִיךְ
הוּא. לְעֵלָּא מִן כָּל־בִּרְכָתָא וְשִׁירָתָא. תֻּשְׁבְּחָתָא
וְנֶחֱמָתָא. דַּאֲמִירָן בְּעָלְמָא. וְאִמְרוּ אָמֵן:

עַל יִשְׂרָאֵל וְעַל צַדִּיקַיָּא. וְעַל־כָּל־מַן דְּאִתְפְּטַר
מִן עָלְמָא הָדֵין כִּרְעוּתֵהּ דֶּאֱלָהָא. יְהֵא לְהוֹן
שְׁלָמָא רַבָּא וְחִנָּא וְחִסְדָּא מִן־קֳדָם מָרֵא שְׁמַיָּא
וְאַרְעָא. וְאִמְרוּ אָמֵן:

יְהֵא שְׁלָמָא רַבָּא מִן־שְׁמַיָּא וְחַיִּים. עָלֵינוּ וְעַל־
כָּל־יִשְׂרָאֵל. וְאִמְרוּ אָמֵן:

עֹשֶׂה שָׁלוֹם בִּמְרוֹמָיו. הוּא יַעֲשֶׂה שָׁלוֹם עָלֵינוּ
וְעַל־כָּל־יִשְׂרָאֵל. וְאִמְרוּ אָמֵן:

(Mourners are seated)

## THE MOURNER'S KADDISH

### Reader

Yis-gad-dal v'yis-kad-dash sh'meh rab-bo, b'ol-mo di'v-ro kir'-u-seh v'yam-lich mal-chu-seh, b'cha-ye-chon u-v'yo-me-chon u-v'cha-yeh d'chol bes yis-ro-el, ba-a-go-lo u-viz-man ko-riv, v'im-ru O-men.

### Congregation

Y'heh sh'meh rab-bo m'vo-rach, l'o-lam ul'ol'meh ol-ma-yo:

### Reader

Yis-bo-rach v'yish-tab-bach, v'yis-po-ar, v'yis-ro-mam, v'yis-nas-seh, v'yis-had-dor, v'yis-al-leh, v'yis-hal-lol, sh'-meh d'kud'-sho, b'rich hu. L'e-lo min kol bir-cho-so v'shi-ro-so, tush-b'cho-so v'ne-cho-mo-so, da-a-mi-ron b'ol-mo, v'im-ru O-men:

Al yis-ro-el v'al tsa-de-ka-yo, v'al kol man d'isp'tar min ol-mo ho-dain kir-ooseh de-e-lo-ho y'hai l'hon shlo-mo rab-bo v'chino v'chis-do min ko-dom mo-rai sh'ma-yo v'ar-o, v'im-ru O-men:

Y'heh sh'lo-mo rab-bo min sh'ma-yo v'cha-yim, o-le-nu v'al kol yis-ro-el, v'imru O-men:

O-seh sho-lom bim'-ro-mov, hu ya-a-seh sho-lom, o-le-nu v'al kol yis-ro-el, v'imru O-men.

# Prayers
## for
# Private Devotion

# Services in the Home

## SABBATH EVE
### KIDDUSH

קִדּוּשׁ

The table is given a festive appearance. A wine cup and a loaf of bread for the blessing are set before the head of the household. The ceremony of ushering in the Sabbath is begun by the kindling of the lights, during which a blessing by the wife is silently asked upon the home and the dear ones. The following may be used:

May our home be consecrated, O God, by Thy light. May it shine upon us all in blessing as the light of love and truth, the light of peace and goodwill. Amen.

*When all are seated, the head of the household says:*

Come, let us welcome the Sabbath in joy and peace! Like a bride, radiant and joyous, comes the Sabbath. It brings blessings to our hearts; workday thoughts and cares are put aside. The brightness of the Sabbath light shines forth to tell that the divine spirit of love abides within our home. In that light all our blessings are enriched, all our griefs and trials are softened.

At this hour, God's messenger of peace comes and turns the hearts of the parents to the children, and the hearts of the children to the parents, strengthening the bonds of devotion to that pure and lofty ideal of the home found in Sacred Writ.

*(The following verses from Chapter 31 of the Book of Proverbs may be added):*

A woman of valor, who can find? for her price is far above rubies.

She looketh well to the ways of her household, and eateth not the bread of idleness.

She giveth food to her household, and a portion to her maidens.

She stretcheth out her hand to the poor; yea, she reacheth forth her hands to the needy.

She openeth her mouth with wisdom; and the law of kindness is on her tongue.

Strength and dignity are her clothing; and she laugheth at the time to come.

Her children rise up, and call her blessed; her husband also, and he praiseth her: "Many daughters have done valiantly, but thou excellest them all."

Grace is deceitful, and beauty is vain; but a woman that feareth the Lord, she shall be praised.

Give her of the fruit of her hands, and let her works praise her in the gates.

*The head of the household lifts the wine cup and says:*

Let us praise God with this symbol of joy, and thank Him for the blessings of the past week, for life, health, and strength, for home, love, and friendship, for the discipline of our trials and temptations, for the happiness that has come to us out of our labors. Thou hast ennobled us, O God, by the blessings of work, and in love and kindness Thou has sanctified us by the blessings of rest through the commandment: Six days shalt thou labor and do all thy work, but the seventh day is the Sabbath hallowed unto the Lord, Thy God.

Praised be Thou, O Lord our God, King of the universe, who hast created the fruit of the vine.

בָּרוּךְ אַתָּה יְהוָֹה אֱלֹהֵינוּ מֶלֶךְ הָעוֹלָם בּוֹרֵא
פְּרִי הַגָּפֶן:

*The wine cup is passed round the table and each in turn drinks from it.*
*The head of the household then breaks the bread and, dipping a piece of*
*it in salt, pronounces the blessing:*

Praised be Thou, O Lord our God, King of the universe, who causest the earth to yield food for all.

בָּרוּךְ אַתָּה יְהוָֹה אֱלֹהֵינוּ מֶלֶךְ הָעוֹלָם הַמּוֹצִיא
לֶחֶם מִן־הָאָרֶץ:

*Each one at the table likewise partakes of bread and salt.*
*Then the parent, with hands upon the head of each child in turn, silently*
*pronounces such a blessing as the heart may prompt, or uses the following*
*formula:*

May the God of our fathers bless you. May He who has guided us unto this day lead you to be an honor to our family. May He who has protected us from all evil make you a blessing to Israel and to all mankind. Amen.

### FOR THE EVE OF THE FESTIVALS
### KIDDUSH

קִדּוּשׁ

*The table is given a festive appearance. A wine cup and a loaf of*
*bread (on Passover, unleavened bread), for the blessing are set before the*
*head of the household. Lifting the cup of wine he says:*

Praised be Thou, O Lord our God, King of the universe, who hast granted us life, sustained us and permitted us to celebrate this joyous festival.

בָּרוּךְ אַתָּה יְהֹוָה אֱלֹהֵינוּ מֶלֶךְ הָעוֹלָם שֶׁהֶחֱיָנוּ
וְקִיְּמָנוּ וְהִגִּיעָנוּ לַזְּמַן הַזֶּה:

## PESACH

Let us praise God with this symbol of joy and thank Him for the blessings which this Feast of Pesach brings to us. Our hearts are stirred by memories of the deliverance of our forefathers from Egypt. The unleavened bread reminds us of the hardships they endured to remain steadfast to the service of God. May their example teach us fortitude. May we feel that true freedom means to serve God by ennobling ourselves and by serving our fellowmen.

(Benedictions, page 379)

## SHAVUOS

Let us praise God with this symbol of joy and thank Him for the blessings which this Feast of Shavuos brings to us. God in His lovingkindness blessed our fathers by entrusting them with the Ten Commandments. Let us renew, on this festival, the promise then made by our sires: All that the Lord hath spoken, we will do and heed.

(Benedictions, page 379)

## SUCCOS

Let us praise God with this symbol of joy and thank Him for the blessings which this Feast of Succos brings to us. May God's providence which cared for our fathers in their wanderings also protect us.

His bounteous hand satisfies all our needs. May our kindness to others show our gratitude to Him whose kindness endureth forever.

(Benedictions, see below)

## NEW YEAR

Let us praise God with this symbol of joy and thank Him for the blessings which this New Year's day brings to us. Happy are we that God has granted us another year of life; and may it be His will to inscribe us for happiness and peace in the Book of Life, for the coming year.

## THE BENEDICTIONS

Praised be Thou, O Lord our God, King of the universe, who hast created the fruit of the vine.

בָּרוּךְ אַתָּה יְהֹוָה אֱלֹהֵינוּ מֶלֶךְ הָעוֹלָם בּוֹרֵא
פְּרִי הַגָּפֶן:

*The wine cup is passed round the table and each in turn drinks from it. The head of the household then breaks the bread (on Passover the unleavened bread) and, dipping it in salt, pronounces the blessing:*

Praised be Thou, O Lord our God, King of the universe, who causest the earth to yield food for all.

בָּרוּךְ אַתָּה יְהֹוָה אֱלֹהֵינוּ מֶלֶךְ הָעוֹלָם הַמּוֹצִיא
לֶחֶם מִן הָאָרֶץ:

*Each one at the table likewise partakes of the bread and salt.*
*Then the parent, with hands upon the head of each child in turn, silently pronounces such a blessing as the heart may prompt; or uses the following formula:*

May the God of our fathers bless you! May He who has guided us unto this day lead you to be an honor to our family. May He who has protected us from all evil make you a blessing to Israel, and all mankind. Amen.

### CELEBRATION OF HANUKKAH

*Hanukkah, or Feast of Dedication, lasts eight days. On the first evening one light is kindled, the number of lights being increased by one on each successive evening. Before the kindling of the lights, the following is said:*

Praised be Thou, O Lord our God, Ruler of the world, who hast sanctified us by Thy commandments and bidden us kindle the Hanukkah lights.

Praised be Thou, O Lord our God, Ruler of the world, who didst wondrous things for our fathers at this season in those days.

Praised be Thou, O Lord our God, Ruler of the world, who has granted us life, sustained us and permitted us to celebrate this joyous festival.

בָּרוּךְ אַתָּה יְהֹוָה אֱלֹהֵינוּ מֶלֶךְ הָעוֹלָם שֶׁהֶחֱיָנוּ
וְקִיְּמָנוּ וְהִגִּיעָנוּ לַזְּמַן הַזֶּה:

*After kindling the lights, say the following:*

Praised be Thou, O Lord our God, King of the universe, for the inspiring truths of which we are reminded by these Hanukkah lights.

We kindle them to recall the great and wonderful deeds wrought through the zeal with which God filled the hearts of the heroic Maccabees. These lights remind us that we should ever look unto God, whence comes our help.

As their brightness increases from night to night, let us more fervently give praise to God for the ever-present help He has been to our fathers in the gloomy nights of trouble and oppression.

The sages and heroes of all generations made every sacrifice to keep the light of God's truth burning brightly. May we and our children be inspired by their example, so that at last Israel may be a guide to all men on the way of righteousness and peace.

## Responsive Reading

(Psalm cxxi)

**Reader**

I will lift up mine eyes unto the mountains;
From whence shall my help come?

**Family**

My help cometh from the Lord,
Who made heaven and earth.
He will not suffer thy foot to be moved;
He that keepeth thee will not slumber.
Behold, He that keepeth Israel
Doth neither slumber nor sleep.
The Lord is thy keeper;
The Lord is thy shade upon thy right hand.
The sun shall not smite thee by day,
Nor the moon by night.

The Lord shall keep thee from all evil;
He shall keep thy soul.

   *The Lord shall guard thy going out and thy coming
   in,*

   *From this time forth and forever.*

(Hanukkah Song, page 92)

### GRACE AFTER MEALS

O Lord, Thou art our Shepherd, and we shall not
want. Thou openest Thy hand and satisfiest the needs
of every living being. We thank Thee for the gifts of
Thy bounty which we have enjoyed at this table. As
Thou hast provided for us hitherto, so mayest Thou
sustain us throughout our lives. Thy kindness endureth
forever, and we put our trust in Thee.

While we enjoy Thy gifts, may we never forget the
needy, nor allow those who want, to be forsaken. May
our table be an altar of lovingkindness, and our home
a temple in which Thy spirit of goodness dwells.

בָּרוּךְ אַתָּה יְיָ הַזָּן אֶת־הַכֹּל:

We praise Thee, O Lord, who in kindness sustainest
the world. Amen.

### PRAYER ON THE CONSECRATION OF A HOME

Except the Lord build the house, they labor in vain
that build it; except the Lord keep the city, the watchman waketh but in vain. (*Psalm cxxvii.*)

Praised be Thou, O Lord our God, Ruler of the
world, who hast granted us life, sustained us and permitted us to celebrate this joyous occasion.

בָּרוּךְ אַתָּה יְהֹוָה אֱלֹהֵינוּ מֶלֶךְ הָעוֹלָם שֶׁהֶחֱיָנוּ
וְקִיְּמָנוּ וְהִגִּיעָנוּ לַזְּמַן הַזֶּה:

O God, we turn our thoughts unto Thee, as we come into this home. Had not Thy blessing rested upon us we should not have prospered; we should not have entered this dwelling with the happiness and peace now in our hearts.

May Thy Providence still guide us. As Abraham stood at the opening of his tent to bring cheer to the wayfarer and help to the stranger, so may this, our home, be a refuge to the distressed and a comfort to the forsaken. May its walls echo words of prayer, of joy, of wisdom, of love and of truth.

Blessed art Thou, O God, whose lovingkindness rests ever upon the dwellings of Thy children. Amen.

### PRAYER ON NAMING A CHILD

Praise and gratitude fill our hearts on this day, as we bring to Thee, Almighty God, the dear child with which Thou hast blessed us. We dedicate it to a life of usefulness, honor and piety. We bestow upon it the name ———. May that name be a token of every virtue. May Thy blessing attend our dear child, to guard it against every evil and to keep it from every danger.

May it be worthy throughout life to be crowned with Thy benediction:

May the Lord bless thee and keep thee.

May the Lord let his countenance shine upon thee and be gracious unto thee.

May the Lord lift up His countenance upon thee, and give thee peace.

יְבָרֶכְךָ יְיָ וְיִשְׁמְרֶךָ:

יָאֵר יְיָ פָּנָיו אֵלֶיךָ וִיחֻנֶּךָּ:

יִשָּׂא יְיָ פָּנָיו אֵלֶיךָ וְיָשֵׂם לְךָ שָׁלוֹם:

Amen.

## PRAYER ON THE ANNIVERSARY OF A DEATH

*(It is customary to burn a small light for twenty-four hours on the anniversary of a death.)*

O God and Father, hear me as I pray with the Psalmist of old: So teach us to number our days, that we may get us a heart of wisdom.

This day, that recalls to me the passing of my dear —————, has now come in the midst of life's daily round of tasks and duties. My thoughts are disturbed, my heart is heavy. O God, teach me the true value of this day, that more of Thy wisdom may enter into my soul.

Help me to feel that my dear ————— is in Thy peaceful keeping.

My dear ————— is gone; but all the goodness, the sweetness and nobility of that life I well remember. As this light burns pure and clear, so may the blessed memory of the goodness, the nobility of character of my dear ————— illumine my soul. May the hallowed influence of this day give me strength to do Thy will, O God, with a steadfast, submissive and loving spirit. Amen.

(Kaddish, pp. 76–77)

# Prayer in the Cemetery

## DEDICATING A TOMBSTONE

All-kind and merciful Father, a thousand years in Thy sight are but as yesterday, and the years of our life are but as a span; yet dost Thou grant us the blessed comfort of prolonging on earth the loving memory of our dear ones.

In Thine unsearchable wisdom, Thou hast taken our dear ———— from us. But the deep and tender love which attached us unto our ———— is strong as death. Striving to soothe the sorrow of our hearts, we dedicate this stone to-day.

In consecrating it unto the memory of the departed, may we at the same time dedicate unto the living the love with which our dear one filled our lives. So may we realize the truth of Sacred Writ: The memory of the righteous is a blessing.

Let us go hence with a deeper and broader love for life and humanity. Then shall we feel that the more nobly we live, the more sincere will be the tribute we shall pay our dead.

In this spirit, O God, we offer our prayers to Thee. Fill our hearts with humility, that we may truly know that Thy thoughts are not our thoughts. Help us so to live that the purity and godliness of our lives may bring honor to the memory of the dear ones who dwell in peace with Thee. Thus shall we erect for them their truest, their lasting memorial among men. May the soul of our departed be bound up in life everlasting. Praised be Thou, O God, who givest life and takest it away. Amen.

(Kaddish, pp. 76–77)

# Scriptural Readings
# for the Sabbath

| TORAH | | HAFTARAH |
|---|---|---|

**Bereshis**

| (a) Genesis | I, 1—II, 3 | Isaiah XLII, 5–12 |
| (b) | II, 4–25 or | Psalm CIV or |
| | III, 1–24 | Job XXXVIII |
| (c) | IV, 1–16 | Psalm CXXXIX |

**Noah**

| (a) Genesis | VI, 9—VII, 7 | Isaiah LIV, 1–10 |
| (b) | VIII or IX | Jeremiah XXXI, 23–36 |
| (c) | XI, 1–9 | Zephaniah III, 8–20 |

**Lech Lecho**

| (a) Genesis | XII, 1–9 | Isaiah XL, 27—XLI, 10 |
| (b) | XIII or XIV | Isaiah LI, 1–16 or |
| | | Psalm CXI |
| (c) | XV | Psalm CV, 1–15 |

**Vayero**

| (a) Genesis | XVIII, 1–19 | II Kings IV, 8–37 |
| (b) | XVIII, 20–33 | Ezekiel XVIII |
| (c) | XXI or XXII | Micah VI, 1–8 |

**Chaye Soroh**

| (a) Genesis | XXIII | I Kings I, 5–36 |
| (b) | XXIV, 1–33 | Psalm XLV |
| (c) | XXIV, 34–67 | Proverbs XXXI, 10–31 |

**Toledos**

| (a) Genesis | XXV, 19–34 | Malachi I, 1–11 |
| (b) | XXVI, 12–33 | I Kings V, 15–26 |
| (c) | XXVII, 1–29 | Proverbs IV, 1–23 |

|  | TORAH | HAFTARAH |
|---|---|---|

**Vayetze**

| (a) Genesis | XXVIII, 10–22 | Hosea XI, 7—XII, 11 |
| (b) | XXIX, 2–20 | Jeremiah XXXI, 1–17 |
| (c) | XXXI, 36–49 | Psalm XXVII |

**Vayishlach**

| (a) Genesis | XXXII, 4–33 | Hosea XII, 13—XIV, 3 |
| (b) | XXXIII | Psalm VII |
| (c) | XXXV, 1–20 | Jeremiah X, 1–16 |

**Vayeshev**

| (a) Genesis | XXXVII, 1–11 | I Kings III, 5–15 |
| (b) | XXXVII, 12–36 | Amos II, 6—III, 8 |
| (c) | XL | Psalm XXXIV |

**Miketz**

| (a) Genesis | XLI, 1–14 | I Kings III, 15–28 |
| (b) | XLI, 14–38 | Daniel II, 1–23 |
| (c) | XLII, 1–21 | Isaiah XIX, 11–25 |

**Vayigash**

| (a) Genesis | XLIV, 18— XLV, 9 | Ezekiel XXXVII, 15–28 |
| (b) | XLV, 9–28 | Psalm LXXII |
| (c) | XLVII, 1–12 | Psalm LXXI |

**Vayechi**

| (a) Genesis | XLVII, 28— XLVIII, 20 | I Kings I, 41–53, II, 1–4 |
| (b) | XLIX, 1–28 | I Chronicles XXVIII, 1–10 |
| (c) | XLIX, 29— L, 26 | Job V |

**Shmos**

| (a) Exodus | I, 1–22 | Isaiah XXVII, 6–8, 12— XXVIII, 6 |
| (b) | II or III, 1–15 | Isaiah VI or I Samuel III |
| (c) | IV, 1–18 or V | Jeremiah I, 1–12 or I Kings XII, 1–19 |

| TORAH | HAFTARAH |
|---|---|

**Voero**

| (a) Exodus | VI, 2–13 | Ezekiel XXVIII, 25—XXIX, 16 |
| (b) | VII, 14–26 | Isaiah XLII, 5–17 |
| (c) | IX, 13–35 | Ezekiel XXXI, 1–12 |

**Bo**

| (a) Exodus | X, 1–23 | Jeremiah XLVI, 13–27 |
| (b) | XII, 1–11 | Ezra VI, 16–22 |
| (c) | XIII, 3–16 | Psalm CV, 14–45 |

**Beshalach**

| (a) Exodus | XIII, 17—XIV, 15 | Judges IV, 1–15 |
| (b) | XV | Judges V, 1–21 |
| (c) | XVI, 1–18 | Psalm LXXVIII, 1–28 |

**Yisro**

| (a) Exodus | XVIII | Isaiah VI |
| (b) | XIX | Isaiah XLIII, 1–12 |
| (c) | XX | Psalm XIX |

**Mishpotim**

| (a) Exodus | XXI, 1–13 | Jeremiah XXXIV, 8–22; XXXIII, 25–26 |
| (b) | XXII, 20—XXIII, 9 | Amos V, 6–24 |
| (c) | XXIV | Jeremiah XVI, 19—XVII, 8 |

**Terumo**

| (a) Exodus | XXV, 1–22 | I Kings V, 26; VI, 13 |
| (b) | XXV, 23–40 | I Chronicles XXII, 1–13 |
| (c) | XXVII, 1–19 | I Kings VIII, 22–43 |

**Tezave**

| (a) Exodus | XXVII, 20—XXVIII, 12 | Ezekiel XLIII, 10–27 |

|  | TORAH | HAFTARAH |
|---|---|---|
| (b) | XXIX, 1–9 | Isaiah LXI |
| (c) | XXIX, 38—XXX, 10 | Isaiah LXV, 17—LXVI, 2 |

## Ki Siso

| (a) Exodus | XXX, 11–31 | I Kings XVIII, 20–39 |
|---|---|---|
| (b) | XXXII, 1–14 | Psalm CVI, 1–23 |
| (c) | XXXIII, 12—XXXIV, 10 | Psalm LXXXI |

## Vayakhel

| (a) Exodus | XXXV, 1–29 | I Kings V, 9–26 |
|---|---|---|
| (b) | XXXV, 30—XXXVI, 7 | I Chronicles XXIX, 9–20 |
| (c) | XXXVIII, 1–19 | II Chronicles IV–V, 1 |

## Pikuday

| (a) Exodus | XXXVIII, 21—XXXIX, 1 | I Kings VII, 1–14 |
|---|---|---|
| (b) | XXXIX, 32–43 | I Kings VIII, 10–30 |
| (c) | XL, 22–38 | I Kings VIII, 54–61 |

## Vayikro

| (a) Leviticus | I | Isaiah XLIII, 21—XLIV, 5 |
|---|---|---|
| (b) | II | Psalm L |
| (c) | V, 14–26 | Malachi II, 1–10 |

## Zav

| (a) Leviticus | VI, 1–11 | Jeremiah VII, 21–34 and IX, 22–23 |
|---|---|---|
| (b) | VII, 22–38 | Hosea VI, 1–6 |
| (c) | VIII, 1–15 | Psalm CXXXII |

## Shemini

| (a) Leviticus | IX, 1–16 | I Chronicles XVII |
|---|---|---|
| (b) | X, 1–11 | II Samuel VI, 1–19 |
| (c) | X, 12–19 | I Chronicles XV, 1–16 |

|  | TORAH | HAFTARAH |
|---|---|---|

**Sazria-Mezoro**

| (a) Leviticus | XII | II Kings V, 1–19 |
| (b) | XIV, 1–32 | Psalm XXXIV |
| (c) | XIV, 33–57 | Job II |

**Aharay Mos**

| (a) Leviticus | XVI, 1–17 | Amos IX, 7–15 |
| (b) | XVI, 18–34 | Isaiah LIX |
| (c) | XVIII, 1–5; 24–30 | Ezekiel XXII, 17–30 |

**Kedoshim**

| (a) Leviticus | XIX, 1–14 | Ezekiel XXII, 1–15 |
| (b) | XIX, 23–37 | Psalm XV |
| (c) | XX, 22–27 | Job XXIX |

**Emor**

| (a) Leviticus | XXI, 1–8 | Ezekiel XLIV, 15–31 |
| (b) | XXII, 17–33 | Ezekiel XXXVI, 16–38 |
| (c) | XXIII, 1–8; 23–38 | Nehemiah VIII |

**Behar**

| (a) Leviticus | XXV, 1–13 | Jeremiah XXXII, 6–27 |
| (b) | XXV, 14–34 | Nehemiah V, 1–13 |
| (c) | XXV, 35–55 | Zephaniah III |

**Bechukosai**

| (a) Leviticus | XXVI, 3–13 | Jeremiah XVI, 19— XVII, 14 |
| (b) | XXVI, 36–46 | Job XXXVI, 3–26 |
| (c) | XXVII, 14–24 | Psalm CXVI |

**B'midbar**

| (a) Numbers | I, 1–19 | Hosea II, 1–3; 18–22 |
| (b) | II, 1–17 | Psalm XX |
| (c) | III, 44–51 | I Chronicles VI, 49–66 |

|  | TORAH | HAFTARAH |
|---|---|---|

### Noso

| | | |
|---|---|---|
| (a) Numbers | IV, 21–37 | Judges XIII |
| (b) | VI, 1–17 | Judges XVI, 4–21 |
| (c) | VI, 22–27 | Psalm LXVII |

### B'haaloscho

| | | |
|---|---|---|
| (a) Numbers | VIII, 1–14 | Zechariah II, 14—IV, 7 |
| (b) | X, 29—XI, 23 | Psalm LXXVII |
| (c) | XI, 24—XII, 8 | Joel II, 21—III, 5 |

### Shlach L'Cho

| | | |
|---|---|---|
| (a) Numbers | XIII | Joshua II |
| (b) | XIV | Joshua XIV, 6–14 |
| (c) | XIV, 26–45 | Psalm CVI, 1–27; 44–48 |

### Korach

| | | |
|---|---|---|
| (a) Numbers | XVI | I Samuel XI, 14–16; XII, 1–8, 19–25 |
| (b) | XVII, 16–24 | Isaiah LVI, 1–8 |
| (c) | XVIII, 1–20 | Jeremiah V, 20–31 |

### Chukas

| | | |
|---|---|---|
| (a) Numbers | XIX, 1–10 | Ezekiel XXXVI, 21–38 |
| (b) | XX, 1–21 | Judges XI, 4–33 |
| (c) | XXI, 1–20 | Psalm XLII |

### Bolok

| | | |
|---|---|---|
| (a) Numbers | XXII, 2–20 | Micah V, 6–14; VI, 1–8 |
| (b) | XXIII, 5–26 | Isaiah LIV, 11–17 |
| (c) | XXIV, 1–18 | Habakkuk, III |

### Pinchos

| | | |
|---|---|---|
| (a) Numbers | XXV, 10–18 | I Kings XIX |
| (b) | XXVII, 1–11 | Judges I, 1–15 |
| (c) | XXVII, 12–23 | Joshua XXIII, 1–15 |

| TORAH | HAFTARAH |
|---|---|

## Matos

| | | | |
|---|---|---|---|
| (a) | Numbers | XXX, 2–17 | Jeremiah I, 1–14 |
| (b) | | XXXII, 1–19 | Joshua XXII, 1–10 |
| (c) | | XXXII, 20–32 | Joshua XXII, 11–34 |

## Masey

| | | | |
|---|---|---|---|
| (a) | Numbers | XXXIII, 1–10 | Jeremiah II, 4–13 |
| (b) | | XXXV, 9–34 | Joshua XX |
| (c) | | XXXVI | Jeremiah XXXIII, 1–16; 25–27 |

## Devorim

| | | | |
|---|---|---|---|
| (a) | Deuteronomy | I, 1–17 | Isaiah I, 1–27 |
| (b) | | II, 1–9 | Jeremiah IX, 9–23 |
| (c) | | III, 1–14 | Lamentations III, 19–41 |

## Voes'chanan

| | | | |
|---|---|---|---|
| (a) | Deuteronomy | III, 23—IV, 8 | Isaiah XL, 1–26 |
| (b) | | V | Psalm CIII |
| (c) | | VI | Zechariah VIII, 7–23 |

## Ekev

| | | | |
|---|---|---|---|
| (a) | Deuteronomy | VII, 12–21 | Isaiah XLIX, 14–26 |
| (b) | | VIII | Isaiah L, 1–10 |
| (c) | | X, 12—XI, 12 | I Chronicles XXIX, 10–20 |

## R'eh

| | | | |
|---|---|---|---|
| (a) | Deuteronomy | XI, 26–32 | Isaiah LIV, 11—LV, 5 |
| (b) | | XIV, 1–8, 22–29 | Psalm XXIV |
| (c) | | XV, 1–18 | Isaiah XXVI, 1–12 |

## Shoftim

| | | | |
|---|---|---|---|
| (a) | Deuteronomy | XVI, 18—XVII, 14 | Isaiah LI, 12— LII, 6 |
| (b) | | XVIII, 9–22 | Jeremiah XXIII, 16–32 |
| (c) | | XXI, 1–9 | Ezekiel XXXIV, 1–24 |

| TORAH | HAFTARAH |
|-------|----------|

## Ki Setze

| (a) Deuteronomy XXI, 10–14 | Isaiah LIV, 1–10 |
| (b) | XXII, 1–10 | Proverbs XXX, 1–9 |
| (c) | XXIV, 10–24 | Isaiah V, 1–16 |

## Ki Sovo

| (a) Deuteronomy XXVI, 1–15 | Isaiah LX |
| (b) | XXVII, 1–10 | Joshua IV |
| (c) | XXVIII, 1–14 | Isaiah XXXV |

## Nizovim

| (a) Deuteronomy XXIX, 9–28 | Isaiah LXI, 10—LXII |
| (b) | XXX, 1–10 | Isaiah LI, 1–16 |
| (c) | XXX, 11–20 | Psalm LXXIII |

## Vayelech

| (a) Deuteronomy XXXI, 1–13 | Hosea XIV, 2–10 (see note) |
| (b) | XXXI, 14–21 | Ibid |
| (c) | XXXI, 22–30 | Ibid |

## Haazinu

| (a) Deuteronomy XXXII, 1–12 | II Samuel XXII, 1–32 (see note) |
| (b) | XXXII, 13–29 | Psalm XVIII, 1–21 |
| (c) | XXXII, 30–52 | Psalm XVIII, 22–51 |

## V'zos Habrocho

| (a) Deuteronomy XXXIII, 1–17 | Joshua I |
| (b) | XXXIII, 18–29 | Ibid |
| (c) | XXXIV | Ibid |

Note: Hosea XIV is the Haftarah either for Vayelech or Haazinu, depending upon which one falls on Shabbas Shuvah. If Vayelech is not on Shabbas Shuvah then it is combined with Nizovim, in which case read the Haftarah indicated for Nizovim. If Haazinu is not on Shabbas Shuvah read the Haftarah indicated above.

## SPECIAL READINGS

| | Torah | Haftarah |
|---|---|---|
| Passover, first day | Exodus XII, 37–42; XIII, 3–10 | Isaiah XLIII, 1–15 |
| Passover, seventh day | Exodus XIV, 30—XV, 21 | Isaiah XI, 1–6, 9, XII |
| Shavuos | Exodus XIX, 1–8; XX, 1–18 | Isaiah XLII, 1–12 |
| Succos, first day | Leviticus XXIII, 33–44 | Is. XXXII—XXXIII—XXXV |
| Shemini Atzeres | Deuteronomy XXXIV and Genesis I, 1–10 | Joshua I, 1–17 |
| For the first Sabbath of Hanukkah | Weekly Torah Portion | Zechariah IV, 1–7 |
| For the second Sabbath of Hanukkah | Weekly Torah Portion | I Kings VIII, 54–66 |
| For the Sabbath preceding Purim (Zachor) | Weekly Torah Portion | Esther VII, 1–10; VIII, 15–17; or IX, 20–28 |
| For Sabbath preceding Passover (Hagadol) | Weekly Torah Portion | Malachi III, 4–24 |
| For the Sabbath during Passover | Exodus XXXIII, 12—XXXIV, 26 | Song of Songs, II, 7–17; or Ezekiel XXXVII, 1–15 |
| For the Sabbath during Tabernacles | Exodus XXXIII, 12—XXXIV, 26 | Ecclesiastes I, V, VII, VIII or XII or Ezekiel XXXIX, 1–16 |

אַתָּה גִּבּוֹר לְעוֹלָם אֲדֹנָי. רַב לְהוֹשִׁיעַ. מְכַלְכֵּל
חַיִּים בְּחֶסֶד. מְחַיֵּה הַכֹּל בְּרַחֲמִים רַבִּים. סוֹמֵךְ
נוֹפְלִים וְרוֹפֵא חוֹלִים וּמַתִּיר אֲסוּרִים. וּמְקַיֵּם
אֱמוּנָתוֹ לִישֵׁנֵי עָפָר. מִי כָמוֹךָ בַּעַל גְּבוּרוֹת. וּמִי
דוֹמֶה־לָּךְ. מֶלֶךְ מֵמִית וּמְחַיֶּה. וּמַצְמִיחַ יְשׁוּעָה:
בָּרוּךְ אַתָּה יְיָ נוֹטֵעַ בְּתוֹכֵנוּ חַיֵּי עוֹלָם:

### SANCTIFICATION
(Congregation rises)

#### Reader

We sanctify Thy name on earth, as the heavens declare Thy glory, and in the words of the prophet we say:

Holy, holy, holy is the Lord of hosts; the whole earth is full of His glory.

#### Choir and Congregation

קָדוֹשׁ קָדוֹשׁ קָדוֹשׁ יְיָ צְבָאוֹת. מְלֹא כָל־הָאָרֶץ
כְּבוֹדוֹ:

#### Reader

Praised be the glory of God through all the world.

#### Choir and Congregation

בָּרוּךְ כְּבוֹד יְיָ מִמְּקוֹמוֹ:

#### Reader

The Lord will reign forever, thy God, O Zion, from generation to generation.   Hallelujah!

#### Choir and Congregation

יִמְלֹךְ יְיָ לְעוֹלָם אֱלֹהַיִךְ צִיּוֹן לְדוֹר וָדוֹר
הַלְלוּיָהּ:

(Congregation is seated)